REAL ESTATE PROSPERITY

by Robert Metz

www.realestateprosperityllc.com
metz@realestateprosperityllc.com

RoseDog Books
PITTSBURGH, PENNSYLVANIA 15238

RoseDog Books
585 Alpha Drive
Suite 103
Pittsburgh, PA 15238
Visit our website at *www.rosedogbookstore.com*

ISBN: 978-1-4809-7864-5
eISBN: 978-1-4809-7887-4

About the Author

Robert Metz received his degree in political science and economics from Georgetown University in 1974 and his Juris Doctorate from New York University School of Law in 1977. He practiced law for many years, owned several real estate brokerage offices, and published a foreclosure and bankruptcy magazine in the 1990's.

Metz has been a principal and consultant in scores of real estate transactions and work-outs throughout New Jersey. He is a frequent speaker at seminars and workshops. He writes from a unique and candid hands-on and academic perspective; authoritative knowledge, and real-world know-how and expertise.

CONTENTS

PREFACE

This Book is intended to serve as a <u>Conceptual Framework</u>, and a <u>Practical, Pragmatic Guide</u> for both the owner / borrower in distress, and the investor / speculator trying to profit from real estate in both short and longer term transactions. My goal is to help the Reader gain a <u>Fuller, Substantive, Functional Working Knowledge and Understanding</u>.

There are endless "how to" volumes and "game plans" out there. My hope, however, is that my Reader will learn <u>Strategies, Techniques, and Methods; Learn about Sources for Deals,</u> and (in a more Cerebral Sense), gain the everyday <u>Working Knowledge</u>, of the <u>Mechanics</u> and <u>Issues which are the subject matter of this Book</u> – as indicated by Chapter titles. <u>I want to enable my Reader to do Profitable Things in the Real World of Real Estate Investment and Speculation.</u>

I have tried to weave a Primer that will send the Reader off to Money-Making, Fulfilling Endeavors (be he an experienced practitioner or a novice), enriched with a Working Knowledge and a Depth of Understanding of the Broader Picture, the Workings of the Market and the Key Aspects of the Industry, so that he can actually do things.

Knowledge, not simply as to Details and How-To-Do, which of course is important. But also Knowledge as to Context, Theories, Approaches, and the Rationale and Underpinnings of the System and the Bases of its Deal-Making.

The point is not to just be a mere walking statistician with blinders; the Idea is to be Perceptive, to be a Doer, to be a Doer whose Understanding Best Empowers him to see the Broader Picture of the Business and a Specific Deal and to Know how to ask the Right Questions and make Good Choices and Sound Decisions.

I caution you: this Book is not one of those shallow pulp volumes crammed with "checklists" and overly-simplistic "steps" and other worthless superficial data and even sillier miracle tales and bravado. It is not to be compared in content or tone to the embarrassing "hype" or theatrics of some of the "flipping" shows on television.

This Book will have achieved its purposes if it Empowers and Enables the Reader and he sees fit to keep it handy for future reference, for re-reading of those passages which may from time to time apply to his own Endeavors and Transactions.

CHAPTER I

THERE MUST (& WILL) BE ANOTHER REAL ESTATE BOOM, & ANOTHER, & ANOTHER

REMEMBER – REAL ESTATE VALUES MUST RISE; DOL-LARS MUST BE CREATED & RECYCLED; OUR ECONOMIC SYSTEM DEPENDS ON CASH-FLOW FROM BLOATED RE-ALTY VALUES, EASY MORTGAGES, OTHER EASY FINANC-ING, & GOVERNMENT 'PUMPS' (WHEN NEEDED), TO MAKE THIS "CONTRIVED FICTION" A REALITY – OVER & OVER AGAIN.

Considering the broader historical perspective, the average American who has come to rely on real estate, or real estate "growth", as his financial savior, should take heart. As this is written in the post-2010 Bust period, the end is certainly not at hand. And not because our economic system and the pivotal role of real estate values and activity are the result purely of the workings of a capitalistic system / free market enterprise, hard work, and good old personal initiative, either. Not at all. It is, quite simply, because the end just CANNOT be here.

The Federal Government cannot permit "prolonged" or permanent downturns; not if there is anything in its power to prevent them. Today our economy is well beyond the chance workings and evolution of natural or innate market systems. The days when market dynamics were driven purely by factors of supply and demand, or steady market growth (& valleys), or by any notion of the ebb and flow of prosperity, (as if these were self-fulfilling norms), are ancient history.

1

Today our System is akin to an "Inevitable Predestination". Not Biblical or Mystical. Not Fatalistic. But perhaps something just as Powerful or, in our lives, even more Powerful – that is to say, <u>THE DYNAMICS OF TODAY'S "ECONOMIC SYSTEM" ='s THE WANTS OF A PEOPLE, PLUS THE NECESSARY ROLE OF GOVERNMENT IN MAKING THINGS HAPPEN</u>.

"Real Estate Booms And Busts", the Cycles of "Boom To Bust To Recovery", the Path to the "New Bubble And Boom", and round and around, are nothing special. Which areas of life and nature do not have their own innate Cycles? Or Cycles, may we say, which have become more pronounced, or exaggerated, by the Hand of Man? The ups and downs, the rise and fall in real estate values and activity, have become much too important a component of the National Bloodstream, to be left simply to chance or the purest workings of the marketplace.

Sure, there's the old saying "What's good can't last, and what's bad can't last." But here the slant on the downside of "can't" is that we cannot, the Government cannot, simply let things meander and take their own route back up. The real estate market cannot be permitted "to work back up", and up a little more, as events, unfettered, would simply evolve at their own speed.

It has to be. We must, and We do, increasingly, help things along. In today's world to satiate the ever-growing appetites of a voracious people, and to grow the System and those appetites, upon any retrenchment, the Process must be Pumped back up – to do it again, and again.

The difference between the Cycles of years past (with few exceptions), and those of today, is the sheer scope, the extremes. Like "the bigger they come, the harder they fall." Effectuating the cyclical swing back to Boom status, which has increasingly become a vital plateau to maintain and grow in our bloated and ever-more contrived and inter-dependent System, requires more extreme tools, more innovative and stronger measures and intervention.

Really, an all-out resuscitation effort by the Feds.

Indeed, *The Times Help Shape The Policies*, and *The Policies Help Shape The Times*.

The need for increasing and more accentuated Government involvement with more novel programs, a broader "middle class" focus, a policy with more creative muscle to stimulate real estate values and activity, is evident today in early 2017, and will continue to be necessary in the years to come if we are to see a real Broad Economic Recovery with backbone in the near future.

Long ago our System outgrew its incubation era of Rugged Individualism, the Up By The Bootstraps Mentality. Today self-help and hard work are only a part of the solution. Modern American Society and its economic fiber are a far cry from any model of pure free market enterprise. Our's is no longer (to the extent that it once was), a truly free market system. Thoreau mused over the ideals of self-reliance and survival, the pure simplicity of needs and life, in "Walden's Pond;" in our world, however, most of the "purity", the old notions, are just matters of intellectual diversion.

For most of us our way of living, our desired standard of living, has morphed into a societal clump of extremes – demands, expectations, perceived entitlements, bloated desires. We hear the rhetoric about sacrifice, community service and charity. But our's is such a smaller world. The Internet. Instant Communication. Technology. Instant Gratification. A far cry from the post-World War II Great Generation of survival, self-reliance, and pride of self- and selfless achievement. More recent decades have borne witness to the proliferation of *The Me, The I Want It Yesterday* Generations.

An Economic System framed by a different socio-economic, a more selfish, populace. A System which has always had its recurring, sometimes mild or more difficult, Cycles. A System which until now had its last seismic disgorging some 80 years ago.

Still our's is a System which has endured and rebounded each time, typically stronger, from its many Cycles. It has been wound ("pumped") and deflated, and reinflated, so many times, most recently having been engorged, as it was DIRECTED, to satisfy the thirsts of an ever-more avaricious population – i.e., the Baby Boomers and their own "very entitled" offspring.

It may seem like ancient history, but scarcely 90 years ago a still tenuous and more simple America was also busy at work gorging the Machine to boost its smaller, less demanding, yet nevertheless quite greedy and conspicuous masses.

The Roaring '20's were not simply the result of a natural evolution of prosperity. Yes, different from the Dawn of our 21st Century; simpler and less extreme; but even then the Government was largely responsible for helping "Pump" things up. The basics of the economic system were less complex, everything was much less real estate–dependent than it would later become. But the essential components of that System were pushed up, and beyond, with help from the Federal Government. Thus was the hyperbole of the Roaring '20's – its prosperity, its gaudiness, its excess.

A Boom To Bust. The Great Depression. The Stock Market Crash. Bank Failures. Dollars Under the Mattress. Gold. Soup Kitchens and Bread Lines. A shocked, distraught People, a Nation in Crisis. Abject Poverty. And Recovery, even in that infinitely more self-reliant, self-sufficient era, was Pumped up by the Government. The crux of the problems and the Bust was not so acutely real estate, as it has been today, for real estate was not the true key to a functional system at that time. Yet values were still deflated and foreclosures rampant.

Federal intervention, or "Pumps", at that time, were directed in a very basic and traditional manner. The CCC – Civilian Conservation Corps – building great public works projects, dams and roads, through the West. Government assistance with mortgages. Reforms in the Banking System, and "new" regulations on Wall Street. Roosevelt's New Deal. The re-creation of jobs, the dollar, values, and commerce. Direct Government assistance to the masses coupled with initiatives for the System.

The path to better times was promoted by Government intervention.

Increasingly, through the last third of the 20th Century the roles of real estate values and real estate activity would become more central to and defining of our overall Boom and Bust Cycles.

The Nixon Years and the prosperity of the early 1970's gave way to Jimmy Carter and the doldrums of the late '70's.

In a New Jersey Foreclosure Magazine which I published some years later I would headline an editorial banner: "Distressed Real Estate…How to Deal With the Problems and Opportunities of Real Estate Workouts & Surplus Real Estate." I continued: "1994?? – No! – an advertisement from a 1979 seminar at New York University."

And the downturn, the Bust, of the early 1980's, when selling a house in the most sought-after neighborhoods became a challenge, would give way to the Reagan Era and sellers' delights of bidding wars and over-asking-price offers. Bidding wars on houses which scarcely a few years earlier had been the proverbial "drugs on the market".

In New Jersey Midlantic Bank, a venerable institution (which a few years later in the next Bust of values and thrifts, would be seized and dismantled by the FDIC and RTC), trumpeted itself as the "Hungry Bankers". Hungry to lend, and ready to offer high appraisals on speculative real estate projects, large or small, to close a loan. And how apropos to our more recent world, the formative years of the early 21st Century, was a January 10, 1986 Time Magazine Cover heralding "The Debt Bomb – The Worldwide Peril of Go-Go Lending!!"

Obtaining Capital for more modest real estate ventures did not necessarily even require a mortgage. Unsecured short-term promissory notes were routinely offered to "qualified" borrowers, including Your's Truly – notes that were "automatically" renewable every six months, often pre-executed in blank for "convenience", the details to be filled in later by bank loan reps. All "for the ease of commerce".

By the early 1990's, when the latest Bubble would Bust, as (then) unprecedented high real estate values crashed, and the FDIC (Federal Deposit Insurance Corporation), became overwhelmed at the task of seizing and liquidating so many failed thrifts, real estate activity again ground to a crawl. The Hungry Bankers were falling all over themselves calling in as many loans as they could. And Midlantic, like so many thrifts across the nation, would ultimately be crushed under the weight of (compared to 2010 standards, anyway), what was a minor wave of "toxic", non-performing, devalued, negative-equity mortgages.

The Government had to supplement the FDIC with creation of the RTC (Resolution Trust Corporation), to help liquidate (auction, sell), the huge volume of foreclosed real estate, good and bad mortgages, and other assets of failed thrifts. In so doing the RTC often functioned as a "Bad Bank".

As I wrote in one of my magazines in the early 1990's: "Gone are the days of ever-spiraling real estate values, equity loans to tap increased values and pay the bills or purchase luxuries. Cash flow for the average businessman, blue or white-collar worker and professional alike, is far from what it used to be. Credit card debt is high, and not many people have the flexibility to keep charging it for tomorrow and living on funny money…Despite the pounding that the economy in New Jersey has taken from the heyday of the '80's, it is hard to believe that bankruptcy filings continue to climb dramatically." Sound familiar? And that was 20 some years ago!!

In 1994 one of my magazine contributors was lamenting "a period of real estate auction activity that this nation has (not) experienced since the Savings & Loan Crisis began. Early reports of trouble surfaced in the mid-'80's, but it was not until 1989 when Congress finally could no longer deny the problem existed and passed legislation creating the RTC…Originally estimated to concern less than 100 institutions representing a possible $100 billion bailout, we now know that these figures were grossly understated – in fact, as of today, the

RTC has handled the resolution of over 744 institutions with slightly more than $460 billion in total assets." *Déjà Vu* (PLUS), Over and Over again!

Then What? The height of the Clinton Years, the latter 1990's witnessed an unprecedented Recovery and Boom period – and, of particular interest, a phenomenal resurgence in real estate values and activity. This, however, was to be a very different sort of Boom.

The now-omnipresent engine for all of this, the Pumps which would be so flagrantly employed by the Government, in part through Wall Street, during most of the Second Bush Era, was Funny Money. Easy Money. New and Innovative Mortgage Vehicles. Securitizations. Derivatives. Bundling of mortgages, to be sold and assigned, to be buried in China and Europe, to be sold to pension funds and investors and investment groups and trusts. Government spending and Pumps leading to high values (augmenting the innate cyclical increases), easy and plentiful money, designed to promote easier and larger equity drawdowns (refinances), and real estate sales.

While it lasted, until things began to unravel Bush, who was being lambasted for just about everything else, would be praised, along with his Fed. Chairman Greenspan, for his "genius" in stimulating economic well-being. And before the clouds started gathering with the initial slides in 2006, which would preview the Bust of 2008, our Federal Reserve Chairman was the acclaimed guru. (As if those "in the know" did not understand the technical levers, the actual dynamics, which make a balloon inflate until it bursts.)

Cycles do indeed bear a certain correlation to, and do to an extent, flow from the diverse philosophical and fiscal policies of a particular Administration. But, they also have and are tempered by a life, an impetus, a timing of their own. And they are framed by external affairs and forces from the world over. Part of the "life", or the inevitable force, of Cycles themselves is the inescapable reality, in today's world, that most of a Cycle has to be the product of Government intervention, or Pumps. This is the case on any upswing, including the Recovery phase. It inflates and then reinflates things, and paves the way for the next Boom.

And unless an Administration wishes to put its head in the sand and deny this now-necessary exercise of Government power, the life of a Cycle, which today must include Government Pumps to right and sustain itself, transcends all other divergent fiscal policies and philosophies.

Indeed, had George Bush remained in Office beyond January 20, 2009, the end results of Government intervention to spur Recovery (some of which we still eagerly anticipate), would have ultimately turned out quite similar – a bit better or worse, a bit sooner or later, than President Obama or any other President would or could have effectuated. The bubbles of astronomical values and funny money just had to, as is always the case, eventually burst. They collapse under their own weight. (Even the ancient Romans would have to relieve themselves, voluntarily or otherwise, after gorging – only to take a breather and then do it all over again. They liked the way it felt.)

And after the Bubble from those heady days of late Clinton and Bush deflated, any Administration, of either Party, would have had to open its fiscal toolbox, and concoct some new tools to add to that box, in order to reinflate things, and to again push the real estate sector, lest the Nation collapse and bring the rest of the world with it into an unthinkable abyss of prolonged Depression and political chaos.

And so, after the 2008 Bust, had Bush and Greenspan remained on the job, maybe with some varying Pumps and perhaps different social objectives and political rhetoric than Obama's, with more, fewer, worse, or better tools, the fix-it scenario would still have been rolled out. Make no mistake about it, they also would have had to get the Machine up and running again. Just as they kept pumping it up through the years of Boom and Prosperity.

And they would have re-claimed their mantels as the gurus of real estate and economic good times – they would not have exited as the "villains" on whose watch it all collapsed. Someone else will receive the accolades when things swing back around. But – who to most people would have been the "villain" had the Bubble burst say, two years after Bush left Office? Certainly not Bush!

The media and politicians may engage in "trash talk". Blame Wall Street. Blame the Banks. Make scapegoats, make ogres. Praise "Joe" and Main Street. Manufacture villains and create "innocent victims". But 2008-2010 was just the peak of an inevitable, harsh cyclical downturn which called for those extreme measures of resuscitation which will, hopefully, be more fully implemented, (not enough having been done as of this writing) by whatever means and in whatever sequence. And it will all be pumped up again. It has to be, the Federal Government does not have a choice. No American President, Democrat or Republican, Liberal or Conservative, has much of a choice anymore. And despite rhetoric of New Responsibility and all the rest, have the initial Obama Programs not simply been newer and larger (albeit not enough, and lacking in needed focus and "umph") variations of those same "tricks" that Bush, Clinton and Reagan rolled out?

IT IS FUNDAMENTAL AND CRUCIAL TO RECOGNIZE THAT "EQUITY SUPPLEMENTS" FROM BLOATED REALTY VALUES MAKE OUR ECONOMY TICK; THE PURCHASE AND SALE OF REAL ESTATE, NEW CONSTRUCTION AND EQUITY-DRIVEN RE-FINANCES ALL PULL MONEY OUT, THEY ALL CREATE DOL-LARS, AND THIS MONEY IS THEN SPENT AND LEVERAGED, RESPENT AND REINVESTED ELSEWHERE AND EVERYWHERE ON REAL ESTATE AND NON-REAL ESTATE GOODS AND SERV-ICES, ALIKE.

During the Clinton-Bush Boom the bloated values which fueled sales and refinancing were promoted, magnified, and accentuated by the prevalence of easy Funny Money. The array of financing vehicles further maximized the mileage which the entire economy received from those inflated values (and "appraisals"). Pumps, creations of the Government, combined with those of the private sector, at times all intertwined, and led to and perpetuated the Boom.

No Down Payment Purchases. 90% First and 10% Second Mortgage Financing =’ed 100% Purchase Money Mortgages for buyers. 106% Financing Vehicles. "Fix-Up" Money back to the buyer at closing. Three Year Adjustable Rate Mortgages (ARM's) to blunt the reality of true carrying costs, to make "more affordable" that which was never affordable in the first place.

Interest Only Mortgages. No Docs, Easy Docs, Balloons, No Income Verifications, "Extra Income" To Qualify, and incomes even in the form of "Projected Rents and Anticipated Income" used to qualify applicants.

And things really took off when Corruption and Ingenuity piled on. Flawed appraisals further magnified already-bloated fair market values. Easy mortgage qualifying terms were pushed over the top with fraudulent data and exhibits and fuzzy underwriting.

Higher values do grease the wheels – they are the drug, the fix, which satiates a Nation's cravings. Human Nature, Needs, Wants, and Greed.

REMEMBER: MOST REAL ESTATE EQUITY IS AN ARTIFICIAL INFUSION OF CAPITAL INTO THE ECONOMIC SYSTEM WHICH SUPPLEMENTS BASIC EARNINGS AND NON-REAL ESTATE SEC-TOR BUSINESS AND INVESTMENT PROFITS.

Our economic system is a hungry, orchestrated, manufacturer; it is, essentially, an artificial merry-go-round of a machine.

Popular wants and "needs" are exaggerated by senses of personal entitlement. Conspicuous Consumption is fueled by both Government and societal forces and mind-sets. Conspicuous Consumption is nothing new; it has just become an ever-more pervasive state of being. Even holidays, the "old" hype of the SUV's and all those gadgets and handheld devices and flat screen TV's, those "must-have" feelings are for the most part a continually manufactured artificial "demand". The result of a social mindset aided and abetted by Government complicity.

"We" all want, we are all involved, we have all been players; we have all been the cheerleaders. Main Street and Wall Street, the Government and the politicians alike. Big Business and Small Business, Joe and the Unions, the CEO's and the blue-collar workers. Who has not appreciated the phenomenon of buying a house with less money down than the deposit required to rent an apartment? How nice to be able to pull those fat, magical equity "incomes" out of your property! Spend. Get. Want. More. 2004, 2006 – Your big SUV riding down the highway, with GPS, satellite radio, blackberry and cell phone in the console, DVD player in the rear, credit card and latte at the ready – the quintessential American Dream, if not reality, for many over the last years. And don't forget the radar scanner on the dashboard – cruising along, living high, and trying to beat both Systems at the same time.

Has not Main Street wanted and sought like anybody else? Work 20 some years, retire in style with most of your salary and benefits, relax, perhaps work someplace else in addition, milk the real estate. Money and its uses. Certainly not the world of Thoreau's Walden Pond. Clumps of generations who know, or knew, nothing of prudent moderation, let alone anything resembling Spartan simplicity.

Yes, our's did become an artificial system rooted primarily in bloated real estate values and other machinations designed to quench heightened expectations at all levels of Society. All sectors of the economy – employers, retirees, Union members, Main Street, Wall Street (like the old junk bond cliques of years past), flourished thanks to Government tinkering, or Pumps. This Economy, like any other man-made machine, must be serviced in order to do its job, to move its cargo, to keep its people happy.

As a result we now have exaggerated gyrations, what will invariably be more pronounced Booms and Busts, with the "need" for ever-stronger Government intervention and ingenuity (when necessary), to Pump it up and keep it up as long as possible, over and over again, so the people may enjoy what they have come to call "prosperity" and "happiness".

While politicians and the media cast blame they have helped fuel popular expectations. For the sake of political expediency they patronize and humor the public, and then they single out scapegoats during a Bust. They tell the people what they want to hear. But we have all been in it, together. We all crave the windfalls and creature comforts. Virtually every segment of the country has been in on the action.

THE MOVEMENT OF MONEY FROM (BY VIRTUE OF), BLOATED REALTY VALUES (BUYING, SELLING, CONSTRUCTION, & EQUITY REFINANCING), MAKES THAT HUGE PORTION OF OUR ECONOMY, COLLECTIVELY CALLED "THE REAL ESTATE TREE" PROSPER. High values and easy financing enhance activity and cash flow up and down the line. This is the line which feeds the masses. It keeps so many so comfortable in their seemingly endless pursuit of those oh so many comforts and must-have "extras", and for others it provides the bare essentials.

The lifeblood of so many diverse professional groups, so much of the financial sector, contractors, service people, material suppliers, manufacturers, retailers, and the import sectors of the economy, is rooted in The Real Estate Tree. Basic, yet complex; intertwined, and very inter-dependent. Big Blocks, Big Dominoes.

The buyer's transaction, and subsequent improvements to the property, throw off a huge and rippling shower of money. As does the seller's side of the transaction, his probable new purchase (be it trading up or down), and maybe even his new-found ability to assist others in their own purchases. Then so many of these buyers and sellers will later refinance, and thus generate ever-more dollar fallout from, and to, The Real Estate Tree.

Who, generally, makes up this Tree? Attorneys, title companies, surveyors, the Government (receiving taxes and filing and transfer revenues), inspectors of every sort, real estate and mortgage brokers, lenders, appraisers, credit bureaus, contractors of every kind, material suppliers, and a veritable host of retailers, repairmen, utility companies, the cable industry, movers, the furniture and homegoods industries, the appliance industry, interior decorators, painters, landscapers, all sorts of trades, and the myriad businesses which market toys for the homeowner – i.e., pools, spas, outdoor furniture, novelties, and games.

Thus it is a given that the massive cash-cow of buying, selling, refinancing, construction, and renovating, feeds not only those specific sectors which comprise the Tree itself, but additionally the many diverse segments of the economy which seem to have little to do with the real estate industry per se.

Real estate <u>Values</u> have emerged as the basis of today's economic model. Gone, or ancillary, are other pillars which were once regarded as fundamental bedrock (at least in America). Heavy Industry, Manufacturing, Export of Hard Products, Natural Resources – even Science, Technology, and War – are still players, but they have taken a back seat.

We make very little; we invent and we create, we think; we look to others (outside) to do; we outsource; we "scheme;" we look to ride the waves; and we look to magically make "prosperity" appear. High real estate values, and easy access to this gold mine, became our not-so-new Core – the "fix", the "solution", the cash-cow, to get us over the bumps of everyday life and toil, to "make" money for us and to be our power to do and get things.

The old traditional intrinsic genuine smellable American economic foundations gradually collapsed decades ago. The System morphed into one of "accepted / expected perceptions". Our younger generations have had little or no idea of what we mean by phrases like the "Gold Standard". Or what it means to back currency with hard gold, stored deep in Fort Knox or under the New York Federal Reserve Bank.

It was a scarce 45 years ago that our domestic money supply still had a quantity of dollar bills, 5's and 10's, in daily use, bearing the old and reassuring inscription "Silver Certificate". The dollar was backed not just by "full faith", or "In God We Trust", but by actual silver, and anybody could take that dollar, or any face value aggregate amount of those bills, go to a Federal Depository and redeem them at the official fixed rate of $1.29 in currency per troy ounce of .999 fine silver and walk away with either a baggie of silver granules or a gleaming rectangular bar, a pure silver ingot, bearing the Official Stamp and Eagle of the United States. And until the redemption windows ultimately closed, the currency of the day having evolved into Federal Reserve Notes, "mere pieces of paper", silver certificates were redeemable at the $1.29 per ounce rate regardless of the actual free market price of silver on any particular day.

(As an aside, it might be noted that the right of redemption was terminated as the open market price of silver skyrocketed to $50.00 an ounce; a lucrative spec. business at the time was to get, to purchase, silver certificates, use them to buy silver from the Treasury at $1.29 per ounce, and turn around and sell that very same silver for almost $50.00 per ounce, or at a discount, on the open market or to middle-men.)

The post-Kennedy and Johnson Years would see recurring bouts of severe inflation. As if trying to convince the country that things were really not so bad, that prices were not so out of sight as most wallets suggested, (it was just our imagination that everything was costing more and more), the spin masters in Washington would periodically change the components of the Consumer Price Index (CPI). Thus could the official read on inflation bear statistics indicating that it was subsiding and "under control", even as it galloped out of sight.

To even begin coping with an over-leveraged, stressed-out System that was starting to spin out of its established bounds and confines, new realities – ever-larger National Deficits, warped Balance of Payments Stats, mammoth deferred bond and retirement fundings, all sorts of creative bookkeeping and accounting standards – changed our financial and economic norms, and the pervasive Rob Peter to Pay Paul psychology took hold in our System. No tight regimen to mark and lasso our currency; just Greenbacks and if everybody would accept them ("accept" was not the word, they would continue to be craved), we would be in business!!

The invaluable role of labor unions in an earlier 20th Century Industrialized America would, more often than not, become an excuse for rampant excess and abuse. Together with some necessary, and some unwise, over-regulation, ever-increasing costs for everything at home, a foreign policy which made it necessary to open our doors to cheaper competition, the dawning and then the rapid spread of technology, and Americans' new-found complacency and softness, Unions ran amuck and led to a further plundering of the foundations of our System – and a changed meaning of old work ethics and what was once known as "Yankee Ingenuity".

Our industrial and manufacturing bases were significantly compromised.

It was a veritable array of evolving realities and social and political forces at home and abroad, which led to the transformation in our economic fiber. It went hand-in-hand with a changing Society and a changing People. Socio-economic trends, an increased number of divorces and single-parent households, different lifestyles, remarkable technology, and heightened desires. So much out there to have, and so many places to go, so quickly, right there in front of us, all for "the asking" and all, in sum, outstripping our ordinary spendable incomes.

Quite a departure from the saving and sacrifice of the Great Generation; and that All-American 1950's and 1960's family, which had often known and been molded by hard times, an up by the bootstraps era. We became a *Me*, a *Now*, a *More* Culture.

Cash purchases and lay-away (buy what you can afford), gave way to the use of individual store credit cards, and increasingly to the general plastic, the everyday all-purpose credit cards. Cheap leases to get that luxury car or the third family car, which we could not afford in the first place. Buy today, pay next year. Rebates on everything. Just mortgage, literally and figuratively, the future; spend what you do not have; use the plastic – just like your Uncle Sam and State Governments do – just like Medicare and Social Security; don't worry about the future, it will take care of itself. Generations of deficits and bonds. More borrowing. All familiar games, just like doctoring the Consumer Price Index components to make things look better than they actually were. Give The People What They Want.

Print more Paper. As long as everybody accepts it, okay. Electronic "money". In a quizzical way, the Federal Reserve Note would come to bear a curious similarity, at least in spirit, to those huge round stones with the holes in the middle that were rolled by two or more people using long poles in ancient Yap. The official currency, the official tender of exchange, accepted and honored by all; this was Money.

The primary thing that remains, and which is viable, meaningful, instrumental in a universal sense and is neither fleeting nor temporal, is Real Estate. It is the modern-day lynchpin which is used to "create" vast wealth. It mints dollars to dump into the System and make it fly. And whenever this catalyst stops bloating and giving and sputters, we need Government ingenuity and ever-more creative and powerful tools to create, to prop, to push and to infuse, until this "private sector realty" again starts churning and "manufacturing" – not a product, per se, but pieces of paper, digits on the computer, for us to swap with. "In God We Trust."

And while things like the Gold Standard once carried meaning for our System, our's has really never been a market fully premised on the security or sanctity of gold. (Or of diamonds or other precious metals for that matter; unlike World War II Eastern Europe and other regions, where such treasures can still be the ticket to survival or free passage in a world of devalued, worthless, and overnight-extinct currencies.)

Surely, gold and jewels are speculative commodities, desirable objects of beauty to many and hawked with zeal during times of economic distress and inflationary cycles. People buy them, wear them, handle them and crave them. But aside from their periodic surges, aesthetic values and ego boosts and somewhat limited practical utility, gold and diamonds have not proven to be stellar investments over the long run.

Precious metals and jewels do not provide income streams, they serve few but aesthetic purposes, they cost money to insure, they are not easy to leverage into; their price volatility and long droughts in appreciation over the past 45 years suggest they are mostly pot luck "investments". If you happen to be on the right side of a price swing, you can make money – as with just about any investment or product or collectible. But as far as being a shrewd long-term, income-producing growth-oriented tax-sheltered vehicle, it is all hype.

Caveat – gold and silver did once have a strong role in legitimizing our currency, but as a real investment, just look at the facts – an ounce of silver today is worth about 30% of what it was decades ago, and gold, when examined by traditional rules of thumb like Appreciation, Ongoing Yields, etc. with its wide and often manipulated price swings is, on an adjusted basis, just marginally more than it was. Even with its recent spikes in price, which can come and go like the wind, gold has been a cumulative dud over the past 45 years.

Real Estate, despite its most recent history: Astronomical growth, plus Income and other Gains along the way!!

We talk about currency. We have never thought in terms of taking shavings from a piece of gold and going to the grocery store or using it to bribe the Gestapo in order to gain our freedom. The dollar is our medium of exchange, "backed" or not. And we "need" more dollars than we typically make in the workplace and the world of daily commerce.

The bottom line is that long-term Government policy is, and shall remain, TO ENSURE THE SURVIVAL, AND THE FLOURISHING, OF THE CORE REAL ESTATE AND OTHER INTER-RELATED COMPONENTS OF OUR SYSTEM. That means initiatives in times of Bust and Recovery, and even during Boom periods. The Government "pumps". And as this is written, we are in Bust / Pre-Recovery mode.

Sooner or later the workhorse will be put back to work. The National Appetite, the nation's survival, needs that cash-flow and the rain-making powers of the real estate sector. Old tools and new tools shall continue to be rolled out. Real estate volume needs to be engorged again. Bloat and activity must return. Direct Pumps in the Real Estate and Financial Sectors, coupled with infusions to other sectors and combined with a certain passage of time and private initiatives, will get things back on track. And with each successive fall, or Bust, each time around, it will take a bit more to reinflate and lead to "Price Recovery".

The old and new Pumps started gearing up in 2008-2011. We have had both the Treasury and Federal Reserve pushing Tax breaks and Rebate checks designed to stimulate spending. Stimulus Packages to help create jobs and a flow, bailouts for Detroit to try to and save jobs and prevent further dominoes from falling. Public Works projects and proposals reminiscent of FDR's New Deal and the CCC Camps of the 1930's.

While the early '90's saw the FDIC and RTC handling the liquidation of failed thrifts and the sale of their assets (efforts to ensure the integrity and viability of the real estate and financial sectors), starting in 2010 we saw the FDIC doing much of the same. (The RTC was merged into the FDIC in 1995 as the '90's Bust crisis subsided.) Today, however, since we have fewer banks and much larger banks than we had 20 odd years ago, the task of cleaning and propping up the banking and mortgage sectors takes on a different tone.

We cannot allow, as they say, certain banks to fail. They are too large and intertwined. The Fed, the Treasury and the FDIC must pre-empt certain failures and infuse, pump, and prop before a failure or during a potential failure.

So we have had new tools evolving and larger aid packages used to pump the Realty and Mortgage Systems in efforts to avoid total disaster. The Tarp. The notion of infusing so much cash into a banking system that the Federal Government buys stock in heretofore "private enterprise" (entities which had been independent and subject to the regulatory arm of Uncle Sam). So much capital that Uncle Sam now calls himself an Investor. So many dollars pumped in that Wall Street is flooded.

The proposition that the Government buy toxic assets (severely discounted or other non-performing mortgages and diverse lender receivables), in order to free lenders of drags so they can make new loans, and to further try to prevent this glut from becoming bank-owned post-foreclosures which are often further dampers on realty values across the board. What is afoot here?

Despite proclamations of "fiscal responsibility" and politicians' for-pub-lic-consumption misdirected scoldings of Wall Street for "forcing" Americans into those big easy loans, which those same Americans had in fact clamored for, we have continued to see the same theories which Greenspan et al. fol-lowed through the '90's and the pre-2008 Bust era! Plentiful money. They may try to scapegoat it. They can say it ain't so. But it is so. All the Stimulus pack-ages, aid to lenders and other Pumps for the real estate market, are designed to make Recovery a reality and Pump things back into another Boom (al-though many pumps have not really gone far enough or been targeted or strong enough to give the real estate sector the dynamite that it still needs in order to stimulate full broadly based True Recovery and Prosperity).

There have been and continue to be plans and programs to funnel Gov-ernment subsidies and other bailout monies in the form of direct aid to lenders and homeowners for foreclosure prevention and relief. We have heard talk of a Bad Bank to purchase toxic mortgage assets from troubled banks and mort-gage lenders.

The Feds have drastically lowered interest rates charged by lenders and they subsidize most mortgage modifications, just as they have reduced the overnight rate they charge to its lowest level in history. Attractive FHA and VA mortgage programs have been introduced, both for qualified buyers and those on the brink of foreclosure. And who is to say that 40 and 50-year direct reduction mortgages may not also soon become the norm?

In an effort which simultaneously involved the Judicial, Executive, and Legislative Branches working in tandem with "private" lenders, agreements were reached, and we almost had legislative enactment of new laws which would have permitted Bankruptcy Judges to alter home mortgages in Chapter 13 cases. A further effort to prevent and resolve foreclosures. As the Associated Press reported on January 8, 2009: "...the change in bankruptcy law would ease the foreclosure crisis that has dragged the economy into the worst reces-sion in decades."

Indeed, this "cramdown" power was designed to prod lenders (a lever over their heads), to be more aggressive in working out modification agreements with borrowers as a preferable solution to the time, cost and other downsides of waiting for a bankruptcy judge to make the call down the line. Still another tool, or Pump, in the Government's arsenal on the Road to Recovery – not law yet, but perhaps in the future.

How curious, how suggestive of the predictable ebb and flow of these histor-ical cycles, and how illustrative of the pivotal role that realty values and ease of borrowing play in the scheme of things, that in 1994 the refrain from Washington ("action must be taken to stabilize values and minimize the damage" from the then-"mini-wave" of foreclosures), was so similar to the rhetoric of 2009-2014!

In early 1994 then-Congressman Jim Moran (D-Va.), was on the House Floor introducing the newly-minted "Homeowner's Equity Protection Act". The Bill was supposed to end the banking industry's control over the foreclo-sure process by requiring that properties with Federally-insured mortgages in foreclosure be sold at "professionally conducted, public competitive auction, after a well-advertised Marketing Program of sufficient length to maximize the number of potential bidders".

Today, just as in prior Down Cycles, Values, Activity and Lending Liq-uidity must all be Pumped up. The elimination of drags on credit availability and property values is part of the process. The scope of Government means, or Pumps, while evolving and expanding, has still not been "enough for this crisis". And Government Pumps do get more expensive and become more in-trusive, in our so-called free market economy.

Enough said: our System is really a Socialism-tinged hybrid form of Cap-italism. With all its theoretical (and real) virtues, the System, in its purest form, just cannot make it anymore. Contrary to how it has been presented in text-books, it can no longer meet the Needs and Desires of Today's Society.

We had to introduce some of the "taboo" into the mix to enable the Free Market to really work. Thus, a strong guiding hand from the Government. The potpourri of initial Federal "stimuli" starting in 2009-2010 bear an eerie, albeit perhaps comforting similarity to the workings of that "ideal" benevolent despot portrayed by the Greek philosopher Plato in his political science stan-dard "The Republic". His was that good-hearted, well-meaning, all-knowing King making the "good" decisions for a desperate flock in need, a flock inca-pable of really governing itself and Doing Right for itself.

Elected, sure, and not necessarily (or always) autocratic, perhaps this is a role that Washington has had to, and increasingly must, take on, often using labels and explanations which are not quite harmonious with its undertakings as the unspoken Absolute Guardian of the Economic Machine. Democracy and Capitalism, yes; Free Enterprise and a Free Market, yes; but along with it, a growing web of Government Dominance and creeping Socialist Overtones.

Even before the initial Intervention of 2008 the tinge was there. There has long been an expanding precedent for the growing use of Pumps, in bad times as well as good. Decades ago this was the case with critical sectors and industries, i.e., Amtrak, the airlines, the steel industry. But now, bigger falls for a sprawling System, larger extremes, deeper Cycles, bigger risks and bigger needs, and much higher stakes, have demanded a more pervasive Government role and presence, and thus we have the Treasury taking proprietary ownership interests in heretofore sacrosanct private enterprise. And this is not an ownership in the sense of an emergent crisis in time of war leading, for example, to nationalization of an industry or a fleet of ships for vital national security purposes. This is much more.

Our's is not a utopia, and we accept it, it's okay, it's just the way things are and have to be. Just keep printing the Green, roll out the new props to get and keep things rolling, expanding, and giving. Literally and figuratively, the Government has been rewriting the rules, norms, and laws of our Economic System, to rescue us from the Bust, to pave the way for the next Boom – indeed, to "protect" us, at least for the moment, from ourselves, and to help us continue to spoil ourselves.

A more jaundiced view would be to call it a variation of our own National Ponzi Scheme. The Stimulus, the new Programs, as with many established programs at all levels, are real enough to all of us. They make things happen. But just like Social Security and Medicare, with the overall psychology of endless borrowing, the printing of more and more money, and the floating of bonds and other deferrals for expenditures which should be funded out of current working budgets, the reality, and certainly any claims to viable fiscal or monetary control, is but a smokescreen. There is an awful lot of punting. We satiate our thirsts for another day – but is any of it real?

Since perception is indeed reality, the answer, as a practical matter, is "Yes". In theory, in truth, of course, the answer is "No". But this is not the issue here. Borrowing enough time, and living on borrowed time, is fine, especially if it seems to be the only way to go. The only means to survive and thrive, as we have continually redefined the words "Survival" and "Prosperity". Create Illusions, but if you create enough of them, and they meet our Needs and Expectations, who cares? Just make the System work – for today – and tinker and cajole, and the System will always live to see another day.

And with the way things in our world are presently constituted, does the Government really have any choice but to make it so? Should we emerge, or re-emerge, someday, with alternate Foundations for the Creation and Expansion of Wealth sufficient to feed the Needs of an exploding populace which harbors its own explosive growth of Desires, perhaps the bases and the means will be different. And perhaps artificial Pumps and our present dependence on Real Estate as the Pillar will change.

But nothing of the sort seems imminent. And even if there were to be new foundations for the creation of wealth, real estate will always remain in increasing demand and grow in value, although perhaps in a more genuine sense. In the meantime, however, it's the Only (Real) Game In Town; so take heart, the nature of our Economic Cycles, and the Sustaining Role of Real Estate in those Cycles, is not going anyplace anytime soon, if ever, at all.

CHAPTER II

YOU MUST INVEST & SPECULATE – IN YOUR HOME
& OTHER PROPERTY – TO HOLD OR TO FLIP

Why? Why invest, or speculate, in bad times or even during good times, with all the negative talk about how real estate has already "permanently" peaked, how it can just no longer climb in value by the leaps and bounds that we have seen in the past?

There are, quite simply, Two Important Answers to this question:

First, there is that strong body of Traditional Reasons To Invest And Speculate. Gains, Growth, "Advantages", and Tax Breaks (Profit Areas). In addition to family-related and other personal non-pecuniary motivations, there are overriding, indisputable Basic Rationales for Prudently Dealing in Real Estate, both for the Short and Long Terms. ("Yields" will be discussed later in this Chapter.)

Secondly, the shrewd purchase and resale, or retention, of real estate, particularly where you try to Capitalize On Market Upswings In Bust-Recovery-Boom Cycles, will additionally lead to huge rewards. Take advantage of future growth, the inevitable gains from the Recovery Cycles. Get ahead. Ride the waves from the Bust. Recoup. Try to be in action on every ground floor and hang in there. Be there when the Market starts to turn back up, with Holdings (from year's past), and hopefully Holdings acquired on attractive terms, at low prices, during the downside of the Cycles. With the massive Government Pumps in play and which must still come into play, this time around the potential gains on the next upswing, (which gains would to a certain extent be inevitable no matter how much or how little Government does), should be all the more dramatic within the next years.

Even during what may seem to be the worst of times, try to hold onto your home and other properties. If necessary or just prudent, attempt to modify (or discount) your mortgage, and partake of other available legal techniques to best position yourself for holding on (Chapter III). And always Buy More, if you can, on the Right Terms during those same Down Cycles.

Remember, down the road, in the end, it is usually your home that will be your primary asset, or equity; even for most business owners, the equity accumulated through ownership of the premises housing their business is typically the largest remaining hard asset of the enterprise when the business is ultimately sold or liquidated. During our lifetimes, we earn, spend, win, and lose – but when the dust settles, at retirement or some other point, the corpus and equity in our real estate holdings will probably be the real key to any future financial security. (And as history has shown, should you be so fortunate to achieve security through wealth accumulation independent of realty holdings, you will still be better off if you also invest and diversify into real estate.)

The Philosophy, the Cardinal Rules, should be clear:

- REAL ESTATE VALUES MUST RISE; DOLLARS MUST BE CREATED AND RECYCLED; OUR ECONOMIC SYSTEM DEPENDS ON CASH-FLOW FROM BLOATED REALTY VALUES, EASY MORTGAGES, OTHER EASY FINANCING, AND GOVERNMENT "PUMPS" WHICH MAKE THIS ENTIRE CONTRIVED FICTION A REALITY.
- BUY LOW, BUY RIGHT (& SELL HIGH); WHEN BUYING / SPECULATING IN REAL ESTATE AND OTHER ASSETS, A CERTAIN PROFIT MUST BE BUILT-IN, UP-FRONT, AT THE TIME OF PURCHASE – BE YOUR PLANS TO HOLD OR TO FLIP, FOR THE SHORT OR LONG TERM, FOR PERSONAL USE OR BUSINESS GAIN.

Being a shrewd buyer, in both good and poor markets, will (1) enable you to gain the maximum advantages from the Traditional Profit Areas of real estate, and (2) to further maximize your gains from Recovery Upswings following depressed Market Cycles. Today's economic climate is ripe, and it will get better. Be aggressive. Search for those under-valued opportunities, the gems and the junk alike (See Chapters VI and VII, Buying).

During a Down Cycle it is obviously easier to buy at UNDER whatever the prevailing prices may be at the particular time. But such a Philosophy is key in any market. Anybody can pay retail, or current value – seldom the wise thing to do, from a business standpoint, anyway. Unrelated over-riding concerns will at times dictate otherwise – i.e., if you "overpay" for a piece of property because your non-real estate business needs just that spot, or if as in the purchase of a home, compelling family or other personal reasons trump the goal of getting the "Best Buy" in favor of the desire for "that house". Blind obsession with absolute top profit maximization is surely not the common denominator in every purchase. But absent compelling personal or non-real estate business reasons which might prompt a particular purchase, the Guiding Rule should always be: BUY LOW, BUY RIGHT, whatever the fair market value may be at a particular time.

And always, be on guard against getting whiplash by buying on the cliff of a Boom Market (even though you may very well later recoup on upward Cycles or through ordinary Appreciation).

The Big Profit and the Potential, call it the Hedge, or the Maximization Factor, or The Icing On The Cake, lies in Buying Low, Buying Right. Get a Good Deal. Then you will be better assured of making it on the short-term spec. deal. Or, if you are in it for the longer haul, you will start out one step up, cautiously optimistic of market gain, (nobody ever knows exact time frames), yet still realistically in control, in a good position, to begin with, on Day One.

The seasoned practitioner will remember Market Cycles and recount his old experiences. But even though that innate magic of real estate must, and will, return (with timing again always uncertain), Recovery will not always mean quick double-digit growth and roaring demand right out of the gate. Patience combined with the up-front Hedge is the way to go. And in our evolving economy, should the present downturn lead to a more prolonged doldrums of lower or horizontal movement, regionally or nationally, before there is a significant upturn, (even in the midst of better indicators and a healthier picture), this Buying Philosophy will always afford the best security and potential.

Prudent purchases and sensible retention and management of your portfolio, (no harm in also profiting through quick Flips), will result in Diverse Forms of Profit over the longer term, especially when accentuated by the pops from market upswings. But nonetheless, there will always be variables – which you can Hedge.

Selling any commodity high, or at retail, is terrific. But it is wise to have that margin from Day One, such that you may also sell at a wholesale price, or someplace in between, whatever the asset or market, and still realize a profit. Ineffective management of holdings, less-than optimal yields or resale prices, market glut, unexpected expenses and problems, must all be anticipated and absorbed. There is always a Purchase Price (Downside) Risk; build that cushion in on Day One. And especially so in our present economic climate and the period of challenges that awaits us before the next large Cyclical Upswing.

A certain resilience is always necessary to succeed in a market such as our's. Plan for the unexpected and the downside while following more positive day-to-day Rulebook Tenets of the successful investor. Look for the good times, for money and values to multiply. But get that Hedge, that security blanket, at the time of purchase.

Buy Low from motivated sellers, Structure your Deal, be clever in your Financing, and then Proceed to do your Short-Term Flip or Longer-Term Investment (See Subsequent Chapters).

Buy Low, Buy Right, find under-valued Deals in a buyer's market. You must know any market in which you are buying, just enough, to know when you spot a Good Buy. A Good Deal, a below market deal, can be right for any number of reasons. You need not make a career out of learning everything about a market. No reason to become a walking statistician. Markets are large, in terms of types of properties, price brackets, and geography – and you need not try to master all data and prices.

Zero in on an area which you already know or decide to learn, and a price range you can handle. Scope out some Sources and initial prospective properties. Do the basic everyday things that one does in looking for real estate – observe visually; scan newspapers, signs, brokers, the internet, the many lists which are weighted with distressed and other below-market priced offerings (See Subsequent Chapters). Get out there and look. Get a feel for the comparables, for asking prices, for the work required, for the pluses and minuses of various properties, and for seller motivations and needs.

Know a value when you see one – through your own learning curve, through your on-the-job empirical experience and through your own growing feel for values. Examine applicable sales comparables with brokers, through online or other records which chronicle recent activity, at the County Hall of Records or with the municipal tax assessor.

Find an appraiser who will accommodate you with conservative broker price opinions (BPO's, mini-appraisals), of properties you may be considering. Speak to local realtors and mortgage brokers about price trends. Read the newspapers, pick up those throw-away realty magazines at the supermarket, get educated by attending local auctions, visit realtor open houses, inquire at "for sale by owner" properties, examine multiple listed properties with your broker.

Check online sites which offer value ranges for specific properties – but understand that such sources are only one "opinion" and not the "gospel".

Buy at below prevailing market prices – how much lower is a matter of judgment which can only be made once you have seen and started to learn a market. Every property must be considered based on price, a myriad of local issues, and overall considerations of its own Potential(s).

You will find Good Deals at below market – to live in, to rent out, to flip, or to otherwise speculate in – no matter how good or bad a market may be. Again, you want to try to sense things and avoid buying on the Cliff of a Boom. You want to learn enough to be able to buy under market, in a good Cycle, before the peak. The best strategy is to do most of your buying at below current market prices in a Bust or Recovery Cycle, when things are at their lowest ebb. Timing and Knowledge are key. You need to get the pulse of any market you are operating in. And never forget: A Great Buy can be had in any market.

Without, for the moment, even addressing Price Gains, or Profits, which result from Appreciation over time, or Profits generated by Rehabbing or Converting a property to a Higher or Better Use (Legally and/or Physically), it goes without saying that every practitioner has stories about making money simply by Buying Low, Buying Right in a depressed market, and then Riding the inevitable Upswing.

I mean the raw gain based on the difference between purchase price and subsequent value, due to mere Cyclical Upswing. Not gains from other factors. Not those gains which are created by the buyer himself or by external circumstances – i.e., socio-economic, transportation, commercial or other changes in a locale. Cyclical Profits, From Smart Buying in Bad Markets. That shot in the arm jolt.

In a buyer's market during the 1980's I bought a primary residence in a desirable suburban North Jersey town. Interest rates were very high, prices soft, the multiple listing was jammed with listings and attractive seller incentives.

And this house was no fixer-upper. Blocks from a state-of-the-art elementary school, located in a choice neighborhood. It was a "for sale by owner" deal, with a savvy seller at that. His family grown, he and his wife were down-sizing to another State, no matter what, and the market was just against him.

My below market bid settled at $170,000.00 and my seller took back a sizeable first purchase money mortgage. (He had paid just shy of $30,000.00 for this "development" style Dutch Colonial not that many years earlier.) And some eight years after my purchase I would sell in a Boom Market, through a broker, within days of listing and after fielding multiple over-asking price offers. After commission and closing costs my net profit was $300,000.00. Not bad for a $40,000.00 down deal, which in the interim provided a comfortable home at reasonable carrying costs. And yes, the only work that I did on the property was painting and floor coverings.

During a serious market lull some years back I purchased a new condominium unit in Central Jersey direct from the builder. A garden-apartment style simple one floor unit, very basic. At the time this was a relatively new breed in the area. The complex of 120 units was located near a mall and growing office and tech facilities, in close proximity to mass transit, interstate highways, the Jersey Shore, and all sorts of commerce.

But it was a tough market. The builder was marking down his remaining units. Like other spec buyers in the complex, I initially found myself carrying a vacant condo before finding a tenant. The builder was one of the largest in the State, substantial and knowledgeable. But this project was built to sell. Having no intention of later selling previously-occupied units, his goal was not to become a landlord. The plans and economics made sense to him only if he could sell out, on the best terms possible, given market conditions.

Caveat – he could "afford" to sell cheap in a bad market because he had bought and developed in accordance with our Cardinal Rules. With foresight, he had obtained the land a few years earlier at well under market. And he saw the Potential and knew the socio-economic trends in his market area. First: Buy Low, Buy Right. And then, "What To Do With It?" He set about his plan of development – on a larger scale than rehabbing or building just a house or two – but using the same overall concepts.

He took his Good Buy, his raw land, and "Converted" it to a Higher and Better Use, Legally and Physically (Chapter IX). And he did it right, so right that he had enough of a cushion to sell, or dump, many units at wholesale prices in a soft market, and still come out with a solid profit. And after the builder's enrichment the stage would be set for the next in line, the little guys, like myself, to play out a similar sequence, this time one unit at a time.

In any case, I closed on one of the last first-floor one-bedroom units, with a dishwasher and painting upgrade, for about $38,000.00 with a mere $800.00 down! I rented it out and had modest success with decent tenants. The rental income basically covered my mortgage and other operating costs, including condo fees, and I had minimal vacancies. But again, this was a prime example of a Prudent Under-Market Price Purchase in a Weak Market.

I ultimately resold at a considerable profit, though not at the peak price the unit would attain during my tenure of ownership. Before 2008 it would be worth $230,000.00. But in the near term after my purchase, on the next one or two market Upswings, it had already jumped in value by $110,000.00.

The story of one local "non-real estate savvy" contractor who did it right, will always stick in my mind. Not for the complexity of what he did, but rather for its simplicity and his gut. Like future generations of his family who would fall into his footsteps, he amassed a real estate fortune in all the right, intuitive textbook ways.

In succession, he and his family "made it" by periodically Rehabbing their properties; by Converting some to Higher and Better Uses (Physically and Legally); by Building on some of their extra land; by being Landlords over many decades; and by Holding and benefiting from the inevitable long-term Appreciation trends. And for starters they made their money by Capitalizing on the Providence of Buying Low, Buying Right during the worst (??) Market Bust in the history of our Nation, the Great Depression.

This "investor" came from Italy and became a mason / paving contractor in Central Jersey during the early 1900's. He started as a laborer, learned some English, but had little formal education – facts which had nothing to do with his business acumen and foresight. Like many immigrants who worked with their hands, he fervently believed in the power of real estate ownership. During and after the Stock Market Crash of 1929, which heralded the Great Depression, he proceeded to buy virtually any local property he could get his hands on and find enough money, or barter, to get into.

Values were low to begin with and he got into most of his properties with little or nothing down, often by just taking over a mortgage. He bought mostly one and two-family homes, some commercial buildings, land, mixed use structures, dumps, and Great Gatsby-like grand homes. And his belief was that you should Hold onto as much as you can.

Starting with the New Deal, and on each successive Market Upswing thereafter, the value of his holdings would explode many times over. During the next 70 years his disparate collection grew into an immense fortune. Its net value would ratchet up during each Boom period, draw back a bit in the lulls and Busts, but each time, in successive Recovery and Boom Cycles, come back ever-stronger at ever-higher numbers. Today the fourth generation of his family still reaps the rewards through Rents and periodic Resales.

Since the 1970's I personally have bought, sold, and retained many properties. Most were bought below their then-current market values, often with attractive Financing terms, in Poor Markets and some during Recovery and Boom Cycles – but key, again, all purchased at attractive prices for the times and with good Financing terms.

With few exceptions these properties have generated the Traditional Categories of Profit and Gain that we expect from real estate investments (See Below), whether I was Holding for the short or the long haul. But invariably the shot in the arm has typically been rooted in getting the Good Buy on Day One – whether Flipping or Keeping, leave your purchase closing with some "real money in the bank", the Built-In Up-Front Equity of your Deal.

And today's market lows will, not to be trite, be tomorrow's bread and butter for new highs. So again, try to Hold onto what you own, get out there and Buy Right, and Maximize on the next Upswing.

HOW HIGH? They Have Always Asked, And Debated, Can Values Go? An old question, during Booms and Busts alike. Akin to the adage where the older generation laments "the young and lazy new generation" with the concern "How Can They Run Things, What Is This World Coming To?"

As far as real estate goes, the answer, quite simply, is "We Do Not Know How High Values Can Go." Nothing, as we like to "understand" our world, is ever so simply unlimited or without bounds. There are, to be sure, different benchmarks and bases of comparison. But here we are not speaking merely in terms of Busts and Recoveries, but instead we are addressing issues of basic long-term growth, through thick and thin, and notions of where it can or will "All End". We are addressing the sheer magnitude of cumulative sum market Appreciation over a long period of time. Not totally esoteric, but a more worldly cerebral question of totality – not Bust and Recovery, not down 2, up 5, down 1, up 2. But the Totality.

One thing we do know for sure, is that the Federal Government cannot, and in the long run will not, promote or permit anything less than a sustained growth, a resurgence in realty values (albeit with the hills and valleys, and with periods of strong or weak Government initiative) into and through the fore-seeable future. That is what the country Wants and Needs. And any comparison of yesterday's to today's, or today's to some future values, as if to say or imply "Stop", "Enough", "We Hit 100, We Hit 1,000, That's It", is no less silly than trying to compare the Wright Brothers to the Mercury Spaceships or today's Space Station. Apples and Oranges. Sure most things and progressions are fi-nite, but not necessarily so when events and assertive policies push them ever further ahead and there is no steel or magical barrier. Like the March of Tech-nology and Science, Real Estate will continue its forward momentum.

I remember way back in 1977 when I owned several brokerage offices in Central Jersey, a seasoned older salesperson in my employ always lamenting and incredulously asking, "How can this be? How high do these buyers think things will go?" He would absolutely insist that those young couples buying the basic 1950's style cape cods at $46,000.00 price tags, just had to lose their shirts down the road, since these same homes had originally sold for $12,000.00. I was only 25 at the time, with little experience, and Stan would preach to me endlessly that "this market" was crazy, that things were just too high. I had been an economics minor at Georgetown, and whether it was macro or micro, I learned little about real markets; but I always did have a sense, perhaps out of a naivete as opposed to Stan's more cynical negativism, that "What did it matter what the price was 20 years ago, anyway?"

Over the next years with market ups and downs, these same houses were selling for $100,000.00, then $250,000.00, and later over $390,000.00.

And not because they had been completely renovated. Not because they were located in areas which had improved. It was a fully developed town which had remained essentially the same. This was cumulative long-term Apprecia-tion. Just like all those other modest homes which saw wild growth in recent decades, with owners buying, selling, and refinancing, pulling those dollars to fuel the Real Estate Tree and the Economy at large, in so many different ways.

Along the way all creating incomes, jobs, commerce, business, liquidity, for the benefit of so many other citizens and private and public entities. The ripples, the dominoes, flesh out the Economy and feed the country – all from those Realty Values and Activity. The necessary Wave, that it has become.

My small examples are but tidbits of what has been universal for so long now. I could cite so many instances, the residential and commercial deals that I have been in, the ones that I handled for others, the ones that got away, the ones that I botched. Buy Right, Hit it Right, and let nature take its course. The self-evident truth is reality. And so is the fact that even the most shot-out, tough urban areas, having fallen to socio-economic forces and other dynamics which are independent of realty Cycles per se, may be trashed and cleared to the ground, only to again bear new and rehabbed properties, which themselves will start the process all over again. Their values will again climb over time. Just like plastic and newspapers, geographic areas get recycled, and start over, they bear new fruit, and they do, and will, Appreciate, over time, Period.

As alluded to earlier, there are essentially <u>FOURTEEN TRADITIONAL BASIC CATEGORIES OF GAIN AND GROWTH WHICH CAN BE ACHIEVED THROUGH THE LONG AND SHORT TERM HOLDING OF REAL ESTATE.</u>

YIELDS – Components of gain, profit or income, in cash, on paper, in kind or otherwise, in the short or long run, in Flip or Hold situations; before, during, and after Boom, Bust, and Recovery Markets. You may calculate, analyze, and ballpark all of the Diverse Facets of Gain and Profit. But no matter how you look at the total of the various Forms of Yield, as they may or may not be applicable to specific properties or transactions, over time, quickly or slowly, you will understand – "What Better Game Is Out There?"

As already discussed, a key factor in real estate Gain is the <u>Up-Front Built-In Profit Angle</u> which results from Buying Low, Buying Right. You are off and running if on Day One you can claim a "positive equity" (fair market value less debt; for our purposes, value less debt <u>and</u> cash investment), in your new purchase. This constitutes real Gain, a genuine Profit.

Many people feel that <u>Cash-Flow or Cash Yield,</u> (net income after all expenses), is the key element in measuring Profit in real estate transactions or portfolios. In the larger picture however, this may be but a small part of total Gain.

The relevant questions: "What is the amount of annual cash return on your investment?" "What percentage yield on your investment (initially defined as down payment plus closing costs), does this income represent?" "What is the projected income (occupancy rent, rent from cell towers, billboards, easements, air rights, and the like), and expense roll?" "Are we dealing with 'an easy to run' or prime property, which based on its purchase price will usually throw off a more modest cash return, or are we talking about a rougher, tougher, workhorse-type investment (based on neighborhood, property condition, quality of tenancy), which should be expected to throw off a higher percentage cash yield (compensating for the owner's enhanced risks and additional work and headaches – a rooming house being a prime example)?"

An annual Cash Yield of $4,000.00 on a $200,000.00 property which required a $40,000.00 cash investment constitutes a 10% cash return on your investment. And should you Refinance the property and pull all or part of your original down payment (investment) out as fresh cash, the true percentage Cash Yield on "investment" will increase dramatically as it is now measured as a factor of your "new, smaller" or even non-existent "investment", post-Refinance.

If, as in this example, after having refinanced the amount of "your" cash now actually invested were to shrink to say, $20,000.00 and net cash income remained at about $4,000.00, the percentage yield on your "investment" changes substantially. $4,000.00 cash income on a $20,000.00 investment equals a 20% cash return – double the original yield AFTER the Refinance has also put "cash money" back into your pocket!

In the real world, however, after "any kind" of Appreciation a sensible refinance of an originally $200,000.00 property should result in more than $20,000.00 net cash being pulled out. Thus, that original $40,000.00 investment would probably be reduced not to $20,000.00, but perhaps closer to $0; with additional cash on top of the $20,000.00 netted out and put into the owner's pocket! Let's say the Refinance pulls out the original $40,000.00 and increases the debt service (carrying costs) somewhat, depending on the actual amount refinanced and any differential from the interest rate on the original purchase money mortgage.

The old $4,000.00 net income might thus be diminished a bit, or not at all, or even increased, depending on any increments in the rent roll since the purchase closing. Maybe the new post-refinance cash income will remain at $4,000.00, or become $5,000.00, or maybe even $3,150.00, for example.

The point is that the owner should now have very little or even none of his own money in the deal – his original $40,000.00 has in all likelihood been pulled out, it is now available for something else, and the entire annual net cash income of the property is "pure profit" based on "no investment!" Can't measure against a zero "down payment". It is an annual income with "no in-vestment" required. (And more often than not over time refinances in all forms of real estate result in a cash surplus being pulled out above and beyond the amount of any original investment!)

One of the key elements in measuring overall Gain on retained property is Appreciation, the primary component of Equity Accumulation. The pertinent questions: "What is the potential for this property?" "What are present and historical local rates of Appreciation?" "How have the local comps fared recently?" And, "Do I start-out with Built-In-Up-Front Equity by virtue of a below market purchase?"

When Holding for the longer run Appreciation is typically where the real money is. A $20,000.00 down payment on a $100,000.00 purchase with 10 % growth in overall value over the next year, for example, translates into a property worth $110,000.00 12 months later, for a whopping 50 % paper profit on the original $20,000.00 investment in just one year. Appreciation is usually an enhanced Gain when measured, and properly so, against a Leveraged Down Payment.

And again, as subsequent Refinancing should result in more post-purchase decreases in the amount of your original investment, (Cash Yield scenario above), the percentage of Appreciation Gain, measured against the (subsequently) lower investment, will also show an ever-larger gain, after you have put cash back into your pocket through Refinancing! Higher value is higher value, whether you are selling or not.

Amortization – Simply put, paying down the principal amount on your mortgage. While some professionals (and novices) stress the importance of "paying off" a mortgage (and in a *prima facie* sense one can always argue the prudence of lowering debt and augmenting equity, by whatever means) – the goal of Amortizing is generally not a sensible primary reason for being in the real estate game.

Indeed, an Interest-Only Mortgage will not be paid down absent sale, appropriate refinance, or cash infusion.

Typically, Self-Liquidating (Direct Reduction) Mortgages, mostly 20 to 30 years in term, wherein fixed equal monthly payments consisting of both interest and principal ultimately satisfy the entire obligation, bear minimal principal reductions in their early years. And such mortgages, for a variety of reasons (i.e., cut short by sale or refinance), do not usually remain on a property for particularly long periods of time.

In the case of Balloon Mortgages, where an interest only or a direct reduction form of mortgage is paid by the borrower as if he were on a stipulated schedule, which schedule is cut short or otherwise punctuated by a lump sum payment(s) of principal on either a single scheduled date or on multiple scheduled dates – the rate of Amortization from actual cash-flow of the property is also usually small.

As a function of a property's cash-flow above and beyond what is thrown off directly to the owner, Amortization certainly constitutes a form of Gain from the investment, albeit usually a modest one. You do not "make" money in real estate through mortgage Amortization. Amortization from a property's cash-flow should be seen as a "plus" to other KEY underlying Yields. As a conscious goal it is not the aim of the savvy investor.

Depreciation – We have all heard about it, we have heard the calls to close this tax shelter and the "reasons" why it is "unfair". But it is part of the Tax Code, and it has been so for so long, in varying forms, and for good reason. Like other benefits, be they actually "earned" or imputed, which Uncle Sam attaches to various investment vehicles, Depreciation is part of the package of incentives which are there to induce both the ordinary person and Big Business alike, to do things, to take risks, to invest, to participate, to help grow the economy for the benefit (we hope), of all.

Depreciation of real estate is, to use the vernacular, an example of a Government Pump, an old one at that, which was designed to help bloat values and promote commerce. (Just as the Depreciation of other non-real estate assets – i.e., autos, machinery, systems, leasehold improvements in a variety of businesses – are Government tools designed to promote commerce and investment in diverse enterprises.)

In its different forms (straight-line and accelerated), Real Estate Depreciation is essentially an artificial bookkeeping device used to create a tax shelter. The benefits of Depreciation flow simply from the fact of owning investment real estate (even if it houses your own place of business). The premise is a paradox. As a piece of real estate is in fact typically increasing in value (Appreciation) over time, the owner is nevertheless entitled to write-off, for tax purposes, the purchase price (excluding land) as a loss; the doctrine of Depreciation says the structure (improvements on the land) is in fact wearing out, it is being depleted and shall eventually be of no value, it shall be fully depreciated or "used up" due to age, wear and tear and obsolescence.

If, for example, based on whatever Depreciation schedule and depreciable value was initially stipulated on a particular property, $20,000.00 per year could be "written off" as depreciated value, $20,000.00 of ordinary income of either the individual or entity owning that property becomes tax free for every year of the Depreciation schedule. This tax free sheltered income works down from the owner's highest income bracket for the particular year.

If, in our example, net cash income, or Cash Yield, from the property in a tax year was $5,000.00, then thanks to Depreciation that $5,000.00 would pass tax free to the owner who would still have an additional $15,000.00 tax shelter for the year. He can thus make the next $15,000.00 of his highest taxable other income tax free, be that income derived from ordinary employment, profit from some other business, interest, dividends, or the like. All due to the fact of owning a piece of property, which in reality is probably Appreciating in value at the same time that it can be claimed as a "loss".

The question becomes: "How can my accountant best advise me on how to maximize the sheltering of all or part of my realty and other income, based on the purchase price of one or more pieces of investment property?" And this goes to the method of Depreciation which should be used in a given case, and the periodically changing nuances in the Tax Code which impact the precise calculations – the province of the professional, and not any consultant or this Book.

Depreciation is a compelling benefit of ownership which historically has prompted many high-earning professionals and others, either individually or as groups, to leverage into high-ticket real estate, even parcels with very modest cash flows, in order to maximize the breadth of their tax shelters for their otherwise highly taxed maximum ordinary incomes. In the right circumstances, especially where it is accelerated and based on higher-priced real estate, this incentive called Depreciation will generate very substantial tax savings, such that the savings themselves become "effective, large cash incomes". Tax free means dollar profit.

This loophole pushes up values and generates activity. While the Depreciation angle also benefits buyers, it "enables" owners to more profitably sell many investment properties, (including apartment houses in marginal tough-to-market urban areas), for prices higher than they could ever dream of were there no such thing as Depreciation.

An owner-occupied residential property on the other hand, brings with it some very different and substantial Tax Breaks and Tax Deductions – on mortgage interest and real estate taxes. Mortgage interest, which again is the lion's share of mortgage charges in the early years of the common direct-reduction mortgage (and obviously it is the entire payment on interest-only mortgages), is a deductible item off the top portion of otherwise taxable ordinary personal income (or Corporate, should the property be held in a Corporate name). The same is true for real estate taxes. These benefits are key in determining the "true" carrying costs of a property and in comparing the costs of home ownership to paying rent.

A $3,000.00 monthly mortgage payment (principal and interest) including real estate taxes, for example, might initially include only $100.00 towards principal. Thus, $2,900.00 of the total payment is tax deductible. $2,900.00 times 12 months equals an annual deduction of $34,800.00 – the top $34,800.00 of this homeowner's otherwise taxable income for the calendar year now becomes tax free.

A loophole, an ongoing Government Pump, if you will, which an endless number of Americans have benefited from in so many ways over so many years. This deduction has helped define and promote the profits from and the prevalence of home ownership. It has augmented values and helped create and sustain markets. It has helped extend the American Dream to so much of the country. It has enabled so many to enjoy "bonus savings accounts" (higher equity and tax-free incomes thanks to their homes), to degrees which would otherwise be hard to imagine.

The stark advantages which such deductions offer is very clear. If an owner has that $3,000.00 mortgage (with $2,900.00 deductible, in our example), and a renter has a $3,000.00 monthly rent payment on his residential unit, the renter first has to pay income tax on the $36,000.00 annual rent that he pays, while the homeowner pays income tax on only $1,200.00 of his $36,000.00 annual mortgage obligation.

Supposing a 25% respective tax bracket, the renter pays his $36,000.00 rent plus $9,000.00 in income taxes, while the homeowner pays his $36,000.00 mortgage and only $300.00 in income taxes on the non-deductible $1,200.00 portion of his annual mortgage (while at the same time realizing those other wealth-accumulating benefits of ownership, not to mention the non-pecuniary ones). In real dollars spent, the renter's $36,000.00 annual obligation costs him $45,000.00; the owner's $36,000.00 "nut" costs him only $36,300.00.

Another way of looking at it is to say that had he not purchased and not been paying that mortgage, after ordinary taxes "the homeowner who wasn't" would nevertheless have given Uncle Sam $9,000.00, meaning he would have retained a net income of only $27,000.00. The Government has long picked up a good portion of the cost of home ownership – a silent partner helping homeowners own and grow equities.

While items such as maintenance costs and property insurance are not deductible expenses in the case of owner-occupied home ownership, insurance, maintenance, management fees, realtor commissions and professional fees are deductible expenses for investment properties. Mortgage interest and real estate taxes are deductible expenses for both the investor and the owner-occupant. Thus, many falsely believe that non-mortgage and non-real estate tax-deductible items also constitute Tax Breaks for the investor / landlord. They do not. They are simply ordinary operating expenses of a business enterprise – in this case, a real estate business (even if it consists of only one property).

No difference from the restaurant owner calling salaries and utilities, advertising and the cost of food, everyday business expenses. Expenses of a going business concern are "true" expenses, they are not profit and by definition they are thus not taxable; they are subtracted from gross revenues (rents, sales), in determining the amount of net profit realized from operations.

Tax Savings or, should we say, Tax Breaks or advantages as applied to the homeowner-occupant, consist primarily of deductions for mortgage interest and realty taxes, and in certain circumstances, include breaks on the Resale of the property itself.

Tax Breaks or advantages for the investor or landlord, on the other hand, lie essentially in the fiction of Depreciation; in certain Resale Tax Savings by virtue of Capital Gains; in the use of Tax-Free Swaps; and in the privilege of being able to Refinance and Leverage Tax-Free spendable dollars out of a property. (The homeowner-occupant can of course also Refinance and pull money out tax free.) And remember, a "Tax Break" is quite different from a mere tax-deductible actual business expense.

Thus, in the context of periodically changing Federal tax regulations (which go to the amount of time a property must be held to qualify and the sum of operative gains), we have a real bonus in the dual concepts of investor Capital Gains and, for qualified owner-occupied residential properties, Resale Exemptions.

For many years there have been demands from certain groups to eliminate Capital Gains treatment for profits in the resale of investment real estate. Absent the introduction of other compensating innovative changes to the Tax Code, the elimination of Capital Gains would, in good and bad times alike, be a disaster for the real estate industry. (As it would be for those other businesses which reap benefits through their own capital gains loopholes.)

And that is just what it is. Like Depreciation, Capital Gains is a form of artificial bookkeeping, a Tax Break designed to promote activity and enhance prices, to encourage the initiatives and risk-taking which are incident to the private sector's Buying, Investing in, Rehabbing, Holding, and Reselling real estate. It is a reward, another Government Pump. In real estate, as in other sectors where Capital Gains are a factor, this break has gone a long way towards building markets and creating wealth.

Loosely defined and subject to periodic changes in applicable regulations – which dictate the requisite term of ownership, calculations to determine taxable profit, and current capital gains tax rates – a Capital Gain entitles the seller (for other than owner-occupied residential), to pay a greatly reduced tax rate on any profit upon resale, after having Held the property for a certain period of time. (Profit ='s resale price less original cost, less transaction costs and capital improvements and certain repairs, plus recapture of Depreciation.) Isn't it nice to pay 15% income tax on your profit upon resale rather than, say, 30%?

Similarly, but in a different vein, a distinct Tax Break for sellers of owner-occupied residential real estate often entitles senior citizens to sell with no tax on their profit, and enables others to sell with a tax-free profit provided they purchase another equally or higher-priced residence within a certain period of time. Capital Gains in the investment sector, and Resale Exemptions for homeowners, are both profit-producing inducements.

A technical tax loophole, commonly referred to as a Tax Free Swap, is too specialized to delve into here and is used primarily by seasoned practitioners, and sparingly at that. These exchanges are best structured by tax attorneys or CPA's having the requisite expertise. But again, Swaps do constitute a force in certain markets, and they stimulate values and deals. The tax savings which they bring to the table usually amount to huge profits.

One of the greatest features of real estate investing (in addition to things like compounded Appreciation, buying with Built-In-Up-Front-Equity and Converting a property to Higher and Better Uses), is the ability to periodically Leverage Out Tax Free spendable dollars, just because you own and have rode the waves to higher values. You can Re-Leverage and further grow and use, live in, rent out, Amortize, and otherwise benefit from your "enterprise" – all the while still owning the same piece of real estate which you have (again and again) borrowed against.

This is called <u>Refinancing</u>. You do a new closing and you pull the money out. Or you may pledge the property on an equity reserve line of credit for future cash drawdowns. Of course, as the value of your collateral increases, you accumulate more and more equity, and more and more room, or ability to Refinance, time and again, perhaps, to pull out more and more dollars. Without question Refinancing is not always an easy feat during Bust Cycles; but in times of Recovery and Boom markets, Refinancing to lower mortgage interest rates, to lower payments, to extend or shorten terms, or to just pull cash out, is often a more common phenomenon than the origination of purchase money mortgages.

Speculators, landlords, and owners of residential properties alike can all Refinance. And since the transaction is a mortgage, the proceeds are tax free; they are not considered income. (The calculation of any taxable profit is deferred until a resale closing and/or the making of principal payments to the refinance lender.)

Refinance proceeds can be used for anything – to pay other bills, for college, for travel, for a down payment on another property, or indeed as a loan or gift to empower somebody else, in his or her own name, to purchase property. In so moving this tax-free money to others, we have a form of "pre-estate planning", a means to raise dollars, tax free, and subsequently transfer them to set the stage for others to create wealth in their own names through their own real estate ventures. As alluded to earlier, the Refinance means of generating spendable dollars from Appreciating real estate is often much preferable to selling.

My father, who grew up during the Great Depression and became a self-made real estate developer and landlord, essentially financed his Accumulation of buildings by Re-Leveraging. The numbers were much smaller at the time, but the principles were similar and a borrower still needed equity margins in order to Refinance. He built his own buildings, at builder's cost, and typically had Built-In-Up-Front Equity upon their completion and rental. His Up-Front equity was the product of Good Buys on the raw land, and saving on construction costs – a variation on our earlier examples of below-market purchase of existing buildings. And subsequent Appreciation would further augment his values.

Some buildings he was able to <u>Refinance</u> several times over. He would pull some of the Accumulated equity out of one building, and use it as the seed, or total investment to build another. And all the while he <u>Held</u> onto most of what he built, he collected rents (<u>Income</u>), he <u>Depreciated</u>, he <u>Amortized</u>, and he saw his buildings <u>Appreciate</u> beyond his wildest imagination.

He always liked to tell the story of a local banker (in his time it was a real live banker deciding whether or not to give you a mortgage), who early on refused to do business with him, concerned, in the words of the banker, that "you're pyramiding", Pyramiding can, of course, be good or bad; just like not pyramiding can be good or bad. But properly thought-out and implemented "pyramids", both literally and figuratively, do stand the tests of time; they do endure.

The notion of "<u>Intrinsic Value</u>", in this sense not just the hard asset itself, but instead meaning certain physical aspects of the asset, specific or subjective indicia of possible future / enhanced values which come with the package ("attached" to the realty), is nothing to overlook. Aside from any other reasons to buy, you might ask whether the Deal carries some sort of "gamble" which may equate with other Ancillary Gain. In buying something you should ask yourself whether you are also testing or anticipating the socio-economic waters, the location, the trends, "changes in the air;" or whether you are looking for something else, perhaps something of a physical nature, that may in and of itself multiply your investment.

"What have I bought?" "Ten thousand square feet of warehouse space at $50.00 per foot with some Built-In Profit or Equity (really worth $60.00), at that?" Or, sensing the extra expensive overhead crane, a unique security system; ultra-close proximity to the main entrance for the airport, or the new storefront or refrigeration system, which may push the replacement or potential value above present market value, you should take it all in and think: "Can anything here amount to something special? What have I got? Might those stained-glass windows or that intricate millwork in the old tudor house mean something down the road – in its use, in a changed use of the property, in Resale or in a Conversion?"

<u>Converting To A Higher And Better Use – Legally & / Or Physically</u>: Above and beyond those diverse forms of Gain which may be gleaned from a shrewd purchase, from the operations of the Market, and from sensible Management of your property – whether you are in it for the Short-term Flip or the Longer Haul – the notion of being able to Better the Physical and/or Legal

Status (codified privileges and benefits), of a piece of real estate is, to me, both intriguing and powerful. Assuming the times and locale are appropriate, and you have the necessary resources and focus for the tasks at hand, the key words – Higher Uses and Conversion – say it all.

"Can the old industrial site become a lucrative discount retail destination? The abandoned, worn former gas station a bustling drive-through? Can the value of the 20-unit apartment house be multiplied by Converting to more pricey Condos? (To sell now, or to rent out?) Will a Variance (a change in legally permitted uses or building guidelines in the local zoning laws), or changes to a stock (standard) building plan for new construction, turn five lots into nine building lots? Which cosmetic improvements might most economically turn a given property into a superior parcel, either in its present or in a different form? What, in short, are the possibilities for a new or different Use, for Legal or Physical Development or Change, which might result in a Higher Value or Yield?"

The goal is to enhance the value and/or utility of the property, be it for purposes of Resale, Rental, Use by the owner or others, or Re-Leveraging. Value can be increased, Equity grown (for purposes of the instant discussion), by performing certain calculated work on the property   clean up and minor touch-up, partial or total remodeling, updating, wholesale renovation, construction of an addition, partial or total demolition, or new construction on the site.

Physical Work, when done literally with the owner's own hands, is often referred to as "sweat equity". (Do not confuse real-world work with those silly, often glamorous portrayals of home renovation as presented on some of the TV "Reality" Shows!)

In trying to make a Deal, hopefully a Good Deal to begin with, into a Windfall, there are also a variety of Legal Changes which can be pursued. Among them: Variances (changes in zoning, permitted uses and building guidelines); Subdivisions (dividing a parcel or tract into smaller ones, for development or for other purposes); Modifications to local Master Plans (which control use and development in a regional sense); Removal of Deed Restrictions which might otherwise prohibit desired uses or forms of development.

And a huge one: Changing the Legal Status of a residential, industrial, or commercial property, or unit(s), from its (their) pre-existing "as is" status to individual Condominium units; (a) so as to augment the overall value of the entire property; (b) so as to split the property and thus be better able to sell everything off, or to just sell some of the new Condo units while retaining others (which would have been impossible to do in their pre-Condo status); or (c) so as to effectuate new development by legally side-stepping potentially large costs and immovable road-blocks which might otherwise scuttle such plans if the division or splits of the parcel had to be accomplished through more traditional means of Subdivisions and Variances instead of the Condo Method.

Additionally, never under-estimate the scope of beneficial changes which can be made to a property's Physical and Legal Status, where an owner merely familiarizes himself with Local Building and Zoning Codes, and proceeds to do his thing by following routine Permit and Application processes in conformity with those Codes, "as is". Many times a desired upgrade or change to a property is, in one fashion or another, already permitted, and all the owner need do is follow the rules, get his permits and proceed. Every brainstorm does not imply such originality that existing Codes never contemplated the possibility!

The astute investor / speculator should always gain at least a Working Knowledge of pertinent local zoning and building Codes (Chapter IX). These substantive and procedural Rules of the Road may require only foresight and ingenuity, along with the assistance of professionals (surveyors, planners, engineers, architects, attorneys), to enable an owner to maximize his parcel's potential.

Finally, on quite another note there is Profit Based On The Quick Flip. Long ago this Genuine Method of Making Money in real estate became the lore of the get-rich-quick hucksters. They perverted it into magic; "make a fortune despite yourself". Over the years we have seen more than enough of those late-night cable TV promotions of tapes and books and "manuals" which promise to make anybody, and everybody, very rich, very easily. The guys on their yachts who will "share" their magical secrets with you. Miracle materials on the Internet. The "gurus". The big fat pulp real estate jibberish volumes which pass themselves off as "books", crammed with useless Generic forms and fantastic claims and stories, which will get you no place fast if you use them as guides to make money in quick turnovers.

But despite how much the denigration and silliness of hyped promotions have hurt investors who pay for and rely on such "guidance", and despite how it has smeared the industry and cast dispersions on words like "Flip", it is nevertheless quite true that a great deal of money can be made on the Quick Flip. (Assuming, of course, right market conditions, prudent buys, and appropriate practices in rehabbing, management, and marketing by a sensible investor / speculator.)

A Profitable Flip can be had by Reselling in essentially "as is" condition, by Reselling after fix-up, by Reselling with or without doing a Conversion, or by Reselling in an up market or in any number of circumstances – as long as the numbers and the bottom line net add up. Again, Buy Low, Buy Right!

In assessing the possibility of a quick turn-around, the basic questions pose some of the same issues which are the bread and butter of the business in general: "<u>Can</u> this property simply be put back on the market and resold for a quick profit? What are the transaction costs? Did I Buy Right? What do the conservative comps look like? Are fix-up, cosmetic repairs, a subdivision, or a variance, called for? Do I need a broker, or can I sell by myself?"

<u>So WHAT, then, is Real Estate? It is REAL; it is Intrinsic, Utilitarian, Necessary, Hard, Enduring, Unique, and Functional.</u>

Unlike many other assets, it is in no way artificial. It is much bigger than any of us, but at the same time it is something that we can have great control over – perhaps not every day of every year, but most certainly over the course of time.

It is not a merely trendy or temporal thing. Land cannot be duplicated or replaced; physical space on our planet, in any locale and for any given strategic or recreational purpose, is finite, limited. Land, property, is really as basic as air and water in an exploding, already crowded world.

<u>And it is the Lynchpin of our modern-day Economic System, and thus indeed of our Society. It is the power and dynamics of our most basic needs and our most outrageous desires. Thus, the resultant necessary Government tinkering will make it go and go, to heights, to values, which the innate workings of the market itself could never achieve, despite periods of drought or down-markets or less-than-optimal Government "promotion". The Destiny is Manifest; it is ever-increasing heights in Values and myriad Yields.</u>

CHAPTER III

GET OUT OF FORECLOSURE – REWORK
YOUR EXISTING MORTGAGE, & OTHER WAYS
TO ESCAPE OR DELAY FORCLOSURE
TO HOLD ONTO YOUR HOME & OTHER PROPERTY

"How do I get a <u>Mortgage Modification Agreement</u>?" The Goal, The Concept, is quite straight-forward: To rework, to adjust, to change the terms of your existing mortgage with your existing lender, by either (a) decreasing or stabilizing the interest rate (changing an adjustable to a fixed rate and thus avoiding future upward rate changes); (b) decreasing, eliminating, or deferring some of the principal amount remaining on the loan; (c) decreasing, eliminating, or deferring the payment of any accrued late fees or arrears; (d) extending the maturity date of the mortgage; or (e) a combination of all or some of the above. The ideal result of Modification negotiations is a document which changes the mortgage terms to reflect a lower principal amount and/or a lower / stable interest rate, and thus a lower monthly payment.

A Modification is appropriate in a variety of Situations: For those in foreclosure; for those in default but not yet in foreclosure; for those who are barely making their unaffordable monthly mortgage payments; for those who have an adjustable rate mortgage (ARM) which has an upward adjustment on the horizon; for those who may still be paying their mortgage but have a negative equity (debt exceeds present fair market value), in their property; and for those who simply want to take advantage of the times and initiatives of lenders and the Federal Government.

Without question since 2008 Workouts in the form of Mortgage Modifications have become much more common than at any time in the past. This includes modifications made directly between borrower and lender which may or may not include Federal initiatives and programs, and those which involve Federal intervention. As further detailed in this Chapter and in Chapter IV, in theory the lender's rationale to modify, to make a deal, indeed to make any sort of mortgage concession agreement, is the result of a number of factors.

Of course where the Government is underwriting or subsidizing all or part of a Modification, and thus any "losses" on the original loan which have been or may be incurred by reason of the default and modification process, it does not take a genius to realize that a lender will be anxious to modify. Generally, however, what it comes down to is the borrower must show his lender that which the lender should already understand even without any "argument" from the borrower (but the lender needs to know that the borrower understands the lender's situation, too) – namely that making a deal today is the most sensible route for the lender in the interests of sound business practices.

A lender must be convinced that a particular proposal is the best (most sensible) net or deal that it can hope for, just as it may at the same time be a good deal for the borrower. And often a borrower can illustrate pertinent facts about the property and his own status which will help a lender better crystallize this option. A deal in the present will often enable the lender to cut its losses, including those accruing costs associated with foreclosure actions, not to mention those which may be incurred in carrying and disposing of a foreclosed property (particularly in a Bad Market) after a Sheriff's Sale.

A foreclosure action can be very costly for the lender. Aside from its internal administrative costs, there are legal fees, filing fees to the Court, appraisal and continuing property inspection bills, and real estate insurance which it must secure and pay for during the foreclosure action in order to protect its interest in the collateral and protect itself against general liabilities. Then there are real estate taxes which continue to accrue, and which the lender must pay out of pocket on a current basis (or later with interest), and which if not paid will ultimately become a lien (with its attendant costs and compounding interest) on the property, a lien which has priority to, which automatically comes ahead of, the lender's own mortgage lien. And through it all, the lender is not receiving any payments on its mortgage.

If the action goes the entire route to Sheriff's Sale, the lender's costs and exposures increase dramatically. There is the deposit and advertising and other fees which must be advanced to the Sheriff in order to schedule a Sale. The costs continue should the lender "buy" (take back) the property at Sale, (which is often the case, especially today, because so many properties which go to Sale have a negative equity, meaning the amount of mortgage and other debt exceeds the value of the property). And who wants to bid at Sheriff's Sale if he is getting a property where he has to pay off so much debt that in the end he may wind up paying over market value for the property? No (few) bidders are so careless or foolish; so in such cases the property will typically "go back" to the lender at Sale.

Post-Sale, the problems and costs for the lender who took a property back keep mounting. Realty taxes and insurance continue to accrue. The now "former borrower" might have to be evicted or given storage money or otherwise paid to move, so that the "new owner" / former lender can resell his property. Legal fees and costly delays may be incurred if the former borrower challenges or otherwise seeks to delay his eviction.

Once it is vacant the lender may discover that his property must be marketed in very poor condition (and thus at a lower price), the foreclosed realty having possibly been stripped of fixtures and piping, or otherwise neglected or trashed by the former borrower or squatters. Or the lender may now have to incur out-of-pocket expenses and further delay to fix the property up in order to get a reasonable resale price.

So there are invariably larger repair or clean-up expenses, a variety of carrying costs – i.e., maintenance (grass, snow), utilities, appraisers, and property inspectors – as the matter drags on.

Once listed and marketed for sale there is the broker's commission and more legal fees to close on a resale. Repair expenses will jump should the lender have to do work or give credits to enable its buyer to meet new mortgage requirements or cure municipal Code violations. And certain debts of the old borrower which, absent its mortgage default would have been of no consequence to the lender, may also have to be dealt with.

We have not even mentioned the time (money) it costs to get to the Sheriff's Sale, and whether the borrower prolongs things and ups the ante through legal opposition or other delay tactics. And vacant, possibly boarded-up, dank, dreary, lender-owned properties marketed post-Sale, do invite the lowest of bids, their values having been further diminished from what they were or "should be".

Moreover, in those cases where there had been a bona fide tenant, or where after a Sheriff's Sale somebody claims to have been a bona fide tenant prior to the Sale, the former lender faces another set of problems, and thus costs. Most States offer substantial protection / rights to former tenants in foreclosed properties. Post-Sale it is much easier to evict a former owner than it is to evict a former tenant of that owner. State laws often entitle former tenants to an extended stay, or a new lease, on "reasonable", somewhat under market terms. This translates into still more delays in efforts to resell, and more losses for the former lender. Lenders typically do not "make" money by being landlords in such situations; often they do not even cover their expenses.

Lenders, as the saying goes, are not in the business of owning or renting real estate – they must focus on banking. Furthermore, there are other implications for lenders who take back properties, and maintaining a glut is only one of the problems. Avoiding the full route in foreclosures, getting mortgages current and back on track, is an important priority to lenders in and of itself. Balance sheets and banking ratios out of control can lead to Government (FDIC) seizure of an institution, or otherwise diminish stock value, lower debt and credit ratings, and cause a host of other problems.

They need to keep their assets, their mortgages, on the street producing. Non-performing assets are a major concern. Depending on market trends and values and the amount of equity (if any), in a property, "interest" which continues to accrue on a mortgage in foreclosure and the "lost" earning power of the lender's funds which are tied up and jeopardized in foreclosed property post-Sale, are usually nothing but bookkeeping illusions. These monies are rarely, if ever, actually realized by the lender.

Poor market trends and variables, depressed and/or declining regional values, a low broker price opinion on the property, a high repair estimate, a high LTV (loan to value ratio), or even a negative equity quote on the property, are all powerful incentives in persuading a lender to entertain a sensible Modification and "get on with life". Particularly in a negative equity situation, lenders often realize that an earlier rather than a later resolution of the problem will best limit their own overall exposures and general liabilities. Present payments in today's more valuable dollars are usually more enticing than future iffy dollars (especially with negative equity properties). Both the lender's realization that there may be no hope of ever doing anything with the borrower absent a reasonable concession, and its desire to minimize the number of underwater properties on its books, are key bottom line persuaders.

Increasingly as the "Great Recession" peaked and leveled off, Government initiatives, call it intervention or "Pumps" in the System, have provided additional impetus for lenders to play ball and modify mortgages. And where called for by market conditions, this trend shall increase. Additionally, as noted in Chapter I, the probable emerging power of Bankruptcy Court Judges to order cramdowns which change payment amounts and other terms of residential mortgages will further help persuade lenders that it can be wiser to do a <u>Modification deal (First Method),</u> with borrowers themselves, deals that might be more to their liking, than to risk more extensive losses and costs by continuing with foreclosure actions and perhaps have a Judge tell them what to do. <u>Modifications have become a key component in the Arsenal of Methods To Cure Foreclosure.</u>

Today the Key Rationale for lenders to Modify is the Federal dollars which have been going directly to lenders and States in the form of bailouts, infusions, general foreclosure help and Modification assistance for individual borrower transactions to help underwrite and subsidize the deals.

Both the Federal Government and the States have rolled out a variety of modification programs and other proposals designed to help stave off new foreclosure filings and remediate certain categories of loans already in foreclosure. Some apply only to borrowers who are current, others apply to those who are not. Certain programs apply to Freddie Mac or Fannie Mae loans. Most impose gross income criteria versus carrying costs as their qualifying basis, and others put limitations on the amount of negative equity or arrears or length of default which a qualifying property may have. And then there are the more general Federal Incentives offered to lenders to encourage and assist the purely in-house lender-driven "Mod. Programs".

<u>The Question – Procedurally and for Qualifying purposes – "How (In The Traditional Sense) Does One Get A Modification?"</u> There are a variety of components, or factors, involved in the process. Both the applicant and his property need to be qualified. Negotiations, good faith dealing, follow-up and follow-through, are all important if you expect to make a deal. The lender (or Government) wants to see a number of things before it will qualify and execute a Modification.

Again, in every case the lender (or Government) must be Convinced That A Modification Is The Most Sensible Route under the circumstances. The "Rationale" for a lender (or the Government) to cooperate must be clearly articulated in both verbal discussions, and in the Package of paperwork which is submitted in requesting and "arguing" for a Modification.

A crucial component of any Package is commonly called the "Financial Worksheet For Mortgage Modification". Upon being notified of a Modification request or often upon any mortgage default, most lenders will automatically send their own customized (or a Government) Package of forms to the borrower. The Worksheet lists income and (hard) expenses, among other data, and should be supplemented with appropriate proofs and a summary of both net (or gross) monthly income and under most of the "earlier" Mod. Programs, what is called monthly gross Discretionary Income. Discretionary Income is the balance after subtracting expenses, including the mortgage payment (whether currently being made or not), from income.

In completing the Financial Worksheet there are certain rules of thumb. Attach Proofs of stated income – i.e., tax returns, pay stubs, W2's, 1099's or letters of verification or promise. Today, promises of employment and rental income – be it from a separate attached legal or illegal unit, from a family member a friend or a genuine third-party tenant, constitute acceptable forms of income for purposes of modifying mortgages. So do benefits such as Social Security, Disability, Unemployment, and the like, and "informal" income like certain forms of "assistance" from household members.

Itemized expenses should be "hard" expenses – not frivolous or unnecessary ones. This includes current mortgage obligations and minimum credit card payments – again, whether current or not – and other basics like food, utilities, tuitions, support obligations and auto expenses.

Under "Disposable Income Programs", an Analysis for the ideal Modification candidate will show his gross monthly income, netted out, less expenses, equals a "surplus", or a "Discretionary Income", of about $200.00 left over at the end of the month. This tells the lender that with current mortgage payments being made, the borrower is just barely "making it", but in the real world he is not making it at all. A $1,000.00 Discretionary Income, on the other hand, indicates that the borrower does not need a break. The lender must be persuaded that the applicant cannot really handle his current mortgage payment, but a reduction in the monthly, of $400.00, or perhaps $900.00, for instance, should make life more bearable and enable the "right type" of borrower to get back on track and start making new more "manageable" payments in a timely manner.

Under the dominant <u>Federally Subsidized HAMP (Home Affordable Modification Program)</u>, however, and indeed under most in-house lender and other Federally Subsidized programs, the trend has been away from the Disposable Income approach, and to what we may generally call the "one-third formula(s)". (Approximately 33 % of monthly gross income should cover monthly mortgage principal and interest, real estate tax and real estate insurance payment.) Under HAMP, which most lenders are participating in as this is written, the Borrower is offered modified terms which typically include an initial 2% interest rate, an interest rate cap of several points higher for the life of the modified mortgage, up to a 40 year payout, forgiveness / forbearance of certain arrears, a principal reduction, and the opportunity to qualify by using lenient income criteria which include a 31% (or so) gross income figure in order to pass muster for carrying a "new" monthly mortgage payment. Successful completion of a trial monthly period of payments will qualify the borrower for a modified permanent loan.

Again, the lender may also want to see proofs of Monthly Minimums and Payoff Statements (balances due), on other Fixed Debts (i.e., credit cards, auto loans).

A brief Hardship Letter must also be submitted. Hand-written or typed, it should be clear and to the point. This explanation of past and/or present circumstances should show that the Hardship has been genuine and significant, perhaps now partially "cured", and it should indicate how the Hardship has hindered ability to pay. It must show why the borrower could not, and still cannot, make the originally stipulated payments. It should show why he is in arrears, or on the edge and paying, perhaps, but just barely so, and about to topple as he is unable to sustain the current payments.

And the conclusion to be articulated is that at this point, having already weathered all or part of his Hardship, the applicant has either bottomed out, is on the rebound, or is treading water with his current payment but in any case can become and remain timely, if the payments are just lowered to a more "manageable" level – i.e., the requested reduced modified figure. Reference to the Financial Worksheet and the Discretionary Income or the One–Third Income Ratio is basic to the Hardship Letter.

Recognized hardships are diverse and sometimes quite subjective. They include: Illness; Death of a spouse or co-borrower; Military duty; Funeral expenses for a relative; Incarceration; Divorce; Separation; Medical bills;

Unexpected expenses; Auto problems or Accident; Failed business venture; Job loss or Relocation; Employment cutback; Any forms of Reduced income; A picture of an applicant who is living week to week with no cushion and rising expenses yet getting by or not getting by at all; or an applicant with an Adjustable Rate Mortgage and higher payments on the horizon or, worse yet, with a Predatory Mortgage.

Lenders may be more motivated to deal when (supplementing their own valuations), they are presented with evidence based on a more complete, or an interior inspection, that the property is worth less than its total debt (Negative Equity, Underwater), or that it has only a bare marginal equity. In this regard a BPO (Broker's Price Opinion), repair estimates, documented comparables, or a brief summary of negative local market conditions (detailing neighborhood blight, boarded-up houses, environmental taint, adverse publicity, or even localized gang violence or problems with the school system) to accentuate low comps are all persuasive. Appropriate pictures and news clippings can also be helpful Exhibits.

The lender will want to review the applicant's Bank Account statements. It is of little consequence what they show in terms of a complete picture, though evidence of substantial cash flow or compensating balances will be suspect and dilute any notion of Hardship which might justify a Modification. The applicant must also submit a standard Authorization form empowering the lender to independently verify data and statements: copies of recent tax returns; an authorization for the IRS to release documents; relevant leases and profit and loss statements; a utility bill proving residence; a Dodd Frank certification; and any number of ancillary documents such as financial proofs and divorce decrees.

The lender is not greatly concerned about where Past Income went (above and beyond information in the Hardship Letter). Any questions regarding the disposition of income which was not spent on mortgage payments or saved for future payments (rarely will this issue arise), can best be answered by reference to the Hardship Letter or the lame, yet common explanation of "poor money management" in the face of problems and cash shortfalls which made it impossible to meet necessary obligations in full. In certain cases, a Modification Agreement may require the borrower to complete credit counseling.

Quite different from negotiating a Short Sale (Chapter IV) where the primary lender (the first mortgagee), is concerned with the ultimate disposition, or pay off of any Second Mortgage on the premises, neither the existence nor the payment of secondary financing is a big issue in the lender's consideration of a Modification request.

In considering a Mod the lender will run a Credit Report on the applicant. This is standard practice, and a low score with negative entries will be expected. The most relevant part of the Report is any evidence of fresh debt, which may either throw the qualifying ratios out of whack or otherwise constitute a stumbling block to an Agreement if the nature or scope of such debt is construed as evidence of bad faith or recklessness by the applicant.

All paperwork should be submitted as one Package, with a brief Transmittal Letter; a Summary Statement of totals, ratios, and the argument; and attached Exhibits.

The Tools, Programs, Techniques and Avenues for Curing and/or Delaying Foreclosure are indeed a Myriad Waterfall Menu framed by both Old and New Initiatives, Trends, Legislation, Judicial Activism, Government and Systemic Policy and Outright Ingenuity.

A quick overview of the primary Federal Programs and Initiatives to Cure and/or Delay and thus Get Out of Foreclosure (overlap of First with Second Methods):

HAMP – Home Affordable Modification Program, discussed above.

HAFA – Home Affordable Foreclosure Alternatives, including a focus on the Short Sale and Deed-In-Lieu of Foreclosure.

MHA – Making Home Affordable Program, since 2009 a major force to help stabilize the markets and assist those who are struggling.

HAUP – Home Affordable Unemployment Program; among other things it can suspend payments for up to two years.

HARP – Home Affordable Refinance Program, to assist homeowners who are current but underwater and struggling.

PRA – Principal Reduction Act

2 MP – Second Lien Modification Program.

Preserving American Home Ownership Act – A proposal to create "a shared appreciation" mortgage via a modification whereby lenders receive a portion of the property's future appreciation in exchange for modifying.

Another Way To Get Out Of Foreclosure is by negotiating an (Existing) Mortgage Restructuring / Reinstatement Repayment Plan (Third Method). Such an Agreement is appropriate in circumstances which are not amenable to a Modification. Indeed, until recently "the old" Restructuring / Reinstatement Method had long been the most common "Cure". These plans are essentially designed to repay the delinquency and resume regular monthly payments.

This process is not to lower interest rates or principal balances. The "break" here is not, as in Modifications, a write-off or write-down by the lender, but rather a negotiated temporary new payment, or repayment schedule, structured to repay (almost) everything overdue, to "catch up", and ultimately to pick up on current payments as originally set forth in the mortgage.

Certain arrears, late fees, and legal costs incurred by the lender in the foreclosure action may be partially paid up front, paid later in one lump sum, added onto the tail end of the mortgage in the form of a balloon, and/or be made part of a new temporary short-term monthly payment schedule (which can initially be higher or lower than that stipulated in the mortgage). But again, this is a temporary revision, it is not a permanent change in mortgage terms. The goal is to reach a point at which regular payments can resume after, one way or another, having either fully cured or made arrangements to fully cure the arrears, in order to Get Out Of Foreclosure.

Most of the salient points which comprise the lender's Rationale to negotiate a Modification overlap in explaining its Rationale to negotiate a Reinstatement.

However, where a property has a negative equity (one of the most important criteria in persuading a lender to Modify), while a lender would certainly be willing to accept full repayment (instead of forgiving or cutting debt, i.e. Modification), such a full repayment (Reinstatement) is a windfall to the lender. Absent other reasons, in a strictly dollars and cents analysis, only the most imprudent borrower would opt for Reinstatement where he has little or no equity in the property.

As this is written the operative mindset is not "Let me repay", or "Let me catch up", but rather "I'm underwater", "Give me a break", or "This is the bailout era, where is my bailout?" (Indeed, even the borrower with positive equity who is able to pay his stipulated obligations is often looking for his "bailout".)

In any case, <u>Reinstatement</u> is the "old" stand-by means of Getting Out Of Foreclosure, and it was the norm long before <u>Modifications</u> became the rage. With the astronomical number of negative equity situations today, however, the <u>Modification Method</u> has become the most viable and appropriate method for the typical borrower. And when the Market Cycle ultimately tips back upwards again, the Reinstatement Method will most likely re-emerge as the more common of the two techniques.

In making the case for Reinstatement, the borrower wants to show the lender its own downside in the event they do not reach an agreement (Rationale). The borrower should paint the most modest picture possible as to positive equity in the property when negotiating a Reinstatement. A lender who senses little equity will feel more vulnerable and be more inclined to negotiate borrower-friendly Reinstatement terms.

In addition to handling the Appraisal / Equity points, again it is incumbent for the borrower to produce proof of Ability to make Regular (existing) monthly payments (Financial Worksheet); evidence of Resources / Sources with which to fund any lump sum or augmented payments; Bank Statements which show (preferably) an adequate cash flow from which to meet obligations; Tax Returns; and a Hardship Letter evidencing improved current circumstances compared to the "recent" hardship period such that the borrower can claim he is back up and running (better).

In essence, unlike the Modification scenario (where there is typically negative equity; a poor market and a borrower who may be "a good guy who means well" but has been "through it" and is on the proverbial wing and a prayer, yet who with that "break" can carry on and save his lender from having to take back still another underwater house), in the Reinstatement situation we probably have positive equity, a lender who might feel a bit vulnerable yet at the same time more in control, and a stronger borrower who has regained his footing to (probably) go forward with his pre-existing payments and either come up with a lump sum or otherwise handle augmented catch-up payments.

<u>The Fourth major Method used to Work Out Of Foreclosure involves consummating an (Existing) Mortgage Forbearance Agreement</u>. Forbearance by the lender may include consent to a delay in the collection of regular payments, a temporary moratorium on legal action in furtherance of a foreclosure, or a delay in setting or carrying out a Sheriff's Sale. Nothing is actually called

off or cancelled. The lender is "giving" the borrower time, or a chance (often for a price) to perform or to Cure.

The lever for the lender is that upon the occurrence or non-occurrence of a certain event or the maturing of a stipulated old or new obligation for the borrower, the lender can halt its Forbearance and pick up on the litigation or its other rights or remedies at whatever point they had been put on hold, and proceed. (And any "price" that was paid by the borrower is typically non-refundable – see below.)

A Forbearance Agreement may be part of, or executed in contemplation of or in conjunction with, an (anticipated) Reinstatement or Modification Agreement, in which case the lender holds off on its action pending the execution of such Agreement or the borrower's performance or compliance with specific conditions precedent for the Reinstatement or Modification Agreement. The borrower is given or pays for the chance to perform, yet the lender has reserved its right to immediately move forward if he does not perform.

Often a Forbearance Agreement stands alone. For a stated Consideration to the lender, the borrower may bargain for an Agreement to hold off a Sheriff's Sale for a given period of time, with or without further guarantees. Similarly, a Forbearance Agreement, standing alone, might simply state that the lender will put a hold on further proceedings pending the borrower's closing on a refinance or sale of the property. Consideration paid for such agreements may or may not be made a credit against the overall mortgage debt which is due to the lender – depending, obviously, on the lender's motivation and position, typically the product of market and equity conditions.

The Fifth Method, an (Existing) Mortgage Reorganization Plan Pursuant to a Chapter 13 Bankruptcy filing, is the primary means used to effectuate a judicially-imposed "legal plan" of repayment. The United States Bankruptcy Court, periodically the butt of barbs and wrath from politicians, interest groups, and the media, has been substantially revamped in recent years. Criticisms of the Court and the System have run the gamut – "The Code favors major lenders; it favors borrowers; it favors the credit card companies; it favors the deadbeat small debtor."

In any case inasmuch as it is Federal Law, The Bankruptcy Code, as its many provisions are collectively referred to, supersedes State Law. On its face it can alter the course of proceedings in any lower court including State Courts which handle foreclosure dockets. While a more detailed look at Bankruptcy provisions is reserved for Chapter VII, in the present discussion it should be noted that the Code's main operative section for purposes of "Reorganization" is "Chapter 13" ("Chapter 11" for Corporate Reorganization).

As Federal Law the mere filing, the initiation of a Chapter 13 case, or Petition, as it is commonly called, places an Automatic Stay, a hold (pending dismissal or completion of the bankruptcy case or other Order of the Bankruptcy Court), on all other aspects of the petitioner's foreclosure action. Whatever the next step would have been, whatever time period had been passing between legal events in the State Court foreclosure action, whatever upcoming Court dates may have been scheduled, and whatever Sheriff's Sale date may have been or might have been about to be set, at any stage of the process all of this, and everything else, is stopped in its tracks, put on hold, pending direction from the Bankruptcy Court.

Even if the Sheriff receives notice of a bankruptcy filing just minutes before the Sale is scheduled to be held, the notice stops the Sale, Period (just like a Federal Court of a different kind, an Appellate Court, ordering a Stay of an Execution previously scheduled by a lower Court in a capital case).

If, as in New Jersey, where the defendant (borrower) has 35 days from receipt of the filed Foreclosure Complaint and Summons in which to file an Answer, he filed for bankruptcy protection on, say, Day 34, without having already submitted an Answer, the clock is stopped; and, assuming the foreclosure matter is not otherwise resolved through the Bankruptcy Court or by other agreement, then upon any dismissal of the bankruptcy case, perhaps two or seven months later, for example, the State clock will start running again at Day 34 and the defendant will have his one remaining day in which to Answer.

Even as he is instantly receiving his Automatic Stay, the "traditional" Chapter 13 case will still require certain subsequent compliance by the Petitioner / Debtor (aka Defendant / Borrower in the foreclosure case), including: (1) Submission of a Repayment Plan which is subject to Hearing and Court approval, or Confirmation; and (2) Commencement of current or revised mortgage payments plus a portion of arrears, on a monthly basis, to be paid through the Bankruptcy Trustee. Historically, the ultimate goal under the traditional "13" has been to Reorganize the debt via a Court-approved Plan which in the end will require the debtor to keep current on his monthly or revised payments, in addition to paying off arrears in monthly installments, usually over 36 to 60 months.

This is called a Chapter 13 Reorganization. It Stays the foreclosure action pending completion of a Bankruptcy Plan. And assuming all of the required payments are made, the debtor will ultimately emerge from bankruptcy, all caught up and current on his mortgage, and the pending foreclosure will be dismissed.

This simplified account has long been the essence of <u>Curing Foreclosure through a "true" Bankruptcy Reorganization</u>. Valid? Yes. Successful and practical as a rule? Not always. Why? Because most borrowers who cannot afford, or who are not disciplined to pay, their monthly obligations, due to legitimate financial issues, other hardship, or lack of proper fiscal management (and the latter has long been the crux of most foreclosure cases), cannot and do not so simply become timely on those same monthly payments and simultaneously pay and keep current on the payment of any additional catch-up, which may be substantial.

In January 2009 (alluded to in Chapters I and II), a trend began evolving in the Bankruptcy Courts (by way of consents from certain institutional lenders), which in certain types of cases would give Bankruptcy Judges the power to alter components – i.e., interest rate, principal, term, and arrears – of residential mortgages. In March 2009 this trend was "almost" codified into Federal Law by the U.S. Congress (both Chambers did not approve).

This new power of the Bankruptcy Courts was to include the authority to order "cramdowns" on residential mortgages. Whenever this notion is codified into law, probably in the not-too-distant future, such a new and improved Chapter 13 process should make "13's" an increasingly popular and effective means by which homeowners can Reorganize their debts on more attractive and realistic terms than exist today. It would also make "13's" a more potent lever, or tool, for borrowers to use in pushing lenders into negotiating more favorable Modification deals outside of, before, or in lieu of, bankruptcy. (As it is today, lenders abhor the delays, costs and variables that a "13" subjects them to.)

It must be stressed that any such impending judicial power which might help compel Modifications would not apply to all foreclosure cases which go Chapter 13. Based on the scope of any Negative Equity, whether the borrower / debtor has "sufficient income", whether the mortgage has a "high" interest rate, the nature of the hardship, and whether there was any taint of predatory lending at the inception of the mortgage, in the scope of judicial discretion a

Bankruptcy Judge can always either approve or deny a Modification request. Modifications / Cramdowns at the hands of the Bankruptcy Court will some-day surely be a remedy, but not by any means a universal one.

Delay – that catch-word associated with foreclosure defense. Delay the onset of the action. Delay the process of the action. Delay the last steps, Delay the Sheriff's Sale.

There are many ways to "deal" with foreclosure through (Sixth Method) "Delay Mechanisms". Delay tactics or "devices", as many in fact really are, are designed and used on the one hand simply to gain more time, free occupancy and use of the premises by the borrower, with neither hope nor intention of ever resolving the foreclosure on its merits. The focus is on dragging the process out as long as possible; call it "free rent".

Delay, however, may also be used to accomplish more strategic "positive" or "cure" objectives – to gain time in order to save money or find capital to get positioned to later negotiate with the lender; to just gain time to negotiate; or to slow the clock in the hope that some kind of "break" will come along later.

Increasingly, in today's climate many debtors feel that if they can string the foreclosure out "long enough", either their present lender, perhaps some third-party lender / investor who may buy their mortgage, or maybe even the Federal Government, will come along with some new program that will better enable them to achieve a positive resolution of the foreclosure. At times, the more that borrowers hear about economic crisis, high foreclosure rates, the plight of mortgage lenders, the number of homeowners with negative equity and the varying Federal programs and proposals to bail out or otherwise aid those in foreclosure, the more they feel that their best course may be to just wait, to Delay, and to Delay some more – indeed, to even deliberately slack off on mortgage payments which they can in fact really make. And there are also many who seek to Delay in order to save for the day that they will ulti-mately be forced to abandon their homes.

Chapter 13 is not always used with the most noble of intentions; instead of simply being a tool for debt Reorganization which also contains a Stay mechanism, it is most commonly used solely as a stall tactic. Yes, sometimes it is used as a Delay maneuver to stay, to hold off proceedings, so that other res-olution techniques may be put into play. This is a positive strategic use. But Chapter 13 is most frequently used to Delay just for the sake of Delay – typi-cally at the end of the game, when all positive methods of resolution have been exhausted, when there is nothing left to do but to try to gain time just to gain time (or perhaps in hopes of a miracle).

Again, the mere filing of the "13" halts everything. And even if the "13" action is not actively prosecuted by the debtor – knowing that he has neither the ability nor perhaps the desire to ever pay and reorganize his debt – a filing in and of itself will halt a Sheriff's Sale for some two to six months in most States. And the debtor can repeat the process of filing (to Delay), sometimes up to three or four times, before the lender's attorney will go to Bankruptcy Court seeking relief on grounds of repetitive "bad faith" filings and have the debtor "thrown out" of bankruptcy and barred from future filings for a stipulated period. Or the Bankruptcy Court itself on its own motion may issue such an Order, which enables the lender to go forward with the Sheriff's Sale or otherwise resume the process at whatever other point the filings had stayed the proceedings.

In the case of joint obligors (borrowers) on a mortgage, husband and wife for example, either debtor may file for bankruptcy with the same legal effect on the foreclosure action. The bankruptcy petition can be filed either individually or jointly. If only one spouse files, and is ultimately barred from future filings, the other can then file in his or her own name, and start the Chapter 13 (repetitive) process all over again. There might be allegations of collusion, which may very well be true in a *prima facie* sense (not criminal to be sure), but everybody is his or her "own" person and files as such, pursuant to his or her own social security number and such filings are a Right.

Note – per present "Rules", where a particular debtor has two Chapter 13 Petitions dismissed within one year, any subsequent "13" filing within that year period will not be an effective Stay against a Sheriff's Sale or continued proceedings in a foreclosure action. The legal and strategic way to handle this is for the debtor who is seeking Delay basically just for the sake of Delay, to organize his legal gymnastics so as to best maximize the amount of time that "13" Filings can give him in the face of the Rule.

To that end: A "13" filing should be prosecuted to its fullest extent, paperwork should be submitted, filing fees paid, adjournments of hearings requested, hearings attended, and every detail handled in a way to enable the "13" case to eat up as much of the clock as possible. Again, by doing very little after filing, the debtor will still gain a number of months in most jurisdictions. But by going through all its steps, perhaps even getting the "13" Plan confirmed and making the first payment or two under the "13", he might drag the case out for the better part of an additional year or more through the Bankruptcy proceedings, alone. Two such cases in one year getting dismissed leads the debtor to Year Two and a second and possibly third bite at the same apple.

Alternate filings by co-borrowers can stymie the One Year Rule. Or one might try to intersperse settlement negotiations or Mediation with the lender or other Challenges to the foreclosure action (see below), between "13" filings, which maneuvers may put the proceedings on at least a temporary hold, in order to run the clock and skirt the One Year Rule. And in any case, to run the clock to the maximum, re-filing of the "13" should be at the last minute before any new Sheriff's Sale is scheduled to take place, as rescheduling can take weeks or months after the prior "13" is dismissed.

Thus, whether or not the debtor wishes to be inventive and aggressive in his "13" filings, especially as an adjunct to other Delay Mechanisms afforded by the System and the often-cumbersome progression of the System itself, there is a significant amount of time, Delay, to be gained through the "13" Mechanism when used to Delay just for the sake of Delay.

Moreover, both in conjunction with and quite apart from the "13" scenario, within the various State Court Systems (where foreclosures absent a Bankruptcy or other Federal Court involvement are typically prosecuted), other Statutory Delay Mechanisms (Seventh Method) are built into the law to benefit and protect the borrower. The defendant / borrower must typically be put on Notice as to certain Rights which he has, including availability of Legal Services to help him cure or defend, and possible Mediation programs, by direct communication from either the Court or the attorney for the plaintiff / lender at the commencement of the action. Where the borrower does not Answer the Foreclosure Complaint, a Notice of Default (and time to cure) must be sent in almost all jurisdictions. Often there are Legal Loopholes in the laws which the borrower may also utilize in Delaying matters. He or his attorney are left to their own devices to already know, or learn, what is available.

The filing of an Answer in response to service of the Foreclosure Complaint and Summons (in New Jersey, again, the defendant has 35 days to Answer), automatically sets the action up on the Court's docket as a contested matter, and thus leads to further legal proceedings. This means the case will drag out longer, whether the borrower can actually prevail in his opposition or not. In most States even vague, frivolous, or unsubstantiated allegations in an Answer will result in considerable Delay.

In a similar vein filing Motions which challenge the Complaint or filing a Counter-Claim to the Complaint, which introduces claims for affirmative relief by the borrower (as opposed to the mere defenses in the Answer), also complicate and prolong the case, and indeed may sometimes result in the award of damages or set-offs against the mortgage for the benefit of the borrower – particularly if the Counter-Claim involves allegations of predatory lending, discrimination or the like. But regardless, the filing of a Counter-Claim in and of itself translates into time, Delay, no matter what its actual merits, if any.

In virtually all jurisdictions by Statute there are various points in the process at which time Notification from the borrower to the lender of "certain things" will halt or slow the proceedings for given periods of time. The New Jersey Fair Foreclosure Act is a Model Standard, codifying and expanding on portions of the Common Law. Written Notice from a borrower late in the process, usually prompted by and in direct response to a required notification from the lender, stating a "belief" that arrears can be cured, for example will, in the case of residential and sometimes even non-residential mortgages in most States, automatically halt the entry of Final Judgment in Foreclosure for at least 30 days. Indeed even the Entry of the Final Judgement which in most States precedes the Sheriff's scheduling of the Foreclosure Sale, can be challenged. And (in New Jersey) in the discretion of the Sheriff, (but a request rarely denied, even if opposed by counsel for the lender) up until the last minute, the borrower can automatically adjourn the Sheriff's Sale for four weeks. The States vary on their Adjournment procedures.

There are other <u>Legal Procedures or Maneuvers (Eighth Method)</u>, which can also be used to Delay. Unrelated to Bankruptcy Protection, Automatic Adjournments or the like, a borrower, for example, may be able to go into State Court on a motion for relief to try to put off a Sheriff's Sale. Certain family situations, illness, other hardships, assertions of unfair dealing, and late-in-the-game claims of new-found abilities to Cure, are typical reasons raised in attempting to secure Judicial Intervention.

There are also the <u>"Less Conventional" Challenges / Forensics (Ninth Method)</u>. A grouping which heretofore has been somewhat arcane, obscure, and seldom–used, but as this is written has exploded in the public domain, such challenges have been reinserted as a tool, a Systemic Pump, to slow down proceedings, to try to make them contested (delayed) matters. The strategy is to blunt the foreclosure process, which improves the chances for the owner to cure and/or get long-term delays. Making the action a Prolonged and/or contentious matter, sometimes on more "creative" or even "whimsical" grounds.

Recent judgments rendered in Forensics litigations where States and the Federal Government have joined as co-plaintiffs in Class Actions against certain lenders have also provided substantial financial and precedent-setting assistance to a variety of foreclosure relief efforts as well as to individual litigants in the Classes.

Forensic Challenges typically go to the Inception or Closing of the mortgage on Day One; to the Chain of Custody of the mortgage; and to Technical Circumstances of the lender's (counsel's) handling of paperwork details in the actual Foreclosure Action. Most Forensics Challenges have nothing to do with the underlying reality that the debt is truly "owed". But they are fodder for Delay games; a means to get on track via settlement or other resolution plans, or to get a mortgage abatement or even outright dollar damages.

In sometimes a quite technical way, a borrower may claim in State Court that the lender has no Standing, or legal grounds, on which to even try to foreclose, at all! The position is that the Complaint is defective to the core and must therefore be dismissed because, for example, the foreclosing lender may have never received from the originating lender or some other intermediate owner of the mortgage, or perhaps may have never recorded, a proper Assignment of the original Mortgage which it is seeking to foreclose!

And this seemingly esoteric game of semantics has proven quite disconcerting to many foreclosing lenders who have mortgages from bundled groupings and securitizations where individual mortgages have been repeatedly sold and assigned and the paper trails to confirm their ultimate ownership may be far from perfected.

The gist of such claims is that the foreclosing lender lacks valid ownership of the mortgage and thus has no right to chase the borrower for money to begin with. The Challenge is to the Propriety of the foreclosure action itself.

The creativity in Forensics Efforts to judicially compel lenders to produce original notes and assignment paper trails has revealed a lot of MIA Documents and many i's not dotted and t's not crossed. The mere Absence of certain

Documents, like assertions of Defective or Unexecuted or Inaccurate Closing Paperwork from Day One, can lead to Delaying Challenges, and Damages.

Other "Rights of the Lender" may also be "Challenged", as can Calculations of amounts claimed to be due and "credits", even post-Answer.

Claims that documents basic to the foreclosure action may have been "rubber stamped" by the lender or its counsel, signatures not properly notarized even on in-house lender documents, numbers and histories not personally reviewed before foreclosing ("Robo Signing"), or files not Audited, have been the rage in Forensics Challenges. Indeed, unless the money is really not due or the documents or default truly fraudulent, such technical errors can always be corrected by the lender or its counsel, and they do not actually go to the heart of the matter, they do not go to the substance or existence of the debt. But again, throwing these issues up against the wall can make for an easy splatter-approach in delaying and getting damages.

Besides allegations of Faulty (i.e. failure to provide accurate current identity or address of lender), or Fraudulent lender Paperwork, the borrower may also argue other points in the process. The non-receipt or Improper Service of notices and other Legal Papers; Assertions of Unfair Dealing; Improper Closing Practices; Predatory Lending; Discrimination; and Misleading mortgage broker practices are all among the "meritorious" claims or allegations used in seeking Delay, and they can be injected into the proceedings at any point and in any variety of ways.

On motion and in the discretion of the Court, with leave of the Court many "claims" can be introduced out of time, especially if a "stranded" borrower in distress piles on the "hardship", and particularly so in a poor real estate market.

Many of the innovative challenges have been about the Government trying to cool down the volcano, with the Government and the private lending sector trying to apply some brakes to the out-of-control train.

Again, <u>Forensics</u> – in both the State and Federal Courts; claims asserted by individuals or private or "public" groups (Classes); to slow or stop proceedings, to recover money for "damages" for an individual claimant or an "affected class"; to reform practices of lenders and/or the Government; to reverse judgments; to obtain justice (and a "break") for the little guy; to abuse the foreclosure system over what may truly be trivial issues when borrowers simply owe what they cannot or do not want to pay; where grounds can be "found" or "invented" and asserted by a little guy or by the largest of entities.

And so while there is room for tried and proven and more novel claims to be made, the Granddaddy of all Forensics Actions was the 2013 Settlement between the nation's largest lenders and servicers and virtually all of the States – bringing $25 billion in foreclosure relief and a raft of procedural reforms and new guidelines.

This massive litigation paralyzed much of the foreclosure / judicial system, gave countless millions of borrowers a free ride, and allowed the tip of the Crisis to cool a bit. The truth is that this was all a lot less of a "concern" with "reform" and "wrong doing" and a lot more concern by the real powers that be over the national angst.

General Assistance (Tenth Method) as it may be collectively called, is an umbrella heading for a variety of means to Delay and/or Get Out Of Foreclosure, including Federal and State programs (and proposals); State programs which are Federally-Funded (primarily through the Troubled Asset Relief Program); and private initiatives and non-profit group efforts.

New Jersey, for example, has had its own plans under its Mortgage Stabilization and Relief Act, legislation (early 2014) to permit the State Housing and Mortgage Finance Agency to buy certain categories of foreclosed homes and convert them to Affordable Housing (eliminating drag on values while providing needed units). New Jersey has also seen legislation permitting expedited foreclosures on vacant properties. Drying up the pipeline of foreclosed inventory helps firm up the market and thus tamp down foreclosures generally.

The Hardest Hit States Fund, a Federal Umbrella which has assisted over 18 of the "Hardest Hit" States, has also provided a variety of direct dollar relief.

To help qualified applicants become current and stabilize mortgages, either in conjunction with or pending finalization of a Modification, funded with a $300 million Federal Subsidy, The New Jersey HomeKeepers Program has enabled the State MFA to provide zero interest 2 year stipends secured by a lien payable upon resale or refinance of the property.

A variety of direct and indirect Assistance has also facilitated Investor Purchase / Speculation in foreclosed properties and mortgages in foreclosure ("Bad Paper") aka "Toxic Assets". Such initiatives are "designed" to get blocks of real estate out of the pipeline.

Caveat – When the private sector buys and starts dealing in discounted assets by doing workouts with owners in distress or by reselling the property or paper to third parties, it is mimicking what the Government, i.e., FDIC of a few years back did with so-called "bad paper" and foreclosed properties, (And it seems quite "Non-Toxic" when later resold in a better market).

And how ironic that these same Government Pumps which we have been told are necessary to rescue Main Street from the "evil doings" of Wall Street, will again in the end fatten up Wall Street! Wall Street buys Toxic Assets. All of which is to say, once more, that we have all been in it together, and Wall Street is only a part of the Circle, the Circle of moving things forward, from the top (Federal Government) down. The For-Public-Consumption political flogging of Wall Street and the "Big Banks" has been one big game!

As in all areas of life and business, bad-faith negotiations (here by the borrower), under the guise of a good-faith reaching out, may be nothing but a premeditated stall tactic. Mediation Programs (Eleventh Method) available through the State and Federal Courts, lenders, HUD, credit counseling agencies, and newer Federal Programs, are a sincere pro-active method of foreclosure resolution, and are also abused by borrowers just to Delay proceedings. Mediation coupled with counseling has become an ever-more widely-used forum.

Finally, at the very end, call it End Delay (Twelfth Method) there is significant latitude for the now "former" borrower / occupant to Delay his departure from the property even after a Sheriff's Sale has occurred. Again, former tenants have superior standing and rights to those of foreclosed former owners. A Chapter 13 filing will gain some time and hold off the filing or proceeding of an eviction against a former owner. A Hardship Petition to the State Court with a promise to pay a carrying charge for a short period of time may also have some success. (Typically with modest chances of success, a former borrower may try to Negotiate a short stay with his former lender.) A Court will also entertain a last-ditch Plea for a bit more time. Indeed, even after the Sheriff's Sale has been held and the former lender has received the Sheriff's Deed, it may not revert to Self-Help to remove a former borrower; if he does not leave voluntarily or in exchange for a modest "fee", often offered by former lenders to expedite matters, the only route for the lender is eviction.

A Refinance Through FHA Or HUD Programs (Thirteenth Method), can in certain situations be a realistic means to Get Out Of Foreclosure and hold onto your property. Although the FHA offers programs and new ones are always being considered and implemented, with favorable rates and a certain leniency towards low credit scores, qualifying criteria nevertheless often exclude many prospective borrowers who are in default on their current mortgages. FHA Refinancing is most likely to work where a borrower applies before his LTV (loan to value) equity ratio falls too low, before he goes into actual default, and before his credit score tanks totally. And as this is written there are specific FHA Programs for borrowers who are current yet have a negative equity in their homes.

A Partial Claim / Related HUD / VA Models (Fourteenth Method), which is a form of Refinance, is a creative mechanism whereby HUD will grant an interest-free second mortgage consisting of past due payments. (VA Refinancing, or Re-Funding, also includes programs which re-amortize the remaining principal balance on VA loans, together with arrears, into a new mortgage at very competitive interest rates.) A recognized Method before Mods became part of our language, we may now group such plans under the broader Heading of Mods.

A recent HUD Refinancing initiative, "The Hope For Homeowners Program", created by Congress to help both those at risk of default and foreclosure and in certain cases those already in foreclosure Refinance into more affordable sustainable loans, H4H, as it is called, is an additional mortgage option designed to keep borrowers in their homes.

With the advent of various Stimulus "Pumps", the FHA, long a haven for marginal borrowers, has become more of a source of loans for those in or at risk of foreclosure. One caveat, however, is that virtually all FHA Programs require the existing mortgage which is in trouble to be Fannie Mae or Freddie Mae; some Programs limit the percentage of negative equity a property may have; some cap the number of months of delinquency or require the borrower to be current; and they all require the property to be a primary residence. All in all, the availability of FHA funding as a source to Refinance Out of an existing Foreclosure, or a precarious pre-foreclosure position, and thus hold onto a property, with or without a discount on the payoff (Modification) from the foreclosing lender, is an important tool.

Conventional Refinancing (Fifteenth Method), of delinquent or foreclosure-status mortgages is difficult to consummate in the current market. During Cycles of upward-spiraling values and easy money, and even during certain down periods, when a property in distress might still be top heavy in equity, the non-Government sector (banks and mortgage bankers and brokers, licensed and smaller unlicensed private equity lenders / investors), is more willing to "put money in the street", even in the tougher cases. The lender's logic is that the high interest rates they are charging, coupled with spiraling values or existing solid equity cushions, will ultimately guarantee their return and protect their stake even if the borrower defaults.

This, as we know, is not the mindset today. Many of these lenders have suffered large losses; they are sitting with worthless or depleted paper (bad mortgages); some have ceased or curtailed operations due to their own non-liquidity; others have just become gun-shy in view of recent events, still-declining property values, and with so many of their potential applicants having little or no equity in their properties. Yet with a "safe", albeit higher risk applicant having "sufficient" equity, under the right market conditions Conventional Refinancing, including the <u>Hard Money Sector (Sixteenth Method)</u> – (new loan will have low LTV, higher rates, up-front points, a short term, stringent lender remedies in event of default) – which before the recent Bust was a vibrant catalyst, can again be a solid Means to Get Out of Foreclosure (see Chapter VI, Hard Money).

<u>Refinancing With The Assistance Of A "Friendly" Third Party Or Investor (Seventeenth Method)</u> is essentially using a <u>Co-Signer</u> to guarantee the Refinance on behalf of a borrower in foreclosure. Stumbling blocks in this scenario may include a non-qualifying or very low credit score borrower, secondary liens which may need to be satisfied in order to Refinance, and the scope of the stake, or "price", if any, which the Co-Signer might demand for his signature. But there are situations in which this type of <u>Co-Signer-Assisted Refinancing</u> is fruitful – especially where the subject property still has solid equity and there is a truly "Friendly" Co-Signer. Caution: In today's market certain lenders will not accept a refinance involving the same surname as that of the borrower-in-default, or even a close family member. Historically we never had this type of "guilt by association". And as market conditions gradually improve this road block will gradually phase-out.

<u>A "Refinance" Solely In The Name Of A Friendly Party Or Third Party Investor, (Eighteenth Method)</u> is another way to Get Out Of Foreclosure. In the right circumstances it can be a terrific idea, though obviously there will be issues: "What is the price for using the signer's credit and qualifications? What will his future stake in the property be?" This method of "Refinancing" involves deeding the property into the name of the third party. The original borrower signs off on the deed. Thus, of paramount importance to the original borrower is getting the property back into his name.

A Supplementary Agreement can delineate the events and payment terms which will trigger the conveyance of the property back from the "Temporary Owner" to the "former-borrower-in-trouble". Such an Agreement should be recorded in the County Courthouse along with the deed to the Signer, in order "to put the world on notice" (one of the prime reasons why real estate documents are recorded), and thus prevent the "Temporary Owner" from reneging on any re-conveyance, or trying to breach the deal and fraudulently convey to someone else.

A threshold issue in assessing the viability of such a "Refinance" deal, assuming the original borrower really wants to "hold on" and get the property back in his own name, is to explore whether a subsequent conveyance back is even realistic in the first place. Will this "former borrower" be able to perform, be strong enough to make the payments, and have sufficient credit, and will the property itself have the requisite equity to sustain still a new mortgage down the road which might be necessary to "retake" the property?

When transferring property to a third party in order to effectuate a "Refinance", enough time must be built into the Ancillary Agreement to allow the former borrower to get back on his feet and truly be in a position to take the property back.

Thus, such a Third Party "Refinance" can be more of a holding pattern; or the new mortgage obtained by the stand-in borrower might be utilized as a more permanent instrument. Such a scenario most effectively deals with the potentially thorny issue of Getting The Property Back. Putting the property in the name of a new entity, an LLC perhaps, instead of putting it directly into the individual name of the Third-Party Signer, permits the new entity to both "own" and "owe".

And ownership of such an entity (Shareholders' Stocks in a corporation, Members' percentages in an LLC, for example), can be divided in some fashion between the former borrower and the Third-Party Signer / "new owner" who will sign on behalf of the entity, and the entity can have an Operating Agreement which specifically defines the respective interests of the parties for the short and long-term, and other financial issues – i.e., "When and on what Conditions can the former borrower get complete ownership of the entity (and thus the property?)" And, "What is the price to the Signer?"

The new mortgage which has been obtained in the name of the entity (with the personal guarantee of the Signer), may remain in place as the entity can continue to own the property or the Third-Party Signer can be "phased out" and the former borrower will thus have a truly viable means by which to "regain" his property. Especially where a property has significant equity, the trade off of a more expensive mortgage (mortgages in the name of a company typically carry higher interest rates), could represent a minor cost if it is "part of the price" to structure a "saving transaction". Such transactions are most appropriate for either commercial higher-ticket foreclosures or those "small" deals where, again, there is significant equity in the property.

A variation on the "Refinance" In The Name Of A Friend Or Third Party Investor might also utilize a "Sweetheart" Short Sale (Nineteenth Method), as the vehicle for a borrower-in-trouble to get his property into the name of his Third Party (individual or entity), in order to secure new financing. The goal(s) – Get Out Of Foreclosure via the Third Party "Refinance", and at the same time discount the debt where the property has a negative or marginal equity. Akin to getting a discount and Refinancing in the borrower's own name, the sequence is to secure a discount via the Short Sale (since title is being conveyed out), and to then "Refinance" the now-discounted sum. (A different kind of Short Sale from that discussed in Chapter IV, where the aim is to "truly divest" the property to some third-party in a "sometimes" arms-length transaction, to just "sometimes get out of it".)

But the principle remains – "a discount of the debt in foreclosure." And here it is not to be funded by some "distant" new buyer, but instead by the financing, the "Refinancing", if you will, of the Friendly Third-Party. A double win – reduce your debt and get new financing – to Get Out Of Foreclosure.

The issues of getting the property back, the Ancillary Agreement, the price of the Third Party, the notion of putting the property in the name of a new entity, are all as discussed above. The difference here is the added kicker for the borrower: he gets a better deal.

A Friendly Short Sale (Twentieth Method), Getting Out Of Foreclosure with a break, a discount, can enable the borrower to retain a *de facto* control or use of the property while it is parked in a third party's name.

The use of Equity Partners (Twenty-First Method), and other variations on the concept of introducing cash investors to the situation is, in a Down as opposed to a Boom market, seemingly less rewarding and more difficult to work out, but where it is possibly the only viable means to survive, it will be a stroke of luck. In any market, and surely in a poor one where new mortgages may not be easy to secure, a Partner's cash can prove more important than his credit. The investor in this case does not necessarily engage in new financing. He uses his own cash or credit lines that he might have available from sources other than the subject property to satisfy the foreclosing lender. (A mini-version of the Government's own Pumps, or infusions, to the bigger players, to the banks.)

Again, in addressing the question of what stake or price an Equity Partner may demand, we can propose a share in the property; interest or other payments; a percentage of profits upon future resale; or any number of forms of consideration, which might include placing a new mortgage on the property in favor of the Equity Partner / Investor.

An additional, albeit a more limited and less frequently used Means (at least when not being perverted by scam artists who prey on victims of foreclosure and lie about the true terms of their deals), for Getting Out Of Foreclosure is through a Sale-Leaseback of the premises (Twenty-Second Method). A type of equity deal in its different forms, it can be an excellent vehicle, particularly with more involved and larger commercial problem situations.

The investor buys the property, does whatever financing of his own to fund the deal and pay off the foreclosure, and leases it back to the now-former owner / new-tenant. As in the above noted Joint Third Party "Refinancing" genres, both title and the legal status of the troubled borrower change. One important difference from those Methods - here the interim arrangement is designed to maintain the original borrower in a "Use and Occupancy" status, tempered by the terms of any Ancillary Agreement, a "Tenancy" which is established pursuant to the Sale-Leaseback.

In Curing a Foreclosure, on its face the Sale-Leaseback will take the form of a basic conveyance and mortgage payoff (together with any other consideration which may pass from the new owner to the former borrower as part of the deal), with no expressed intentions other than that the new owner is renting the premises back to the former borrower on stipulated terms, thus maintaining him in the property, but clearly not in title. This gets him out of foreclosure and gives him continuity in the premises.

Or the Sale-Leaseback May Be Coupled With A Re-Purchase Agreement or Option (Twenty-Third Method). This version is less permanent than the Refinance Methods and has a different legal structure, yet in certain respects it is similar. It is a Means to Get Out Of Foreclosure, with or without a principal discount from the foreclosing lender (of course the <u>Sale-Leaseback can also be made part of a Sweetheart Short-Sale Package</u>), and the new landlord / owner will ultimately be obliged to convey title back to the original owner on stipulated terms.

<u>Assistance (Twenty-Fourth Method)</u>, can be another route to Get Out Of Foreclosure, but no matter what the private or public sector may offer, it is clearly not a panacea. Federally-sponsored Assistance Programs have come and gone. There are also a variety of State programs around the country, some of which are Federally-funded. In New Jersey for example, the Home Mortgage Finance Agency has a program called HomeKeepers, courtesy of a $300 million Federal grant, which in certain situations can give unemployed or under-employed homeowners up to $2,000.00 a month for 24 months, or a like lump sum, to assist in subsidizing payments or bringing a mortgage current, either in conjunction with a Modification or pending Modification negotiations, through a no-interest lien on the property re-payable upon resale or refinance.

Direct Federal Assistance to borrowers in foreclosure, in whatever form, is a Federal Pump – like subsidized FHA Refinancing, incentives to lenders to Modify, and Government Subsidized / Private Sector purchases of "bad paper" (toxic assets).

(Caveat – <u>Repeat</u> – when the private sector buys and deals in such discounted assets, either workouts with borrowers in default or reselling the paper to third parties, historically it realizes huge profits, i.e., in the past buying "bad" assets of failed thrifts from the FDIC. And down the road this Paper won't seem all that "toxic!")

<u>Redemption (Twenty–Fifth Method)</u> of the property from the successful bidder at Sheriff's Sale (third party or former lender) will permit the debtor to "hold onto the property" and, in a round-about-after-the-fact manner, Get Out Of Foreclosure! Absent any post-Sale discount, terms would include satisfaction of the debt on the foreclosed mortgage plus reimbursement of costs and related charges incurred by the former lender in the Sale process.

Thus if the Sheriff's Sale has already been held, the now-foreclosed-upon owner has one last chance to "hold on", provided he can get the money and pay up. Redemption Periods vary from State to State (in New Jersey it is 10 days from the date of Sale). The Redemption Period is the period of time after the Sale during which the borrower has one last statutory opportunity to Cure and avoid the finality which after this Period would otherwise include conveyance of the Sheriff's Deed to the successful bidder.

A source of capital must be arranged if the tolling of the Redemption Period is to be avoided. The assistance of a Third Party to secure the cash is usually necessary in such scenarios. (Caveat – as with so many of the matters discussed in these pages, analytical insight will invariably lead to ever-more questions, issues, possibilities and openings.)

Let's assume a situation in which the Redemption Period is drawing to a close (again 10 days in New Jersey), and the borrower feels he can raise the necessary money to pull it out of the fire. But even at this very late date, he still "needs a little more time". Let's further assume that he (or any co-borrower) can still legally file a Chapter 13. Even at this "12th hour", such a filing will stay the progression of the Redemption Period. And pending any dismissal of such bankruptcy, the "foreclosed" borrower has once again bought some time, some wiggle room. For example – file the "13" on Day Nine of the Redemption Period, get thrown out of bankruptcy in four weeks – 29 more days to try to do something! And should there still be sufficient positive equity in the property, all may not be lost.

A few years ago I received a call from an old friend, who I did not know was in foreclosure, mid-afternoon on what he promptly told me was the 10th day of his Redemption Period. "What could he do?" he wanted to know. Fortunately, he still had about $50,000.00 solid equity in "his" $200,000.00 one family bread and butter, albeit somewhat run-down cape which was located in a desirable suburban Union County, New Jersey town. I met him within the hour and gave him the most basic barebones pages of a bankruptcy petition which would get him in the door of the nearest Bankruptcy Court (30 minutes away), so he could file and get a Case Number. He filled out the package within minutes, and along with a money order for a minimal initial partial filing fee ($20.00), he was on his way to the Federal Courthouse in Newark, New Jersey.

He had the papers filed and stamped just before the 4:00 P.M. deadline. Along with a one sentence letter of explanation, he then faxed a copy to the County Sheriff's Office and the lender's attorney. He was now officially in Chapter 13, the remaining time of his Redemption Period was on hold (at least for awhile), and he had gained some breathing room.

The question then, was "What could he do, and what would he do, during this new 'grace' period, to try and 'resolve' things?" Absent any resolution on his part, the "13" would have "only" delayed the date on which the Sheriff would tender the Deed to the winning bidder (former lender or third party; in this case it was a third-party speculator, which itself bore witness to the fact there was real equity in the "foreclosed" property). If no other positive Curing would come of this extra "free time", it would have still gained him a number of additional weeks in the premises before the new owner gained the right to evict him.

I referred him to a local investor who I knew was renovating another house in his neighborhood. Based on its equity, the property's potential value after rehab, and my friend's need more for the cash than to remain in the house, the plan was to have the investor Redeem the property by paying off the mortgage in the name of the borrower, who would then retain ownership for the moment (which he still technically had despite the Sheriff's Sale having been held, since he was still stuck on "Day Nine"). Then he would immediately obtain a voluntary dismissal of the bankruptcy (making it legally possible for him to execute a deed to the investor), he would tender the deed and have the foreclosure action dismissed and the Sheriff's Sale would thus be officially cancelled. (Meaning the Sale Deposit tendered by the "winning" third-party bidder at Sale would be refunded by the Sheriff, and all rights of the winning bidder voided by the Redemption.)

The deal between the investor and my friend left him with $17,000.00 in "salvage" equity proceeds – $17,000.00 more in liquidity than he had had to his name before, and it left the investor with a property to Rehab and Flip for an even more Substantial Profit. Knowledge (or initial lack thereof), Advice, Use of a Legal Remedy, plus some basic common-sense Negotiations combined to achieve a much more palatable outcome than the bleak foreclosure morass my friend had been facing.

Call this a Redemption coupled with a Sale. Given a different borrower, it could have been a Redemption with a continuity of ownership. Other third parties could have become involved in our example had the premise been to keep my friend in title; with a different mindset, different personal qualifications or access to resources (and smarts), he could have kept himself in title through a Redemption and thus retained a property with good equity and an even better upside through future rehab.

In any case, this was a classic example of how a borrower can Maneuver and indeed how an investor can Maneuver to make or to keep a dollar. A seemingly lost cause was turned around, as so often they can be, and The Real Estate Tree bore fruit for all involved!

Oddly, my friend had done nothing from Day One of the foreclosure action to try and <u>DELAY</u> or <u>CURE</u>. He was aware of my real estate involvements, but never called me before the end. If it was embarrassment, he could have reached out for somebody else. But he had done literally nothing. And in the end I was able to help him and as it turned out the investor who I "introduced" him to was an old high school classmate!

<u>Some people will do anything to SURVIVE and RECOUP; others just seem to have their own ways. But such is the essence of Real Estate Success and Failure, Skill and Chance; and this case bears testimony to the fact that there are literally endless Opportunities out there for the Knowledgeable and Enterprising Practitioner, be he an Owner or Potential Investor!</u>

CHAPTER IV

"PROFITABLY" SELL YOUR HOME WHILE IN
FORECLOSURE – EVEN WITH A NEGATIVE EQUITY

There are essentially <u>Seven Major Reasons Why A Borrower In Foreclosure may opt to sell his property as his own "best way out scenario" rather than try to Hold on</u>. A desire to still <u>Try To Realize Something</u>, perhaps something substantial, in net proceeds from a sinking property is usually the paramount reason. "Is it a negative equity situation, or is there still some real owner's equity (fair market value less debt) left?" Less so in today's "Post-Bust" period than in the past, even well into the process and beyond many properties in foreclosure nevertheless retain a chunk of equity, which a pro-active owner can cash-out on, even absent the benefit of a lender discount, after a full payoff. All he needs to do is to literally do something about it! Go out and properly market the property for sale.

(As detailed in the next pages, there are <u>Four General Frameworks within which to sell a property in foreclosure; (a) Short Sale with a lender discount on the mortgage; (b) "Sweetheart" Short Sale; (c) Short Sale with a "Courtesy" lender discount on the mortgage; and (d) Straight Sale with no mortgage discount.</u> Variations include: <u>Auctions, Raffles, Selling to a Charity, Sale-Lease-backs, and Deeds In Lieu Of Foreclosure.</u>)

The Second major Reason why a debtor may want to Sell, regardless of the anticipated amount of available net proceeds, is so he can "<u>Move On And Get On With His Life</u>". To start over in a different environment. To get away from bad memories and bad times. To make daily life and finances more manageable, more comfortable. Sometimes an illusory form of reasoning or perhaps a necessary or self-fulfilling form of Closure, such thoughts sometimes prove to be a pragmatically useful means for turning the page and becoming more productive and happier. In the end it is just a personal choice, a personal decision. Yet the notion of "moving on" can prove a powerful persuader even where the borrower may in fact still find a viable means through which he can Hold onto his property.

For some there is also the consideration of wanting to avoid the prospect of a Sheriff's Sale, a bankruptcy filing, or other events or delays incident to a foreclosure action which could more adversely affect their already damaged Credit. Regardless of the potential for an outcome which might actually result in a more or less favorable credit score, some are just concerned about <u>Salvaging What They Can (Think They Can) Of Their Credit, Now</u>. For those who purchased with good credit, the prospect of also losing this asset along with "everything else" might prove overwhelming. At the point of default some most acutely feel the importance of having decent credit in the future. And they might come to think that this is what they must focus on salvaging in hopes of trying to rebuild their future.

A variety of other factors can also influence such a decision: Age; Education; Profession; The extent to which the borrower may be in the public eye; A concern with the bearing of credit status on employment or future endeavors; The prospect of a significant future inheritance; and The need for better credit in the short term.

A desire or need for <u>Credit Rehabilitation</u> is often a major concern. The reasoning is that a prompt resolution of the foreclosure will result in a credit report which shows the problem was a short-lived aberration, and the mortgage was either paid in full or amicably settled (discounted). Depending on other credit issues immediate payoff can be a quick start at credit rehab. Indeed, in a Short Sale / Discount the deal with the lender might even be negotiated to include a provision for a "favorable" explanation on the credit bureau entry.

Understanding that it is one of the worst and most enduring of credit smears, some will want to sell, no matter what, at whatever price, just <u>To Avoid The Possibility Of A Sheriff's Sale</u>.

Or, they may want to sell, to cut it all off, out of <u>fear of having a Deficiency Judgment</u> levied against them. A deficiency is the difference between the total mortgage debt (principal, arrears, late fees, legal fees, other costs, advances for taxes and insurance), and any lesser net realized by the lender from Sheriff's Sale or other discounted settlement of the mortgage. A Deficiency Judgment is a personal obligation of the former borrower in favor of the lender which results from a lawsuit in which the lender seeks full repayment based on any personal guarantee in the Mortgage Note.

A foreclosure is an "in rem" action, an action against a piece of real estate; it is a lawsuit which seeks to compel sale or other form of seizure of the real estate, the collateral, as a means to obtain repayment of the (entire) obligation. Many times a foreclosure is completed and, depending on the net realized from the property, it will result in only partial satisfaction of the total obligation.

The lender sues the owner of the realty, be it an individual or entity, in a foreclosure action not to obtain a personal judgment against them (in most States), but rather to get to the property to try to obtain a Judgment In Foreclosure which entitles the lender to have the property sold in order to satisfy all or as much of the debt as possible based on what the property realizes. It is akin to the repossession of a motor vehicle (a repo being done on the papers, not by lawsuit, though), in order to get the collateral so it can be disposed of to fully or partially satisfy the obligation in default.

And in order to assert or collect on any Deficiency from a former owner who had signed to be personally responsible for the mortgage debt (such personal obligation evidenced by the Note), in most States a lender must commence a new, a second legal proceeding after the foreclosure has been completed, this second action being an *in personem* action. This is a suit against the person or legal entity in their individual capacity. It seeks a personal dollar judgment for the deficiency amount. Such a Court award is called a Deficiency Judgment.

Although the borrower's name will appear in both public records and credit reports as the defendant in a foreclosure, again it does not personally obligate any borrower himself or itself to pay money. A Deficiency Judgment, on the other hand, imposes a dollar liability on the named defendant.

A personal judgment must be satisfied if the debtor hopes to own or transact other property in the future (at least in his own name) or to rehabilitate his credit. If a judgment debtor owns other property in his name at the time a judgment is rendered against him, or thereafter but before the judgment has been satisfied of record, it also automatically becomes a lien on such property. Long after a foreclosure judgment, damaging as it may be in the credit context starts fading, an unpaid personal judgment will still accrue interest and be a continuing drag on credit. Such is a Deficiency Judgment.

Of those borrowers whose major fear is a possible Deficiency Judgment, some, where there is sufficient equity, will wind up doing a full mortgage payoff, while circumstances will have most doing a partial or discounted Short Sale payoff. A borrower may bargain for a Hold Harmless Agreement from the lender – a forgiveness of any deficiency, a "no-chase" guarantee on any deficiency. In reality, however, as a matter of policy most lenders do not give such assurances, and often cannot give them in a Short Sale or otherwise. Usually the "lender" with whom the borrower deals is just the loan servicer, having no authority to give such guarantees, as the mortgage is owned by some other entity.

Caveat – guarantee or no guarantee, for the most part it is moot; lenders typically do not sue to obtain Deficiency Judgments, so while the concerns of some borrowers may seem logical, in the vast majority of situations their thinking and thus their motivation to sell is flawed and will seldom prove productive.

A second lawsuit seeking a Deficiency Judgment after the foreclosure entails more legal fees and costs for the former lender. It is time consuming. And lenders understand that most former borrowers who have just been hurt or wiped out in foreclosure do not typically have a lot of money with which to pay a new unsecured Deficiency Judgment.

Moreover, it is understood that they may always later file a Chapter 7 bankruptcy and wipe out any Deficiency Judgment anyway. Actions chasing deficiencies are usually reserved for cases where a former borrower or co-signer has verifiable substantial assets (and few do; if they had had such assets, they probably would have enlisted them to Cure the foreclosure). Nonetheless, some borrowers are motivated to sell, to get it over with quickly, while there may still be some equity in the property, precisely out of fear of that Deficiency Judgment and any attendant complications down the road.

A potent motivation for some debtors to opt for the Sale Route is their dread of and desire to avoid, extended Embarrassing Local Publicity And Family Trauma, which they feel will be incident to the progression of a foreclosure action. There are the newspaper advertisements, notices posted at the property, inquiries from investors and others, public data on the internet, the gossip of local realtors and the like. So in addition to perhaps just being tired and wanting To Get On With Their Lives and turn the proverbial page, some are concerned with cutting off negative publicity, as well. After all, aside from the more general Embarrassment, gossip and publicity can impact younger children; affect a borrower's employment or local business; taint his involvement in political, civic or professional matters; and impact other sensitive personal and business concerns. Some sellers believe that a voluntary Sale will stop all of this and represent a Comforting Security and Certainty with respect to their resources and future direction.

Sometimes a decision to Sell while in foreclosure simply reflects the conclusion that this is the <u>Generally Best Resolution</u> of the problem, given the borrower's overall circumstances / personal issues; financial abilities or lack thereof; needs; plans; and sheer fatigue or lack of will to tough it out and deal with the demands and vagaries of a foreclosure action.

The <u>First</u> and today increasingly the most common <u>Method of Selling While In Foreclosure</u> is through a <u>Short Sale</u> – wherein the lender takes a discounted payoff – and this is also a sensible approach when trying to sell in negative or marginal equity situations, generally.

As a result of our most recent Boom to Bust Cycle in values – with high LTV ratios of most Purchase Money Mortgages which were closed during the last Upward Cycle; a similar spike in high LTV Refinances which were based on exaggerated values to begin with and then rubber stamped by appraisers and underwriters who often approved most anything and further inflated valuations during the Boom; and further LTV problems occasioned by subsequent accruing arrears on these Mortgages – we wound up with a glut of properties in foreclosure having little or no equity. These properties are "underwater".

Again, the primary qualifying criteria which a lender looks at when asked to pass on a Short Sale: First and foremost, the lender must conclude that it is a negative or marginal equity situation. Secondly the lender must be convinced that the defaulting borrower does not have sufficient income or resources with which to cover his monthly payments and arrears in any way, shape or form. And a Hardship must also be documented and remain uncured when the Short Sale is applied for.

The lender, as it were, likes to see multiple problems with the property value, with generally negative market trends, and with the borrower himself. The lender should be persuaded that the borrower, as he presently stands before him, in combination with his property, presents a hopeless situation. (Opposite of the Modification scenario.) The lender must be drawn to conclude that nothing can be done, he can't pay, he won't pay, and the property is a net negative and still sinking. Finally, if there is secondary financing ("behind, after") the lender's first mortgage, the lender will want to be assured that, should it approve the requested discount on its first mortgage, any such lien will receive only the proverbial pennies on the dollar in settlement.

If the first mortgage lender senses that a second mortgagee might receive "too much", it will deny the Short Sale request. The logic is that since this is at best a marginal equity situation, if sold at Sheriff's Sale the property would not generate sufficient proceeds to even satisfy the first mortgage debt. Thus, in the event of a Sheriff's Sale any Second will get nothing, it will be wiped out as a matter of law by the Foreclosure Sale. (Proceeds from a Sheriff's Sale go to satisfy liens in order of their priority, passing to the next in line only after the lien ahead of it has been paid in full. Real estate taxes and the first mortgage obviously come before any Second.)

So, the first mortgagee asks, "Why should a Second get anything at all in a Short Sale?" The reasoning is that the Second should consider anything to be a gift. And that is usually true. But it is also true that a Short Sale will require any Second to sign off. And while the alternative would in all certainty produce zero for the Second, it can nonetheless be difficult for any secondary lender to simply green-light a deal in which a defaulting borrower, who is Underwater, gets something; a purchaser is probably getting a good deal; and the primary lender is probably getting a good chunk of its debt satisfied and in any case probably doing much better than it would have done at Sheriff's Sale; yet the Second is being asked to take a virtual total hit when its signature may be the key to the entire deal and the gains of all the other parties.

So there is a tension, sometimes a challenge to get the Second to sign off. Most first mortgagees will not approve a Short Sale where documents submitted for review during the approval process show anything more than a token payment, perhaps $1,000.00, going to the Second. (Release of secondary liens is of course required for the buyer to get clear title.)

There are some very specific things which the parties must do if they hope to get their Short Sale approved. Regardless of who is actually facilitating the paperwork – attorney, broker, buyer, or seller / borrower – it must all be done in the name of and with the written Authorization of the borrower. First and foremost, a credible Broker's Price Opinion (BPO) or mini-appraisal along with supporting comparables should be submitted to the lender. If appropriate, a contractor's Repair Estimate should also be introduced to help substantiate any "low" valuation and premise of negative or marginal equity.

Additionally, the seller / borrower must submit a proposed Closing Statement showing (on paper, "at least") only a "modest" net coming to him at closing. If there are secondary liens, the proposed Closing Statement, accompanied by Payoff Letters as proof, must also show the nominal amounts to be paid to such lienholders.

Other components of the Package submitted for approval: (Similar materials to those submitted for a Modification, but of course with different content and criteria): A Financial Worksheet showing income and expenses with the net (opposite to the Modification requirement) indicating a clear inability to pay any real portion of the mortgage; A Hardship Letter showing an uncured hardship; Copies of Payoff Statements for fixed debts; Copies of Bank Statements (preferably not contradicting stated income claims); and a Transmittal Letter and Summary Statement highlighting the Financial totals and Argument in favor of granting the Short Sale.

In furtherance of the review process, the lender's Rationale for Consent must be squarely addressed. The lender must be able to conclude, in reviewing Proofs and Exhibits of the borrower and in view of its own business policies and profit and cost structures, that in the current market it would be a good business decision to agree to the Sale. And again the lender's Rationale to deal, to agree to a Short Sale, overlaps some of the same considerations of and mirrors the Modification review.

Once the lender approves, the seller / borrower can move forward, in accordance with his contract with the buyer, in standard fashion to a closing, with transfer of title by seller's deed and disbursement of closing proceeds, including the stipulated payoff, through an attorney or title company trust account. Having thus received its discounted payoff, the foreclosing lender cancels the mortgage of record and the foreclosure action is dismissed. There is a new owner, the foreclosure is history, and the now-former borrower moves on. (Note – again, the Short Sale technique is also useful where there is no pending foreclosure action, but there is a negative or marginal equity and other attendant criteria.)

A Second Method Of Selling While In Foreclosure involves what, in a different context, has previously been referred to as a "Sweetheart" Short Sale (Chapter III). In essence this technique enables the borrower to sell in the

Short-Sale genre yet realize more than the nominal proceeds which a lender would normally permit (per the Closing Statement) in such a scenario.

The transaction: to obtain the lender's discount of the mortgage; to then "sell", preferably to a truly "friendly" third party or "friendly" third party-for-a-fee-investor and, by way of separate agreement between seller / borrower and buyer, to participate in some form of resale or other transaction or use of the property at a later date and thus generate further profit for the "friendly" investor and the seller / borrower. And of course the steeper the mortgage discount on Day One, the more room for additional future profit for both parties.

Thirdly, a borrower in foreclosure might sell when there is still "some" equity in the property, perhaps not a great deal, and through another variation of the "strict" Short Sale <u>Method</u> can attempt to negotiate a hybrid type of settlement with his lender – a modest "Nuisance Value" discount in an informal less thorough type of Short Sale review process – <u>A Short Sale With A "Courtesy" Discount</u>.

The lender's Rationale for dealing is basically as outlined earlier. And even where a lender feels there really is adequate equity such that the borrower will net "sufficient" proceeds absent a discount, market conditions do help persuade lenders to "chip in a bit", anyway. This is always a subjective judgment call, with the "right lender" at the "right moment" overlooking some of its own strict guidelines for Short Sale approval. Even large institutions will be flexible and look the other way, approve a "contribution" not entirely called for by their underwriting criteria, and just get a deal done in the interests of sound business practices.

By far traditionally the most <u>common Fourth Method of Selling While In Foreclosure</u> has been via a simple transaction, borrower to new buyer, with a full mortgage payoff. The <u>Straight Sale Method</u> presupposes an equity cushion, a positive equity in the property. No discount is required. And based on the numbers, the lender would not give one if asked, anyway.

The lender's position is that there is no need to compromise in solid positive equity cases. It is owed the money, there are resources with which to pay, and there will still be some money left over for the defaulting borrower. The tension – if the borrower wants to Sell to Get Out Of Foreclosure and to also net something, he had better just proceed, sell, pay up, and not drag things out too far, since accruing carrying costs and fees on the lender's side will continue to eat up potential proceeds.

The concern in selling a property in foreclosure via the Straight Sale Method, as indeed it is when selling any rundown, distressed or negative equity real estate, is to avoid the appearance of a "fire sale". Whatever equity may remain, especially where there is a thin margin and longer marketing may be necessary in a less than stellar market, can quickly evaporate if buyers perceive a "must sell at any price" property. The best defense is prudent marketing (See Brokers, below).

Historically, though less so today than in the past, many foreclosure cases end with a Borrower's Sale prior to a Sheriff's Sale, wherein the borrower will often walk away with a reasonable sum and his buyer can get a good deal at the same time. Determining factors, again, include the amount of equity, market conditions, how early in the process and how quickly the borrower acts, and how well he avoids a marketing fiasco that smells of distress.

Auctions can be an effective Variation on the Methods of Selling While In Foreclosure (as they generally are in all markets). To some the word "auction" carries a certain mystique; to others, it means bargains; to still others, it conjures up images of either pricey gems and exotic collectibles, or surplus junk. But the word "auction" typically connotes action, it connotes a burst of buyer activity, pulling them out of the woodwork, as it were. And an Auction, with the auctioneer at the helm, who may be the seller himself, or preferably a licensed professional (be it an absolute or reserve bid auction), is in fact designed to stir things up, to get action, to get attention, to create an event, to set this piece of property apart from the others, to focus individual import and a certain level of excitement on the subject property, to maximize its price, to move it quickly.

The hoopla, the sometimes raging buyer's psychology, the buyer's mentality, often ends with even some savvy and well-healed buyers bidding more than they had intended at Auction. As with other auctioned commodities, real estate will often sell at over "asking" or over market, due primarily to the Auction mentality. Whether the Auction is serious business or just for fun, if well enough attended its bidding frenzy can resemble a gambler feeding the slot machines. And so much the better for a strapped borrower who is trying to bail out.

Depending on the situation it may be wise for the borrower to negotiate the parameters of a possible post-Auction discount, or hypothetical Short Sale, on behalf of any potential successful bidder prior to the Auction.

The Auction vehicle can be viable regardless of the amount of equity in a property, though based on initial costs in setting it up and the work involved, this Method is most rewarding when there is still at least a reasonable amount of equity left.

By way of background, the allure of drawing buyers through Auctions is far from new and the underlying attraction is not entirely the product of modern marketing, either. Auction history is intriguing. In 500 B.C. ancient Greece, potential husbands acquired their brides at public wedding auctions. Imperial Rome developed a highly successful system of commercial trade which was based in part on the auction method. In fact, our modern English word "auction" is derived from the Latin root *austos* which means "to increase".

The Thirteenth Century English King Henry VII enacted a law which required a license to sell by "public outcry", and thus did the word "auction" first appear in Edward Phillip's "New World" in 1658. The first advertisement for an auction which was devoted exclusively to land appeared in The London Evening Post in the 1740's. Naturally, as more and more immigrants came to American shores, the auction concept would follow. And it would not be long before auctioneers occupied an important place in the financial ranks of the New England States.

Before the outbreak of America's Civil War, auctions were already a fully developed concept; and during the Civil War, the property of vanquished rebel partisans was regularly sold at auctions presided over by Union officers of the rank of "Colonel" or above. Today, licensed auctioneers still hold the honorary title of "Colonel".

Modern day Auctions are a sensible viable marketing tool which can help a seller realize the greatest return in the shortest possible time. However conducted, and particularly in down markets, local and national real estate brokerages promote their Auction capabilities as effective means of quickly and profitably marketing a property in foreclosure. The Auction must be well-publicized and held preferably with on-site access to a mortgage broker and pre-qualification packets, and be presented as a Reserve Auction – meaning prospective bidders are advised there is a certain minimum bid, it is not a give-away distress sale.

Although seldom used, <u>Raffles</u> and <u>Selling To A Charity</u> also bear mention as Methods of moving property. In those States where it is legal for others besides the Government or charities to hold Raffles, anybody may "market" real estate through a Raffle or Lottery. This can be an innovative attraction. The fun nature of the process, the extra attention that it can generate (particularly with the prospect of a huge payday), can quickly get a property out there in front of everybody. After all, depending on the price of a ticket or chance (perhaps $100.00 or $500.00), with a reasonable cap on the number that can be sold, entrants will have relatively good odds of being able to "win" a valuable piece of real estate, free and clear.

Dealing a property to a <u>Charity</u> is a narrow avenue and relatively esoteric undertaking. But depending on the type and location of the property, the price to be paid by the Charity and tax implications for the right seller / borrower, it can be a workable Sales approach for a certain range of borrowers.

A <u>Sale-Leaseback</u> arrangement (See "Getting Out Of Foreclosure" while remaining in the premises and trying to regain title), can also constitute an effective means of Selling Outright, as part of a Short Sale or in the Straight Sale scenario where there is a positive equity. It permits the borrower to make his break and fulfill other personal or business needs (i.e., in the case of commercial property) by remaining in occupancy as a short or long-term tenant; it permits a transition period, a continuity, and for the buyer / landlord an immediate income stream.

Unlike those situations where a Sale-Leaseback is used to bail out while "Holding Onto The Property" pursuant to an Agreement, a potential path back for the seller / tenant to regain title (Chapter III), this is a pure tenancy relationship.

A <u>Deed In Lieu Of Foreclosure,</u> a term often bandied about yet largely ill-understood, is a viable means for a borrower to wrap things up and get out; it is a conveyance, essentially giving the property in foreclosure to the lender, which typically results in very little if any cash proceeds to the vacating borrower who wants to "sell" to Get Out Of Foreclosure. It will allow the borrower to quickly proceed on at least marginally improving his credit status; it will avoid any possibility of a Deficiency Judgment, no matter how remote one might be; it will usually be coupled with a lender's Hold Harmless respecting possible future legal claims; and it might contain a guarantee of "benign" credit reporting related to the forgiven balance and also address concerns borrowers may have about avoiding further embarrassment.

Where there is substantial equity lenders will still contact borrowers and suggest a Deed In Lieu Of Foreclosure, but in such situations the proposition is absurd. And although a Deed In Lieu will close the matter out regardless of how negative the equity may be, it will still be more negative than a Short Sale resolution on credit reports. This is because with a Deed In Lieu the borrower is actually surrendering the collateral to the lender and saying he has completely failed to fulfill his obligations.

The Deed In Lieu satisfies most of those concerns in a lender's Rationale to negotiate in a foreclosure situation, but here the lender does wind up in title and must resell his collateral. Ownership of deeded real estate is not the average lender's goal; but it is still part of the business, just like taking back at Sheriff's Sale. The lender who takes the Deed has concluded that despite the new headaches of carrying and reselling, the good outweighs the bad, the downsides of dragging the foreclosure out.

Before accepting a Deed the lender must determine what if any secondary liens are on the premises. If the foreclosure were to continue through Sheriff's Sale, secondary liens would be wiped out, and should the foreclosing lender take the property back at Sale, they would thus be irrelevant when it goes to resell. If however the lender takes the Deed and there are other outstanding liens, since by definition it is stopping the foreclosure action the liens cannot be wiped out in a Sheriff's Sale. They are thus of great import to the lender and must be satisfied for the lender to give clear title in any resale. Depending on the amount of equity in the property and the sum of its mortgage and other lien debt, acceptance of the Deed can be either a net plus for a lender or such a costly morass that it would be preferable to not take the deed and instead go to Sheriff's Sale or seek some other resolution. Conventional wisdom is that a lender will not take a Deed In Lieu where the presence of secondary liens makes the numbers "too close".

Furthermore, where there are concerns over environmental problems on the premises (usually industrial sites and raw land), or costly local property Code violations or hazards (most commonly in multi-family dwellings), lenders will be reluctant to take a Deed. Not only does the Deed put them in the real estate business, but in such cases it will also burden them with expenses, exposures, delays and possibly even corporate or individual criminal and civil liabilities as owners. Liens and problems, after all, do go with the land!

(One reason lenders insist on certain standards and evidence of Code and environmental compliance at closing, is precisely for their own protection in the event they ever face the prospect of taking the property by Deed In Lieu or at Sheriff's Sale.)

Finally, in discussing options available to a seller / borrower the question of whether to employ a <u>Broker</u> or to try to sell as a <u>For Sale By Owner</u> is basic. Absent a "Friendly" or other investor-in-waiting, one must decide on the best way to market the property. While a fuller discussion of pros and cons of using a Broker is reserved for Chapter V (many reasons favor using Brokers), in the case of a seller in foreclosure who is making the choice, there are several additional observations.

First, unlike many other Seller scenarios, in foreclosures the seller is invariably in a difficult personal and emotional state (distress, sense of loss and attachment, family issues, financial and other pressures), and the assistance of a competent professional who is removed from the problem may prove invaluable in an intelligent marketing effort. (Cutting counter to this logic however, is the fact that some people do their best under pressure and function in a clear business-like fashion.)

The second caveat – and this may seem to cloud my own personal favor for generally using Brokers – is that great care must be taken to ensure that a seller-in-foreclosure is not, if you will, sold down the river by his Broker or some co-broker. Sure, there is that legal, fiduciary, ethical, professional role of the Broker which goes to the heart of most State regulatory laws and canons of realtor ethics. The Broker is there to make a commission, but he is supposed to make his living as he also does right, his best by his client.

Yet we are dealing with Human Nature – greed, opportunity, self-serving motivations, the desire for quick convenience. It can be tempting for a Broker to accidentally or deliberately push the property as a distress sale, a bargain, a quick deal. This makes his job easier, makes for a faster commission and turn over, and may even position the Broker to direct the property to his own stand-in straw buyer or other associate at a lower price than he should really be trying to get for his seller / client. And once a seller and his property are "pegged" on the multiple listing system, among local offices, at open houses, and in print ads as being desperate or a "must-sell", the stigma will stick.

My advice – unless a seller is unusually savvy and firm, he should choose a respected, aggressive local Broker and make it clear on Day One that he wants his property marketed intelligently and aggressively, not as a fire sale.

CHAPTER V

HOW TO SELL YOUR HOME (OR OTHER REAL ESTATE) IN A BAD MARKET… AND, FROM ANOTHER VIEW, SOME TECHNIQUES FOR BUYING IN A BAD MARKET

There are many times when a homeowner, investor or speculator is faced with the difficult prospect of needing or wanting to sell in a poor market. Whether dictated by financial or other business necessity, personal needs or desires, the financially secure, like the more desperate, must often make choices to sell regardless of market conditions. This is not to say, by any means, that in the larger picture the choice to sell in a Bad Market is necessarily a foolish decision. The realities of life, health, marriage, and business do not always wait for the Boom Markets. Whatever dictates a Sale, take the most intelligent approach to effectuate it in the most rewarding manner possible. It does not have to be a disaster just because the times are not the best.

What, precisely, is a "Bad Market?" There are <u>Four Essential Indicia, Or Qualifications</u>, which, broadly speaking, can be used to identify or quantify a "Bad Market". (And a combination of the Four will usually most accurately characterize such a Market.) <u>A Tightened Availability Of Credit</u>, accompanied by the Second element, <u>More Stringent Qualifying Terms</u> to obtain financing, are chief among the hallmarks of a poor real estate market.

When lenders become overwhelmed with non-performing mortgages and other types of "toxic" loans, when they perceive the end of a Bubble (Boom) with delinquencies rising and values generally deflating, they will restrict the amount of Money which they put into the System (lending) and tighten the Criteria (down payment, amount and proof of income, credit score), for an applicant to qualify.

In a circular spiral, lenders have historically impacted the vitality of real estate markets by choking off the dollar supply (decreasing volume of loans and/or tightening qualifying conditions, the two being independent yet inter-related).

Indeed, Federal and State over-regulation or unrealistic regulation, of the banking (lending) systems, can pose undue negative risk, exposure, and an un-attractive yield scenario for lenders, which itself will in turn lead them to curtail mortgage originations.

Just as the Federal Government can employ policies to Pump the System up, so too can Governmental regulations in and of themselves dampen or paralyze mortgage and real estate markets, and lead to Bad Markets and Bust Cycles. Unduly restrictive usury (interest rate) ceilings imposed on lenders, for example, particularly during eras of otherwise high floating free market interest rates, can absolutely kill markets.

Where mortgage originations might be damped by Government regulations, innovation and ingenuity can still make a deal happen (though this is certainly not a substitute for making an entire market vital), as I found out some years back when I was trying to close deals and lenders were just avoiding, at all costs it seemed, originating First and often even Second mortgages.

At the time banks and money market funds (such as Merrill Lynch, then still an American icon), were paying higher interest rates on deposits, even short-term certificates of deposit (CD's), than Federal Law permitted them to charge on new mortgages which they wanted to give. How could they lend money if their cost of funds exceeded what they could charge? The real estate market was Bust, and Bust very badly.

So how did these institutional lenders do even a modest amount of new lending? The maximum allowable rate which they could charge on Second mortgages was higher than what they could charge on Firsts (typically the case in any market due to risk allocation), and at a certain point, was still high enough to permit a profit spread in the origination of Seconds (but not Firsts).

If the loan officer at the bank (or mortgage broker at the mortgage company) felt he could "work" with the parties in a transaction, or preferably with their attorney or broker in confidence, he might help them structure an acceptable deal: the crux would be to have the seller or some third party "take back" or "place" a nominal ("fictional", though real on paper) first mortgage of, perhaps, $1,000.00 on the property. This would legally put the "real lender" in position to make a secondary mortgage loan. And the Second would be for essentially the entire financing that was needed – purchase price less down payment and the $1,000.00 "First". The lender could thereby make its spread, and the parties could close.

As long as originating a Second was profitable for the lender, a Second it would be. And indeed, the risk traditionally inherent in secondary lending would be academic in such cases, since a subsequent default triggering a foreclosure would be no big deal for the Second as foreclosing on this Second would, in dollars and cents, not be much different than foreclosing on a First, because the First – which would have to be satisfied by the Second – would be so nominal as to never really matter anyway.

And when the maximum rate that lenders could charge on Seconds later dropped below their cost of funds and there seemed to be no way for them to make a profit in either First or Second mortgage originations, in clever concert with buyers, sellers, and their representatives, some lenders would still find ways to make deals happen.

After having had some routine loan requests turned down by what was then one of the country's largest equity / Second mortgage originators, The Money Store, I received a call from a senior manager with whom I had some prior dealings at their corporate offices. My own initial cluelessness notwithstanding, I caught on to his request: "As a condition of any new loan, have your clients purchase some (expensive) life, health, or disability insurance, and have them agree to maintain the coverages through the life of the loan (with the lender or an affiliate acting as the insurance broker), and the loan will be granted." Their commissions on high insurance premiums would be their real profit!

Attorneys for some of the mom and pop lenders at the time (mom and pop in comparison to today's super-lenders), who also happened to sit on loan committees or otherwise had (due / undue) influence in decision-making, would help push through loans which they were closing, especially on larger commercial transactions where the borrower's "price" was inflated review and closing fees.

Lenders have also made originations profitable by imposing heavy Points at closing, or making a loan a Balloon Mortgage.

Points, subject to Federal and State Regulation, are up-front "fees" paid by the borrower at closing or time of commitment; "pre-paid" interest by a different name. Seven points, or seven percent of the principal amount of a new mortgage, charged at closing, for example, translates into a lot of interest when amortized out – especially in view of the relatively short life of most mortgages, regardless of what their maximum stated term may be.

A Balloon Mortgage is a loan granted for a set term, 15, 30 years or whatever, which loan is to be re-paid as if it were on such a set term or direct-reduction (self-liquidating) basis, with monthly payments pursuant to its fixed term schedule, but with the provision that at some stipulated earlier date(s), the balloon date(s), any principal balance still due (in accord with the full mortgage term), must be paid in full.

For instance, in the case of a 30-year direct reduction mortgage with a five-year balloon, the payments are made more palatable since they are based on the 30-year schedule, and at the same time the lender's interests in limiting its outward-exposure on interest rates are served as the loan can be called at the earlier balloon date. At such time the lender may still decide to extend (rewrite) the loan, perhaps at an adjusted interest rate and/or with additional fees or points, as part of the price of a refinance.

In those markets where it has been good business to create interest under a different name, points and other up-front fees have also been charged in conjunction with balloons, and they further enhance the lender's yield and limit its exposure. "Non-interest" mortgage income can be considerable.

Other dynamics which restrict, cause or contribute to Bad Markets, and which thus further contract available liquidity and the parameters (more or less restrictive criteria) for qualifying, involve a range of Federal Monetary and Regulatory Policies. These include, but surely are not limited to: General directions of the Fed; Consumer and Mortgage interest rate policies; The prime rate; The overnight rate charged by the Fed to banks; Directives on the money supply; Federal deficit policies; and, of course, The many "Pumps" discussed in this Chapter and in other pages of this Book.

Flat, Declining, or Depressed Real Estate Values, usually combined with a glut of Foreclosures, is a common and our Third Indicator Of A Bad Market. These circumstances typically go hand-in-hand with problems in the mortgage sector – rates, availability, etc. It should be noted, however, that trending lower Values are sometimes indicative more of a regional than a national issue.

Localized depressed or flat Values, regionally poor markets, in the midst of a wider-spread national prosperity are common. Regionally depressed indicators are often rooted in specific economic sectors such as manufacturing or agriculture. (Detroit and autos, Pittsburgh and steel, the Midwest and corn.) They may be the result of temporal local natural disasters; or stem from disruption of an economy due to socio-political, trade or technology issues, or new environmental regulations (mining, fishing, smokestack industries, energy and the like). So New England may be booming, with Mississippi and Louisiana in the doldrums.

Finally, the <u>Fourth</u> general indicator of a Bad Market is a <u>Sluggish Level Of Activity</u>. Mortgage money may be out there, Values constant or edging up, yet Activity can still be stifled.

<u>But when all Four Indicia of a Bad Market co-exist (Tightened Availability of Credit, More Stringent Qualifying Terms, Low Values, and Poor Activity), we clearly have a Bad Market – or worse.</u>

<u>What then are some of the Keys to "Success" when Selling In A Bad Market? (Or "Where, In All Of This, Are Some Of The Keys For The Shrewd Buyer?")</u> The savvy seller, with a thoughtful professional in his corner, should always initially try to determine <u>what Incentives or "Tricks" might help sway an otherwise less-than-motivated lender to originate</u> a loan. Having identified such a lender and its probable terms, the seller should direct prospective buyers to this lender, and attempt to build into his sales price at least part of any augmented freight (costs), which might be incurred in making a loan happen.

More substantively, <u>Various Forms Of Seller-Financing Or Seller-Assisted Financing (AKA Creative Financing) are basic tools to always explore when Selling In A Bad Market. (Other Purchase Money Financing Methods are discussed in Chapter VI.)</u> There are <u>Eight Primary Forms Of Seller Or Seller-Assisted Financing</u>, each with its own elements and pros and cons for a seller to consider.

<u>First</u> is what some refer to as <u>"Take-Back" Financing; Taking Back The First Mortgage.</u> In this scenario the seller ("mortgagee") grants the mortgage, a First and possibly the only mortgage to be placed on the property in connection with the sale, to his buyer (the "mortgagor"). Such structuring is possible only if a buyer's cash down payment is sufficient to enable the seller to pay off his own mortgage (if any), and other liens and closing costs, (unless the seller is bringing money to the closing in order to satisfy liens and thus convey clear title – subject to the new mortgage being executed in his favor). Provided the down payment and/or other resources will allow for sufficient cash at closing to clear title, the seller must feel comfortable and protected by

the financial and other personal qualifications of his buyer and the "good faith" amount of any down payment.

The overall financial position of the seller, his cash position, the amount of his equity in the property, the amount which will be required from the down payment and/or other finds for closing, the issue of any immediate need he may have for net cash proceeds from the deal, his plans, all affect the feasibility of Taking Back The Mortgage.

The seller will want to be comfortable not only with the sales price, the amount of the down payment, the integrity of the property he is selling, and the present and anticipated future strength of the local market such that in the event of a future default by the buyer he will have an adequate cushion to minimize potential losses to his mortgage principal, but he should also be confident that in the event of default he can survive with an interruption in his income stream from mortgage payments. Business terms of the mortgage must comport with the seller's anticipated plans and needs.

The legal boilerplate in any Take-Back should be stringent – i.e. as to grace periods, events triggering default, late penalties, right to inspect the property, and requirements for property maintenance by the mortgagor. The interest rate should be a function of the strength of the deal, prevailing rates (go lower), any real estate market weakness in general, the sales price compared to fair market value of the property, other mortgage terms, the buyer's ability to pay, the seller's motivation, and the neighborhood.

On balance, the seller must decide if his financial situation permits a "Take-Back", and indeed if other personal considerations truly make such an ongoing future "involvement" a wise choice.

In considering the pros and cons, where there is a properly structured transaction, where the neighborhood is not in the throes of terminal decay, where the mortgage is paid in a timely manner during its initial period and it survives whatever market Down Cycle was occurring at its inception, (if possible a "trial period" of initial non-mortgage payments as a pre-condition to actual closing may be a good idea), the seller with the means to Take Back who is determined to sell will generally find that the rewards outweigh the risks.

Besides facilitating sales, depending on their term, actual payoff date, interest rates and ancillary terms, Take Back mortgages can be decent investments in their own right. Particularly in upward market cycles, they are usually paid off well before their maturity date(s), through either resale or refinance by the new owner. But again, regardless of where a market trends in the immediate years after a Take-Back is granted, with the decision having been made to sell in a Bad Market, the essential goal is to initially meet the needs and desires of the seller through Creative Financing.

A Second Version of Seller Take-Back Financing via a first mortgage is the First Take-Back Mortgage Of Longer Duration, Coupled With One Or More Balloon Payments at stipulated dates or upon the occurrence of stipulated events through the life of the mortgage. Both Direct Reduction (principal and interest) and Interest-Only Take Back mortgages with Balloons, offer the buyer a longer term (an attractive hedge, especially where there is no pre-payment penalty), and at the same time still somewhat insulate the seller / lender by virtue of one or more pre-maturity principal reductions and the probability of a pre-maturity complete satisfaction.

Paradoxically, as the Longer Term Coupled With A Balloon offers something to the buyer, its simultaneous role as a limiting factor on the seller's own exposure is accentuated by its ability to help "persuade" the buyer to refinance earlier rather than later in order to satisfy looming balloon payment(s). Such impetus is a huge plus for the seller who has already done his deal, and a few years later is itching to cash out. So the carrot may have helped land a buyer in the beginning, it sweetened the deal and perhaps resulted in a higher price, and it may later help the seller untie himself from a mortgage that he does not want to hold any longer than he has to.

The Third Variation of Take-Back Financing assumes a new third-party purchase money first mortgage which will permit the seller to place his own secondary financing on the property at closing, a Take-Back Second Mortgage, constituting a portion of the purchase price. The amount of any such Second will usually be much smaller than a First position Take-Back. This technique is useful in tight mortgage markets characterized by conservative appraisals. The considerations involved in granting a First apply in a more limited sense when deciding whether to give a Second.

Clearly this scenario assumes a qualified buyer who can secure outside primary financing. The seller can provide incentives besides offering the Second, such as breaks on its interest rate and the sales price. With a tight First, a willing buyer and seller make up the balance of the price (less down payment), through the Second.

It is usually easier for a seller to offer a smaller Second than a larger First. On the one hand being in Second position to a fairly large First poses greater exposure, though at the same time the extent of any such exposure is minimized by the relatively modest amount of any such Second and the broader context of the transaction.

Again, in order to give a larger First the seller must have "sufficient" equity in the property and/or discretionary funds which he is willing to bring to closing if necessary to bridge any difference in his own payoffs. He must have a minimal need for cash from the property and be willing to go forward maintaining a larger involvement in his former property.

So it is usually more feasible to give a modest Second rather than a large First. Again, it is true that Second position carries enhanced risk. But provided the buyer performs, sells, or refinances and/or the market swings back, a Second Take-Back is usually a sound position. And besides, if taking that Second enables the seller to accomplish his original objectives in a difficult market, that fact alone, coupled with any cash realized at closing should, in a soundly structured deal, outweigh any negatives.

Many times the principal of the Second will be nothing more than the icing on the cake – an enhanced sales price which never would have been to begin with absent seller participation. Granting a modest Second in a Bad Market in order to close a solid deal at a decent price is a smart move.

It should also be noted that, depending on market conditions and "the quality of the Paper" taken back, there are those secondary markets in which the seller / lender can immediately or in the future sell his new asset and turn the receivable into cash. He may be able to sell at a premium (over face amount of principal), at par (equal to the principal amount), or at a discount (less than the principal amount).

Again, all of this is a function of the value of the mortgaged property, the priority position of the mortgage, the loan to value ratio, the interest rate and other mortgage terms, the strength of the borrower, and the climate of the secondary markets in which these Securities are bought and sold. Depending on those markets, there will be larger or smaller pools of investors and mortgage brokers to facilitate the sale of such Paper at any given time. (A mini-version of Wall Street's securitizing, bundling, buying and selling of mortgages originated by institutional lenders!)

The Fourth Form of Seller-Financing is by Assumption Of An Assumable First Mortgage which is already on the property. By their terms, most recently-originated Firsts, except VA (Veterans Administration) and FHA (Federal Housing Administration / HUD) loans are usually not automatically assumable by a new buyer. Assumption of VA and FHA mortgages, and these have become more and more common, multiplying in the recent downturn, requires a minimum of paperwork and a small transfer fee. Depending on the amount to be assumed, either the down payment alone or the down payment combined with secondary financing from either a third party (more difficult to arrange in a poor market) or from the seller must bridge any gap in order to satisfy the purchase price.

Most often the primary issue is whether the Assumable balance is sufficient to make the Assumption a practical vehicle for doing the deal. The volume of recent and anticipated FHA Refinances and Take-Back Purchase Money Mortgages will contribute to a resurgence in Assumptions, especially if the mortgage markets remain somewhat constrained; we will have a lot of Assumable FHA Paper down the pipeline carrying balances which represent 95-100% of current values on many, many properties.

The original obligor (signer) / seller remains responsible on the assumed obligation. But this should seldom be a deal-breaker. True, in the event of subsequent default or foreclosure and (particularly with the FHA), the extremely unlikely prospect of a Deficiency claim should a foreclosed property not cover the debt, the original obligor and his credit will get tangled up in the web. His credit may also be compromised by late payments from the successor mortgagor. (And a timely payment history will, conversely, enhance the seller's credit.)

Where the successor is a responsible person and qualified to handle the payments and has a new buyer's motivation (as most do in legitimate deals) to perform on his low-interest "gift" mortgage, and the Assumable Mortgage was probably the key to the seller's ability to sell (and usually at a higher price), the seller's actual Downside is relatively modest.

But it should be stressed – in most situations a decent down payment and satisfactory credit report on the buyer should be pre-requisites to any Assumption deal. And should the seller still have concerns about possible default by the buyer, he can obtain an added layer of protection if the parties execute and record a Supplementary Agreement entitling the seller to stated remedial rights and control over the property in such event.

A Protective Agreement might even grant the seller / obligor the right to step in and keep payments current, or to sell the property before it reaches foreclosure status. While this is all hypothetical and undoubtedly not the type of ongoing involvement the average seller would relish, the mere fact of the seller having such rights can be very useful in appropriate cases. Even absent such elaborate safeguards the bottom line is that a higher principal lower interest Assumable loan is often a boon for a seller in a tough market and the benefits of an Assumption will typically outweigh its downside.

A seller may help facilitate the <u>Assumption Of A Non-Assumable First Mortgage, our Fifth Form of Seller Financing</u>. For Consideration and upon given terms, which usually include the requirement that the original borrower "stay on the paper", Assumptions which are not a matter of right can at times be negotiated with the lender. Conditions for granting such Assumption(s) might also include changes in the interest rate or term and payment of new points, and obviously a prospective buyer with strong credentials can better negotiate down a lender's demands.

While certainly a more complicated matter than the residential case, at least in terms of legalities and business elements, negotiating an Assumption of a commercial mortgage can often be a more valuable accomplishment and more of a deal-maker. Commercial financing is quite difficult to originate in Bad Markets. Fortunately for parties trying to negotiate a commercial Assumption, unlike the vast majority of garden-variety residential loans, commercial paper is often retained by "smaller" or at least more accessible local and regional institutions with whom face-to-face or quick negotiations are more possible. And it is the commercial sector where deals can be most dependent on Creative Financing during Cyclical Downturns.

<u>The Sixth and a hybrid variety of Seller-Financing is created where an Existing Non-Assumable Mortgage Is Not Assumed But Is Instead "Left In Place"</u> to facilitate a deal. This is a legal way to take advantage of the terms of the old mortgage and use it "to finance" the new deal.

Where a mortgage is not assumable (absent lender's consent to Assumption) and it is not assumed but is simply Left in Place, an outright transfer of title to a new buyer will typically trigger the due-on-sale clause of the mortgage, meaning the lender can foreclose.

However, a seller may nevertheless utilize A Non-Assumable Loan for the benefit of his buyer (i.e., himself), by tendering the deed to his buyer, which puts the buyer in title, and also including his own name as a grantee on the deed, thus keeping him in title, also, in a limited defined ownership capacity as spelled out in the deed. Thus, the original borrower / seller remains an "owner" and, strictly speaking, has thus not triggered any due-on-sale clause; he is simply Adding The Buyer's Name To The Deed. It is almost as if the buyer bought "subject to the mortgage".

This is a legal fiction designed to circumvent restrictive non-assumable terms (spelled out or not) of an existing mortgage. Just, so to speak, "telling" the lender, should it ever get wind of the transaction and try to act on it, "I am still the (an) owner, no violation, your consent was not necessary, we just added a name". And the mortgage note, which makes the original borrower personally responsible, remains untouched – but again, the note becomes relevant only in the event of foreclosure and resultant deficiency, and the unlikely case that the lender ever moves to be made whole by suing personally for any deficiency.

With the seller retaining an interest in the property, perhaps even less than 1%, the respective legal and financial obligations of the parties should be delineated in an Ancillary Agreement recorded with the deed. Points to be addressed: Clearly define in dollars or by formula the parties' present and future Ownership interests; Responsibility for payment of mortgage and other expenses; Respective remedies in the event of default by the buyer; a Termination date for the relationship and a Maturity date for the mortgage if it is to be earlier than set forth. Also a permanent Power of Attorney giving the buyer qualified authority to sign on behalf of the seller with respect to subsequent resale, lease, or refinance of the property should also be executed and recorded.

Clearly this Method will have ongoing involvements – but if executed properly with adequate safeguards, it can prove a valuable means to effectuate a transaction and thus enable a seller-in-need to liquidate his equity in a property when market conditions might otherwise stand in his way.

An essential vehicle and the Seventh Form Of Seller-Financing is where the Seller Co-Signs for his buyer on a new third-party mortgage – a First or Second, the mortgage standing alone or in combination with other financing.

In this Form, only the buyer will be in title, and both Buyer and Seller / Co-Signer (Co-Obligor) will be on the mortgage, note, and ancillary closing documents. The new mortgage is granted based on the joint income and credit profiles of both parties. However, triple-A credit and solid income on the part of the Co-Signer in and of itself will still not overcome an extremely poor credit score of the buyer.

The rewards for a seller are obvious in those cases where his signature can make a deal which he wants, or needs, happen. True, he gets tied into future credit exposure almost as if he was the borrower. Delinquencies and defaults will adversely affect his credit, just as a good payment record will enhance it. Issues affecting both parties can be handled in a Hold Harmless / Indemnification Agreement in favor of the Co-Signer, and/or through an Agreement which simply delineates the Co-Signer's remedies in the event that omissions (inaction) or actions of the buyer might adversely affect him.

Somewhat related to this Form of Seller-Assisted Financing, is the Installment ("Land") Contract, our Eighth Way to effectuate a "sale" in a Bad Market. The experienced real estate practitioner can do wonders in structuring an Installment Contract – the less "professional" actor may invite disaster if left to his own devices or level of Knowledge in drafting such documents.

An Installment Contract is a detailed agreement which conveys a Proprietary Interest in a piece of real estate to the buyer, while for an initial period of time maintaining the seller as the legal owner of record. Such a "conveyance" is made in accordance with terms and conditions of the Contract, and the Interest thus conveyed is to remain a Proprietary one and not an actual Legal Ownership In Fee, until a specified point in time or the happening or non-happening of a stipulated event, at which time the contractual relationship between the parties will end, and the deed will be transferred from seller (or from a contractually-designated third party escrow agent). In the event the Contract is voided, title will never be conveyed to the buyer.

This is a way to do a deal, to get a buyer at least "partly in" and to get a seller at least "partly out" while circumventing any need to close a new mortgage (which may not even be available), without need to assume an existing mortgage (which may not be assumable), and without need for the seller to commit resources (which he may or may not have or may or may not want to commit), to paying off an existing mortgage in order to ultimately convey clear title through a clever Form of Seller-Financing.

The key to the pliability, indeed the key to using the Installment Contract, is the premise that title is not conveyed, a deed is not to be tendered at any "closing" either simultaneous with or immediately after the signing of the actual Contract. And by its very terms this Contract is no ordinary sales agreement. The Installment Contract is drafted to function as a longer-term contractual relationship which contemplates a deed, a closing of title, at some future date. And this is why the Installment Contract must be properly drafted to best address the salient issues and reasonably secure the divergent interests of both parties over this longer period of time.

Sometimes referred to as a "Land" Contract due to its origins, primarily in the Midwest where such forms of contract took hold mostly in the sale of farms and other tracts of land when neither a lot of cash nor financing was readily available, the Installment Contract was most commonly used in the mid to late 1900's. But it remains a viable technique for both small sales and larger commercial deals alike.

The risks and rewards flow on both sides of the Contract. Installment agreements can be useful where there is either a large or small equity in the property; where it makes sense to leave the existing financing in place; where the existing mortgage cannot be assumed and financing is needed and not otherwise available; and where the numbers for the deal fit only if the existing mortgage can remain in place. Installment Contracts are most useful where the seller can close and offer his buyer Seller-Financing in the form of an actual new mortgage, seller to buyer, but prefers "to wait and see", he prefers to keep title in his name for a certain period of time and not immediately give the deed and grant a new mortgage. Why?

Because where the seller gives title and grants a mortgage and the buyer subsequently defaults, the seller (lender) always runs the risk of encountering those problems which are incident to any foreclosure action. Under an Installment Contract, however, a buyer default in payments to his seller (whether the monies being paid represent purely seller's proceeds or also include reimbursement to the seller for ongoing payments he is making on the property, perhaps for a mortgage that has been left in place), entitles "the seller-under-contract" to more immediate and less costly remedies than he would have in a foreclosure action. No mortgage to foreclose. No collateral (property) to try to get back and sell or get sold at Sheriff's Sale.

The seller still has title. The buyer has a contractual interest in the property, and by its terms the Contract has built-in self-executing remedies in the event of default. Notice requirements and remedies are spelled out in the Contract. Typically, in the event of default which is not cured, the seller can cancel the Contract, cause a forfeiture of the buyer's rights and down payment and other investment, and/or exact other penalties from the defaulting buyer.

The underlying issues as to respective rights, liabilities, and purposes of the Agreement should be settled in the Contract. Before signing the seller should make adequate inquiry – credit check, etc. – so that he is confident of his buyer's character and ability to perform. And so should the buyer have confidence that his seller will be fair and perform according to Contract. Both parties are making considerable investments of time and money in this Contract; and remember, the buyer is placing real trust in the seller, as the seller remains the legal owner.

Among the contractual points: Purchase price; Amount of down payment; Amounts and terms (and allocation) of subsequent regular (monthly) payments; Terms of any balloon / final payment(s); Particulars as to existing third party mortgages which are to remain open and how and when they will be liquidated as a portion of the purchase price; Seller's rights and remedies upon default by buyer in payments or other terms; Buyer's rights and remedies upon default by seller, particularly with regard to seller's continuing obligation to pay any outstanding mortgage; End (or balloon) date for Contract to close and merge into conveyance of a deed and the terms for such closing.

Due to the nature of the ongoing relationship, the Contract must be specific in delineating performance and liability issues, in even the most routine of everyday matters – i.e., "Who handles, Who collects from, and Who makes decisions respecting any tenants in the premises?" Both parties have insurable interests and the Contract must qualify matters which concern insurance payments and the content of insurance policies. Responsibility for routine maintenance, improvements, major repairs, Code compliance, management and daily decision-making, and tax and utility payments, are among the topics which must also be covered.

As a measure of protection for all concerned, the Contract should direct that documents which will be important down the road, including the deed, affidavits, authorizations and powers of attorney, be executed along with the Contract and the originals be held in escrow by an attorney. An Escrow Agreement detailing the ultimate disposition and use of the escrowed documents, their release, cancellation, or recording, per the Contract, should also be executed and held by the attorney.

Some years ago I handled an Installment Contract preparation and eventual closing for a large rooming house in an urban New Jersey city. The buyer and seller were two of the most unlikely and opposite of characters; I do not know that either fully understood the import or details of the Contract, but both were honest and businesslike, both abided by the Contract, and five years after its inception they closed. By the time of closing the seller's old mortgage had been paid down considerably. The market had improved. The value of the property had Appreciated. Its rent roll had jumped. The buyer had modernized the structure. And by the closing date the buyer was in a position to secure what after the previous five years now seemed like modest financing, which would satisfy his balloon to the seller and thus permit the seller to receive the balance of his profit and pay off the balance on his old mortgage.

This transaction had every element imaginable. When the Contract was signed the seller had been trying in vain for almost a year to market the property. He could not find a buyer with sufficient cash or one who could get a mortgage. (Mortgages are always difficult to place on rooming houses.) He was not in a position to come to the closing with cash and pay his own mortgage off, either. His attorney did not want him to convey title with only a small down payment, or continue to be involved with his buyer and a non-assumable mortgage. The primary fear was the buyer would take title, milk the building, let it deteriorate further, not pay the seller or the existing mortgage, and down the road leave the seller to take back a debt-ridden, depleted mess.

The Installment Contract did the trick. The seller could no longer manage the property and he was able to get his money out and retire. The buyer, who all these years later still owns the rooming house, now has a gold mine that he has completely refurbished and re-Leveraged a few times over, and its considerable income has allowed him to trade in his lunch truck for the business of a "working landlord".

Without question there are clearly some very practical and effective ways to work around things and make Deals happen even in Bad Markets. Without some Ingenuity and Creativity, many Deals will and do end up as nothing more than Lost Opportunities.

And as mentioned in Chapter IV, the <u>Raffle</u> or Lottery Variations of Selling (where permitted), and the <u>Auction</u> concept, can prove effective when utilized by a seller as attention-grabbing shrewd "stunts" in Bad Markets. Auctions may or may not require third party financing, but both Auctions and Raffles stray from the Box and ignite Notice, Publicity and Buyers.

The dynamics of Auctions also tend to bring bids which often exceed offers drawn from more conventional marketing routes. <u>Sometimes you have to</u>

Think, Shake Things Up, and Not Simply Follow The Crowd or Give in before you have to, if in fact you will ever have to give in at all.

A major question, particularly when Selling in a Bad Market is whether or not to use a Real Estate Broker and if so under what circumstances and with what understandings between Seller and Broker. When your back is up against the wall, when the market, the times, and the numbers, are all against you, when things are tough, when the profit margin may be thin, when the stakes are high and matters a bit out of your control, is no time, especially if you are a novice seller, to try to market a property without trying what can be done to Maximize Prospects.

Listing a property for sale with a licensed real estate broker (a licensed salesperson works for the broker, the broker owns the office and/or supervises the salesperson, and the commonly misused term "realtor" simply refers to membership in a professional organization), should involve an exclusive listing agreement. The form describes the property and gives the designated broker the exclusive right to sell (or lease) that property (the listing) – at the listed price or such other price as the seller (or landlord) might subsequently accept – for a stated period of time (usually three to six months), for an agreed compensation to be paid to the broker upon closing of the transaction (usually 5 to 7% of the sales price or aggregate rental).

Unless there are specific "exemptions" noted in the listing agreement, "exclusive" means that whether the seller, the listing broker, or any other broker causes a sale or lease to be consummated within the listing period, the commission will be due and payable to the listing broker – to be apportioned according to any splits between the listing broker and co-operating offices with whom the listing broker has reciprocal agreements.

A properly negotiated listing with the "right" broker is usually the best course – and far preferable, for all but a few, to taking the "for sale by owner route". But list with the "right" broker. Not some office that promises the impossible.

You do not really want a broker who will "yes" you to death just to get your listing – who will agree with you no matter what and try to convince you that he will get an over market price for the property, "absolutely", regardless of a poor or mediocre market. If you foolishly insist on listing at a ridiculous asking price – thereby pricing yourself out of the market, losing prospective buyers, paving the way for your property to become shopworn or a local joke – only if your Broker had initially advised you to be realistic and then listed at your overpriced number after having first cautioned you – should you regard him as being a "Right" Broker.

Educate yourself, learn a bit about your Broker's track record, as well as that of your individual salesperson. Know them. Get References. See what they have on the multiple listing service, see what they are currently marketing or have recently listed and sold in your area. Assure yourself that they are aggressive and closing deals. You do not want somebody who will ignore your best interests or even sell you down the proverbial river, do nothing or permit the property to become known as a steal or distress sale. A Broker can easily do irreparable harm to your sales effort by either over-pricing or not fully cooperating with other offices which attempt to show your listing. The seller's broker is supposed to look out for the seller's interests.

Request a Written Guarantee from your Broker, either as an addendum to the listing agreement or by separate document, specifying what he will do to market your listing.

When I was just graduating from law school in 1977 I owned two real estate offices in suburban Central New Jersey. That was still the era of primarily mom and pop offices, with today's regional and Inter-State multi-office firms and diverse franchises still in their infancy. And a good part of the ingenuity which grew my two offices from nothing to profitable entities within less than a year was my practice of volunteering a written guarantee of what we would do for our listing sellers. (We guaranteed some then-innovative services, commission structures, and publicity in our own quarterly advertising magazine – a very uncommon form of broker promotion at that time.)

So, get a Written Guarantee that your exclusive listing will be placed in all appropriate multiple listing services which serve your area. (A multiple listing system is comprised of brokers who share their listings and show each other's listings under a pre-determined commission split between the listing and selling offices.) Be sure that your Broker clearly specifies on your listing the commission split which he is offering to cooperating offices – preferably giving the selling office more than 50% of the gross commission.

When listing push your Broker, and especially so in a poor market, to offer incentives to other offices in order to best induce them to focus on, to show your listing whenever they have a customer who might be a candidate. A 60/40 or even 70/30 split of the prevailing (do not go lower) gross commission rate, in favor of the other ("selling") office, is advisable.

The seller's cause will also be advanced where the listing Broker offers creative inducements such as a lump sum dollar bonus to the office that sells the property by a specified date, and if the listing Broker is cooperative in facilitating showings by other offices (i.e., making the key available, promptly returning phone calls). Your Broker must focus the attention of other offices on your listing, your Broker must set it apart from the other properties on the multiple. Get an edge. Get action. Generate attention, get more showings, better your chances of receiving a better offer in a shorter period of time

Other services which a Broker should itemize – placing a sign on the property, holding a minimum number of open houses, type and frequency of advertising, printing brochures for more expensive properties, and utilizing internet sites. You need a Broker who will push the listing not only in his own office, but and often more importantly, one who will push it through the many other offices on the multiple listing system.

You should be guaranteed use of all available avenues which can create the maximum exposure for your listing. Your listing Broker should be able to tell you, as I would tell many owners who listed with my firm, "our office will probably not sell your property, but we will see to it that it gets sold as soon as possible and on the best terms possible". Your Broker's job is to make sure you get the desired Deal – through somebody.

Intelligent, Professional, Aggressive Marketing, especially in difficult times, is the seller's best assurance that he will come out on the best possible terms. The "right" marketing by the "right" listing Broker. The results, the best bottom line, are what count. Even after netting out a commission, most sellers do realize a higher bottom line with less hassle when listing with a Broker than if they had tried to sell as a "for sale by owner".

Especially in a Bad Market, when a seller's financial needs are probably the greatest, and he is pressured, a 'for sale by owner" campaign will not only likely net less than a Broker effort, but it will also prove a difficult daily experience and probably prolong the marketing effort. The "chase" will also divert the seller's attention from other pressing personal and business concerns.

A seller is often too involved personally, emotionally, and financially. He might appear to be desperate to a buyer, which will invite bargain-hunting. His own tensions may put a damper on a buyer's visit and interest. A seller who shows his own home also tends to focus his commentary on the less important things in his property which may be of interest to him, but which are not selling points. He may be prone to showing off that makeshift paneling job in the den; or the cracking concrete slab with stones in the rear yard that he passes off as a fantastic patio; while the prospective buyer is on an entirely different wavelength, mentally trying to figure out how much it will cost to redo or replace the homemade "workmanship". Many sellers are also too defensive in answering legitimate buyer's questions. Moreover, the average seller will rarely be the best person to negotiate or try to structure financing on his own.

The bottom line – aggressive no-nonsense marketing by a Broker will attract more buyers and usually more qualified buyers, which translates into more possibilities and thus a better shot at success.

And use your own business and real estate Smarts, with the input of your attorney and mortgage broker, in conjunction with the marketing efforts of the "Right" real estate Broker.

Caveat – sellers often think they are clever in promoting their property through an "open listing", which is basically publicizing it with certain offices and offering them a commission in the event they consummate a sale, without signing an exclusive or multiple listing. Such a seller may feel he is shrewd and getting the best of both worlds – exposure through certain brokers while still preserving his flexibility to sell on his own and "save" on commission. The argument to the broker is that he can keep the entire commission if he sells, so therefore he should be happy with an open listing and push the property.

But such an offer of a "full" commission holds little water, at least in the residential field. The listing needs to be in the multiple. It must be promoted by a Broker who has a vested interest. Cooperating offices need to see that you are motivated and "for real". The listing must be out there, in the standard industry format, with the Brokers knowing you have a proper listing agreement which will protect them if they bring in a buyer. With the exception of certain commercial listings, in most markets brokers often discard and rarely show open listings.

So too is it foolish to sign a one office non-multiple exclusive listing; opting for one office instead of hundreds to work for you for the "same price" does not make sense.

Aside From Your Method Of Marketing, Asking Price is also an important consideration. My advice – not too high, not too low (usually). In a Bad Market it is often best to ask in the middle range, based on current comps. (Of course in Boom Cycles, over-market asking prices many times bring still higher over-asking price offers.) Know your market, know the current comps, know what's on the market. And should your listing linger – Reconsider, Recalculate just what the Market is bringing. <u>Pricing, Expectations, And Negotiations</u> are all functions of your own Needs and the Realities of the Marketplace.

The <u>Appearance</u> of a property and <u>Access</u> for showing are also vitally important. Budget and Time Constraints, Condition of the property, the Type of property, the Amount of Equity in the property, the Desired Net and a concern with possibly Diminishing Returns from further "investment" in the property, are all Appropriate Factors in deciding what, if anything, should be done to "Spruce Up" before Marketing. A savvy Broker will assist with considerations of whether or not more Mundane Cosmetics should be done, whether or not the property should be Staged, and how such seemingly minor yet often important issues like Clutter and any need for Professional Cleanings should be handled.

<u>Yes, you can Definitely Intelligently and "Successfully" Sell in a Bad Market, just as you can Intelligently and Successfully Buy in a Bad Market</u>.

CHAPTER VI

BUY FORECLOSURES – TO HOLD OR TO FLIP

In the Introduction to a Foreclosure Magazine I was publishing way back in 1994, I wrote something which was very true then, which has been true in Boom and Bust Cycles before and since, which is true today, and which will certainly be apropos in the future, also: "The purchase of properties in the process of being foreclosed or, for the sophisticated practitioner, the purchase from the lender of the mortgage instrument itself which is in foreclosure, represents a proven method to succeed on a quick turnaround, to accumulate equity, and/or to create cash flow. Opportunities abound for the Knowledgeable shopper of residential and commercial properties, land, and more exotic parcels…

We list properties in foreclosure within an appropriate number of weeks of the action being filed. We publish the listings six-sixteen months prior to the Sheriff's Sale. That gives you, the Investor, ample time to explore the particular property and to negotiate a deal with the owner and /or the lender."

No matter what the current market may be, regardless of what the immediate trends may be, the bottom line is there has always been, and there will always be, a Great Deal of Money to be made in Buying and Selling, Holding, Fixing, and Renting, Foreclosures.

As discussed in Chapter II, absent other compelling personal, business or sentimental reasons for making a purchase, the Guiding Rule for the shrewd investor and speculator is to Buy Only When A Measurable Profit Is Already Built-In Up-Front. Buy Low, Buy Right – (and Sell High). Elementary. And by definition, buying foreclosures is at its heart a form of bargain hunting.

Whether Holding, Flipping, or Rehabbing, whatever you do with it, the purchase price must be good enough, "as is", on Day One. Visible to the novice naked eye or clear only to the more experienced – "Something Extra, That Edge," which makes a property "A Deal", must be there. And "that" something is what makes dealing in <u>Foreclosures</u> a special opportunity – in its own way "more special" than the sum total of the lucrative "<u>Basic Yields Package</u>" which is inherent in real estate generally (Chapter II), which Yields should be basic to any purchase over the course of time.

Know your Market; Do your Due Diligence!

Only a few years back successive eras of free and easy money and repeated Boom-to-Bust or Boom-to-Down Cycles, helped inspire a wave of hucksters and other promoters to start equating the buying and selling of foreclosures with the "magic" of multi-level marketing schemes and other "miracle" cash cows. But as good as it can be it is usually neither. Their pitch has been simple: "No knowledge. No money. No credit. No work. No risk. No nothing. Just listen to me, buy my tapes and books, and you are set. Just sit back and collect."

With varying intensities of promotion since the late 1970's the hucksters have been preaching their nonsense on cable and late-night TV and the internet; and as things turn around many more will re-surface; both pre-and post-Internet it has been a campaign to get everybody "involved". And the huge market Appreciation over those years – so many novice "investors" with such scant knowledge, making so much profit from foreclosures and just about any kind of purchase – did convince too many (but certainly not the promoters themselves!) that maybe their outrageous claims were really true! Today, most of these self-styled high-flying gurus and their ilk of "motivational speakers" have temporarily taken a back seat.

<u>For the most part Making Money in Foreclosures, and real estate generally, requires some Knowledge, Prudence, Effort, Pragmatism, and Perseverance, along with some Money and/or Credit – either your's, your bank's or your partner's</u>. It is a lot more than those glorified "boot camps", late night infomercials which portray the casual new investor out on his yacht or swinging a sledge hammer as he magically demolishes walls, and all of those promotions and (non) seminars which promise endless riches if you just buy their "how to" products.

In periods of spiraling Appreciation and Demand, Amateur Hour can be very misleading and give the wrong impression that the "no knowledge, no nothing" approach really can be the way to make it.

Luck notwithstanding, and aside from those times when almost any purchase can turn a quick profit, in order to really "make it" there is a bit more to speculating. (In the longer term, however, there is something to be said for Accumulating Capital and racking up Diverse Yields through the sheer passage of time.)

What, then, is the basic anatomy or definition of <u>Foreclosure</u>? As noted earlier, Foreclosure is an "in rem" – Latin, the root of most legalese – action. It is a legal proceeding, a lawsuit in the appropriately designated State Court. It names as defendants to the action the obligors (individual or entity) on the mortgage and any successors or lienholders who had, have acquired, or may have, a legal or equitable interest in the property. The lender (plaintiff) may be either the original lender or a successor who purchased the mortgage as an individual security instrument or as part of a block of bundled mortgages. (Banks, mortgage companies, investment funds, and "Wall Street", just like the Federal Government, buy and sell mortgages as securitized commodities, discussed earlier) at a discount, at a premium, or at par, depending on their "quality", interest rates, performing status, and market conditions.

A Foreclosure is designed to enforce payment of the mortgage balance upon default as specified in the mortgage. "Default" may include failure to make required payments to the lender or a third party; failure to perform certain other specified acts or duties; or actions or non-action constituting forbidden acts or conditions. The real estate is the collateral.

A lender may be more than happy to work something out – a sale of the property by the borrower or some sort of loan revision – in order to recoup all or part of its debt or otherwise restore the mortgage to performing status. And while most lenders typically prefer to avoid foreclosing, it is part of their business and sometimes the only or most effective means to get the collection process off dead center, to conclude the process.

The logical extreme of a foreclosure action, the Sheriff's Sale, is the ultimate step, the culmination of the process, at which time either the lender takes back the collateral to later resell (with the hope of recouping as much of its debt as possible), or a third party buys it at Sale and pays off the entire debt (or some lesser portion stipulated by the lender prior to Sale). Lenders may not relish being in the real estate business, but it is often inevitable.

In discussing foreclosure properties, many in the industry juxtapose the terminology, resulting in common misnomers. Once the Lis Pendens and

Court Action have been filed, the property is "in foreclosure". It comes "out of foreclosure" only when the lis pendens is discharged and the legal action dismissed. This ends a foreclosure action, be its conclusion by owner's sale of the property, by refinance, by Sheriff's Sale, or by a mortgage workout.

An action which is terminated by Sheriff's Sale concludes in a different fashion than any other resolution. Here the property has been "foreclosed upon". The lender becomes either the "new owner" (takes back at Sale), or the "former lender" awaiting payment of net Sale proceeds from the successful bidder through the Sheriff's Office. In either case the foreclosure action and mortgage become history by operation of law as the mortgage and lawsuit merge into the resultant Sheriff's Deed and are extinguished by cancellation.

The literature and common parlance often refer to properties in active foreclosure as "pre-foreclosures". They are not "pre-foreclosures". They are "in foreclosure". Properties which have gone the route through Sheriff's Sale have been "foreclosed upon", and in those cases where the former lender takes them back, they become Bank-Owned Property (REO-Real Estate Owned), and not, as many refer to them, "a foreclosure".

While different States employ a host of procedural rules to prosecute fore-closure actions (Strict, Judicial, and other jurisdictions), there are certain common basic steps in the process. The impetus for the action is a Default in the mortgage which goes uncured. The mortgagor has breached his Contract with the mortgagee.

Default will typically mean non-payment but again, in accordance with the operative terms of the documents it could also include a variety of other actionable breaches – i.e., property maintenance and use violations, failure to make tax and insurance payments. If not cured in accordance with the mortgage terms, Default entitles the lender to proceed with an Acceleration of the mortgage (demand for immediate re-payment of the entire debt in full). Should the lender's assertion of this legal remedy per the mortgage for the specified breach go unanswered, the lender can go forward with its action. And the purpose of this action, again, is to get things back on track, either by persuading the borrower to pay up or otherwise settle or comply instead of risking the loss of his property, or to satisfy the debt by causing the loss of the property via Sheriff's Sale.

The lender will first serve the borrower with informal letters and ultimately the Final Notice to Cure, which warns of the impending action. An explicit Final Notice served in a specific manner is typically a condition precedent to filing for foreclosure. And as with other Notices and Pleadings in the action, in order to be valid the Final Notice must contain certain precise information, deadlines, and language; each State's Civil Rules of Foreclosure Practice specify their particular forms and content.

The initial Notices are usually a series of letters which build in intensity. Prior to filing the lender will probably also have an Asset Manager make personal visits to the property and attempt telephone contact in final efforts to persuade the borrower to perform, settle or sell.

Also before filing the lender will conduct a title search and make other inquiries to determine the chain of title and to be sure of the identity of any possible interested parties who may have any sort of legal or equitable status in the property, and who therefore must also be named in the foreclosure Complaint as co-defendants. Most States require the lender to join with the named borrowers anyone who may have any interest in the property, including judgment and other creditor lienholders of record, tenants, and known or possible spouses.

The Lis Pendens is filed in the local office which handles the recording of documents affecting real estate, usually the County Clerk or Register, and its filing signals the formal announcement of the action in the sense that it is the requisite recorded Notice of the pendency of a foreclosure lawsuit.

Like other recorded documents respecting real estate, this filing "puts the world on notice" of the in rem action which is about to start and which shall affect the described piece of real estate. This legal procedure automatically cuts off any party who may thereafter "acquire" an interest in the property. The legal theory is that anybody who may subsequently become involved with the property will, or should, do a title search, and thus find the Lis Pendens Notice in the official County property records and thereby be Put on Notice as to the impending action. Whether they intend to purchase, lease, lend, or otherwise obtain an interest in the property, they should be guided accordingly. Thus does the lender protect, or perfect, his impending action.

Any interests of record prior to the Lis Pendens having been filed are named co-defendants; and by virtue of the Lis Pendens, any subsequent interests, be they presently unknown, suspected, or unsuspected, will thus *ipso facto* be "joined" into the action, not individually on paper, but as a class by operation of law. If the matter goes to Sheriff's Sale, any such subsequent interests will have thus been cut off and "foreclosed" themselves, as it were, from having any stake in the property.

A Deed or Mortgage recorded after the Lis Pendens, for instance, or a Mechanics Lien, a Contract, or a Docketed civil monetary Judgment will not complicate the foreclosure as they do not have to be "added on" later as additional co-defendants, and they are rendered a nullity with respect to the action.

The actual lawsuit is initiated with the Complaint in Foreclosure. It recites the names of the parties to the action, the basis of the action, the relief sought (collateral, and perhaps rents during the prosecution of the action), and the terms and parameters of the debt-mortgage which is in default.

The Summons is the legal instrument which formally serves the Complaint (Notice of commencement of the action) on the named obligor(s) and joined co-defendants. It is attached to the Complaint as a companion piece of paper in the Service of Process. The Summons and Complaint must be served on all defendants in accordance with local Court Rules, either in person or by other designated means, which may include advertisement. Where the plaintiff wants to reserve its right to possibly seek a deficiency judgment (to recoup any balance on the debt which may not be covered by proceeds from the realty) at some later date, the legal papers must almost always be served on the obligor(s) personally.

The lender need not join superior lienholders as co-defendants. Such superior liens – "superior" because they are primary to, ahead of, the foreclosing lien due to their priority as a matter of law, as in the case of real estate taxes, or due to their priority resulting from the date of recording of the lien – are not concerned with what a junior lienholder may be doing (the junior lienholder in this case being the first mortgage). The superior lien comes first, and it must be made whole, it must be satisfied in its entirety before monies from any disposition of the property can flow to the foreclosing lender (again, which in this case would be a junior or secondary lienholder, even if it is a First Mortgage).

Taking the analogy a step further, where a second mortgage holder files for foreclosure, any (pre-existing) first mortgage still open of record need not be named as a defendant in the Complaint either. The rights of a First are not normally affected by a foreclosure action of a Second. The actions of the Second cannot diminish the entitlements of the First; the First must be satisfied before the foreclosing Second can get a dime.

In filing for foreclosure the lender must make certain decisions regarding any tenants in the premises. As noted earlier, in most States even tenants with verbal leases possess Statutory rights which require the lender or successful third-party bidder at Sale to recognize them and extend a certain latitude permitting them to remain "for awhile" at a reasonable market rental.

Where a tenant's lease precedes the recording of the foreclosing mortgage and neither by its terms nor by any other satisfactory writing signed by the tenant is it subordinated to that mortgage, then the foreclosure action may have no legal effect on the rights of such tenant. This issue is a function of applicable State law and the facts in each case. Even if a lease is executed after the mortgage or otherwise subordinated to the mortgage the lender may still prefer that a tenant remain, at least during the prosecution of the action (but typically not for long after the Sheriff's Sale), as a positive presence in the property.

Note – Most leases contain boilerplate language subordinating them to (superseding) rights of any existing or future mortgages, meaning that the mortgage will have priority over the lease with its rights tempered in favor of giving "some sort of latitude" to the tenant only by virtue of State law.

The lender does not want to get well into an action, let alone complete a foreclosure, only to have it deemed procedurally or substantively defective, a finding that will certainly lead to delay and additional expenses and a need for corrective measures, possibly even a redo of the action.

So, the Summons and Complaint having been served, the lender will have a second title search done to ensure that the necessary parties have been given proper notice and were properly joined in the action. This second search will also make sure the borrower has not made a "midnight" sale of the property in an effort to derail the lender.

Assuming no corrective steps are needed, the action proceeds – at different speeds, with varying procedural steps, and with stipulated legal opportunities (Notices), at given intervals for the borrower to cure. The States have their own particular procedures by which a lender obtains a Judgment in Foreclosure. This is the litigation phase, when the lender, like any plaintiff, must do certain things and the defendant has given rights to challenge and opportunities to otherwise act to Delay the action. (See Chapter III – i.e. Answer the Complaint, File a Counter-Claim, Challenge plaintiff's Standing to sue, Submit Filings which result in Automatic Stalls.) Most foreclosures are uncontested actions which consist essentially of filing and serving sequential paperwork.

Either before or after the Final Judgment in Foreclosure is obtained and entered and acted upon, which Judgment permits the lender to proceed to Sheriff's Sale, there are final Statutory opportunities for the parties to try to negotiate an amicable settlement. Literally until the Sale is called, they can work to Reinstate the loan, Modify it, Close on a Straight or Short Sale, Secure a Refinance or other Resolution, or Arrange for a Deed In Lieu Of Foreclosure. In New Jersey and certain other jurisdictions, the borrower has until the Final Judgment is entered to Cure and thus end the action merely by tendering the arrears and costs, even if the lender objects.

And again, there are the final Statutory Delays (as to the Sale, etc.), and those which can be negotiated. Legal maneuvers in other arenas, such as Chapter 13's, State or FHA Mediations, can of course also impede the progress of the Action both substantively and procedurally.

Absent prior or subsequent resolution, the Final Judgment In Foreclosure sets the stage to schedule the Sheriff's Sale. Different States have their own requirements for requisite advance public advertising of a Sale – legal notices to be of certain form and content, placed in designated newspapers at specific intervals and/or otherwise posted immediately prior to the Sale date. The Sale is usually scheduled by the local Officer of the Court, typically the Sheriff, after the plaintiff has submitted its Final Judgment and a copy of the proposed ad and the required deposit to advertise and hold the Sale.

Typically pre-Sale ads must identify the parties, set out the legal description of the property, state the amount of the debt, list the identity and amount of other (superior) liens which must be satisfied, and give the date, time, and place of Sale. Advance publicity is designed to ensure that the public is given an opportunity to bid, to ensure that all parties to the action are afforded a "means" to attract attention and thereby promote bidding, and to ensure that the defendant(s) are given abundant notice.

Where a Sale is actually held, depending on the jurisdiction, it may be in the form of the stereotyped public event on the steps of the local Courthouse, or it may be a simple business-like gathering in a small room at the Courthouse.

The Sale is usually administered by an Officer of the Court, such as a Judge, Sheriff or other official. In certain States the lender itself can conduct the Sale. For the most part Foreclosure Sales are Reserve Auctions (meaning the successful party must bid at least a certain stipulated minimum), and sometimes Absolute Auctions (where the highest bidder becomes the buyer).

Bidders must be very careful to ascertain if there are Superior or other forms of Obligations affecting the property which they must later satisfy or assume – such as primary monetary encumbrances, construction clouds or problems, open Property Code violations or penalties, pending environmental regulatory entanglements or remediation problems, etc.

At most Sales (Auctions), the properties are called and the "upset bid" for each property is announced. The upset bid is the minimum amount that the lender will accept, be it the entire Judgment or a lesser sum set by the lender. Again, a successful bidder must satisfy either the entire Judgment or any announced lesser minimum in the more common Reserve Auction. Absent a sufficient bid, the property will "go back" to the lender.

In the event the lender takes the property back, or if a successful third-party bidder does not bid sufficiently above the amount necessary to satisfy the foreclosing lien (including costs of the Sale), so as to "pay down" junior liens, all or part of any named junior lienholder's debt is wiped out.

A winning bid, and there can be bidding wars at Sheriff's Sales, which more than satisfies all Foreclosing Debt and Sale Costs, will result in a "Surplus" which, in order of priority and where appropriate will go, in a pro-rata fashion, first to the Junior Liens and, provided all such liens are satisfied, to the Former Owner.

Depending on the State, the successful bidder must deposit 10 to 30% of his bid, and tender the balance, usually within 30 days, or risk forfeiture of his deposit. In order to bid, prospective bidders must come with sufficient bank funds in hand to cover the estimated deposit on any parcel they went to buy. Sales are open to the public, and anybody can show up and watch.

The successful bidder must then wait out the Redemption Period – typically ten days – during which the borrower has the opportunity to pay off his entire debt to the foreclosing lender and thus cancel the Sale and retain his property. Assuming there is no Redemption, the lender who "took back" simply waits for delivery of the Sheriff's Deed; any third-party winner must pay the balance and within weeks will receive a similar Deed. Then it is time for the new owner to start dealing with the property itself.

If it is still occupied any bona fide tenants must be honored or dealt with as aforesaid. A former owner who remains in physical possession must be persuaded, or "bribed", to vacate, or an eviction may be the only route to removal; and as noted earlier, an occupant can delay his exit through a "13" filing or other tactics.

Then comes the actual day-to-day management. Utilities, maintenance, fix-up, carrying costs, perhaps marketing.

The objectives of a third-party buyer? Keep and use the property in some fashion; simply live in it; rent it out "as is" or "fixed up"; sell it "as is" or "fixed up"; or undertake some sort of rehab. The goal of a lender who has taken his collateral back? Maintain it, and (usually) get rid of it on the best and quickest terms possible. (Note – today most lenders prefer to vacate their foreclosed properties prior to reselling them.)

In the event there is a Deficiency between the debt (plus costs incurred by the former lender) and the amount realized at Sale, or between the debt (plus costs incurred by the former lender) and the former lender's net from subsequent resale of a property taken back at Sale, the former lender, as discussed earlier, may elect to undertake what in most States is a second legal action against the obligors individually. In some jurisdictions the Rules permit an anticipated Deficiency claim to be included as part of the actual in rem foreclosure action. But in most States, New Jersey included, the Deficiency claim is a second lawsuit, an *in personem* action; unlike the foreclosure action against the property, this action being the garden variety liquidated damages (dollar) suit against a person or other entity.

Again, most lenders are loathe to start a second expensive lawsuit against a possibly wiped-out, maybe hard-to-locate former borrower, chasing dollars that he will most likely be unable to ever pay. Unless the lender sees strong and clear assets, a Deficiency action is rare.

As already discussed, there have been many proposals and discussions about expanding existing safeguards to better protect borrowers facing foreclosure. And in recent years, even during the Boom Cycles, many States have initiated foreclosure reforms designed to enhance borrowers' rights and streamline the actual process – reflections of more general societal and legal thinking which is geared to improving "the lot of consumers" generally.

We have seen the legislation (codification) in many disparate statutes and judicial decrees which, aside from those incident to recent Federal Anti-Bust Initiatives, constitute broad Foreclosure Reforms. Some examples of Federal Pumps which simultaneously address the Economy and reinforce the pre-existing trend towards making State foreclosure practices more "consumer friendly" include: Foreclosure Moratoriums; Moves to use "13's" to compel Cramdowns; Federal Subsidies for certain Modifications;

Court-Sanctioned Mediation Programs; and Mandatory Forensic Reviews of foreclosure paperwork.

New Jersey's Fair Foreclosure Act, referred earlier, a case in point, has been hailed as precedent-setting legislation which has brought substantial relief to borrowers in default. It was officially described as "a measure which enables the lender to expedite the actual process of foreclosing in those cases where the owner is not offering a defense (and at the same time) a measure which enables the owner to have more of a chance to reinstate the mortgage and thus hold onto the property" – by granting additional time from the date of default to bring arrears current without the necessity of paying off the entire mortgage.

As The New Jersey Institute For Continuing Legal Education observed upon its enactment: "The new law is designed to provide additional protection for homeowners facing foreclosure, and to help lenders return defaulted mortgages to performing status." Their Commentary continued: It is the "first step in the complete reform of the mortgage foreclosure practice in New Jersey".

And in the immediate future the anatomy of a foreclosure will probably assume new and more borrower-friendly characteristics and procedures nationwide. This will be effectuated through changes in substantive State Laws and Rules of Civil Practice along with (superseding) Federal Statutes.

Such changes have implications for the speculator and everyone else involved in buying, selling, and rehabbing foreclosure properties. But in the end none of this means that (many more) foreclosure actions will necessarily be resolved more favorably for the average debtor. There will always be more than enough Deals for all to pursue. Not to be crass, but it is inevitable that certain people will be hurt in real estate as others profit from their losses.

It is the same principle which is at the heart of the overall realities of Economic Boom and Bust Cycles, various problems with individual sectors of the Economy, the rise and fall of retail chains, and indeed the average going-out-of-business sales where the loss on one side will translate into gain on the other. Good Buys will always be out there. As with other distress or sub-market opportunities, when dealing with foreclosures it becomes irrelevant for us to try and ascertain the root of any specific individual problem – greed, poor management, personal or general economic problems. Once the ripples from a problem situation have reached a certain stage, there will be a "bargain" property out there, and in most cases someone will lose and someone will win.

No need to "justify" buying foreclosure properties. Just as there is no need to explain why or how somebody can buy all sorts of personalty from, say, an Estate or a defunct restaurant, and profit by the Deal.

One of the central questions in the Field is "How Do We Best Find, Locate, Foreclosures Which May Be Good Buys?" Some 15 years ago the best method of prospecting was by combing Lists Of Recently Filed Actions, lists which were most readily available in monthly foreclosure publications or through faxed weekly update services. Increasingly, the focus shifted to the Internet, where today a speculator has a seemingly endless array of listings in any State at his fingertips, in areas so vast that he could never begin to digest or follow-up on a fraction of the information.

Today's data providers typically list actions which were filed within 24 hours of their posting, together with actions docketed within the previous two or more years. Standard monthly subscription rates for such services range from about $30.00 to $200.00, with these at the lower end of the rate scale providing more than enough listings and adequate depth of content.

These listings can be reviewed online, sometimes printed out, or retained with labels run for bulk solicitation mailings. They typically contain as complete a legal and factual picture as can be gleaned from the filing of an action. Some providers supplement the basic data which they obtain from the Foreclosure Complaint with relevant information of their own such as comparables and market trends, to further assist the speculator. Thus, the salient information in most of these listings will usually include: Owner's name and address; property address and legal description; mortgage balance, original amount, interest rate, term, and, possibly, date of default; name of plaintiff's attorney and contact information; details as to other liens; and sometimes a price opinion for the property.

Such summaries are excellent starting points, as complete an overview as one can get before actually going out and seeing the property, making contact with the owner, studying comps and local market trends and, if need be, negotiating with the lender and/or owner. Not usually available in these listings, however, is a vital piece of data – direct contact information for the lender. Lenders have regional offices and often servicing companies and asset management firms handling their workouts across the world. The lender is a key party who the speculator will want to contact and, many times, negotiate with directly, and their account number, contact person and telephone number will all be found on collection letters in the possession of the property owner.

In addition to using published Lists, other basic Ways for finding properties in foreclosure, or possible foreclosure candidates which may not yet even
be in default, Potential Deals, include: Maintaining a Network of Professional
Contacts / Referrers (attorneys, real estate brokers, appraisers, mortgage brokers, accountants and financial consultants); Routinely studying the local Multiple Listing System "for what seems to be interesting" and Doing Visual
Inspections and Other Routine Observing and Reading with an eye peeled for
potential properties, and Simple Word of Mouth and following Legal Advertisements in newspapers – the standard (free) source for best tracking upcoming Sheriff's Sales.

Should you be fortunate enough to have one or more "Birddogs" feeding
you tips about possible Deals, it is a good idea to also have a standing profit-
sharing or other fee or commission arrangement with them. You want people
in the Know (and those who are in the Know are astute and aggressive, and
may also have contacts with other speculators), to have a reason to bring Leads
to you, and not to the others.

In trying to Make Contact With Owners Of Properties In Foreclosure,
Or Properties Which May Be Foreclosure Candidates, it is best to initially
send the owner a general introductory "Solicitation Letter". These letters can
be sent to selected individual owners or in bulk to groups of owners who you
may choose as possible "Ideal Targets" from Lists, by geography or according
to price range, depending on the manner in which you wish to focus on Potential Deals.

They should be simple, short, clear and respectful. While arguments can
be made for the "Best Time Windows" in which to send Solicitation Letters
(see below), with such a vast number of Listings at your disposal, having chosen
your areas and price ranges (not a necessity), you should set a regular schedule
for sending either select or bulk mailings to owners in foreclosure, both old
and new cases.

It is often hit and miss. The month-old listing might not be in the mood
to talk, he may be looking at other options or be inundated with letters from
other speculators, attorneys and mortgage people. But the ten-month-old listing may have exhausted some opportunities to cure with no success, he may
be tired, he may have been misled by others, and he may be anxious to jump
at your offer when perhaps five months earlier this same owner would not have
even responded to you. Sometimes there is no rhyme or reason as to who will

bite, when, or why, despite those gospels which purport to "explain" what is the "best time" to solicit.

The goal of the Letter is to elicit a response, to enable you to speak briefly with the owner on the telephone and arrange an appointment to meet with him at the property. You need to get in the door to inspect the property, to review the owner's notices and paperwork, to get a sense of his needs and goals, and to be able to market yourself as a ready, willing, and able buyer who is credible, respectable, understanding, and businesslike.

There is no harm in sending Follow-Up Letters if the first one brings no response, or in trying to reach the owner by telephone – although the prevalence of unlisted numbers and cell phones makes this difficult. Uninvited visits to the property, showing up and knocking on the door, are not only often counter-productive in a basic business sense, but are also rude and dangerous, and in many cases may constitute illegal trespassing.

<u>Once you have located a Prospective Deal, the Key is to be able To Negotiate A Transaction – Buy Low, Buy Right</u>! Negotiating is not a unique art, and making the Deal is often a Process, an Uncharted Course.

And while different approaches and techniques may better suit one individual or personality than another, and may ultimately result in the same outcome anyway, an important thing to keep in mind when Negotiating with a borrower in foreclosure (in the context of other principles which should also guide your Negotiating Approach), is that in this type of situation you are dealing with a "seller" who is probably under a great deal of stress. As one individual to another, and as a smart business person, show respect; not conceit, not a haughtiness, not a condescending demeanor; but do not show a meek or wimpy persona, either. Show Competence and Confidence, but in a Personal and Understanding way. (Chapter VIII addresses Negotiating in General.)

The Ultimate Goal in dealing with the owner is to buy the property from him, pay what must be paid to the lender and any other creditors, and move forward. As noted in Chapter III, foreclosing lenders have many reasons (their Rationale) to deal with the owner / borrower and any third-party buyer whose involvement may help effectuate a desired resolution of the foreclosure action. So too (see Chapter IV), we must understand and remember the Rationale which may motivate owners in foreclosure to want to Deal, to dispose of their property before a Sheriff's Sale (as opposed to the owner who may want to Hold Onto His Property).

In the <u>Short Sale</u> scenario you Negotiate with both owner and lender (not the lender's attorney); you should be the one to facilitate efforts to persuade the lender to discount the debt; you must work with the owner to complete the paperwork which the lender may require; you should take the lead in Negotiations with the lender. You make your Deal with both lender and owner, who you pay through the closing / settlement as you also tender the discounted payoff to the lender, and you receive your deed from the owner.

Again – sometimes a Short Sale is accomplished by discounting both a First and a Second Mortgage; the viability of such a Deal depends on the amount of equity and the willingness of both mortgagees to discount sufficiently such that the transaction can be made profitable. And as discussed earlier, the First will always have an issue with the amount you pay to satisfy any Second.

With the basic <u>Straight Simple Sale,</u> in situations where the total balance plus arrears and costs will essentially be the payoff figure, or where there is only a <u>Token Discount</u>, for the most part negotiations are with the owner. The scope and extent of Negotiations with owner or lender will be a function of the amount of equity in the property and the structure of the transaction. <u>A Tight Short Sale</u> scenario requires the most interaction with the lender. Where no appreciable discount is sought or to be expected, the focus is basically on making your Deal with the owner.

The most <u>Lucrative Deals are typically those where there is still some solid equity in the property, the Straight Simple Deals</u>. Short Sales, which generally have tighter margins, are more difficult to accomplish and tend to be less lucrative – but there is still plenty of money to be made here, and they should never be overlooked as an Avenue.

<u>Buying At Sheriff's Sale</u> is usually not the gold mine that many envision and, with exceptions, is usually the least lucrative and most difficult Way to Make Money In Foreclosures.

Again, there are a number of reasons why Buying At Sheriff's Sale is often the least desirable Way to speculate in foreclosures – notwithstanding the fact that with money in hand, the Sequence leading up to securing a deed might seem easier, on the face of it, than the Negotiating Process with an owner or lender. In bidding at Sheriff's Sale, hopefully you will have first done your Due Diligence, and any winning bid you make at Auction will constitute a Good Buy, and you will wait out the Redemption Period, pay the balance, and get your deed. Less hassle and fewer steps? Yes. The issue, however, is "What Kind Of A 'Buy' Did You Get?"

We know that many properties which go to Sale are already too far gone before the Sale is even held. Most have been picked over for potential deals during the preceding year or more since the foreclosure action began. By any Sale date many are hopelessly Underwater. And unless the lender adjusts its Upset Number at Sale so that the property "acquires" some sort of equity (which may still not be enough to create a sufficient profit for a bidder), many properties at Sale are simply Negatives.

Moreover, the Auction Mentality attracts novices and can promote a buying frenzy which tends to push prices over market value or to otherwise non-profitable levels. Negative Equity, Marginal Equity, and Over-Bidding do not make for Good Deals. Again, you can make a windfall from Buying At Sheriff's Sale, but do not expect this route to routinely hand you Bargains.

A case in point: A few years back I bought a lower-priced vacant "fixer-upper" from a local attorney who had bought the house two years before at Sheriff's Sale. Under the mistaken belief that he was actually out-bidding another buyer on a much more expensive parcel at the Sale, he in fact paid well over market for this particular house! It was his first Sale, he and his wife went "to strike it rich" but they bought the wrong house.

Stuck, he spent the next two years digging a deeper hole for himself, thinking he could do a rehab without knowing what he was doing, and contractor after contractor took him to the proverbial cleaners. Ill-equipped by background and hampered by his own temperament and unwillingness to learn, he should have taken his first loss and just resold after the Sale. I do not know what his total loss turned out to be, but I got a decent Deal, I did a quick Rehab, and I turned a modest Profit.

There are other Financial Issues to contend with when Buying At Sheriff's Sale. The 10 to 30% Sale Deposit (depending on the State), which is forfeited if the Balance is not paid within the Statutory time period, usually thirty days, is a major concern. Such risk requires strong financial ability and calls for a Good Deal in the making. Furthermore, with a quick closing and limited or no access to the property for pre-Sale or "pre-closing" bank appraisals and structural inspections, the Average Buyer's Ability To Fund this type of purchase by putting new initial financing on the subject property is limited.

It is rare that a potential bidder can do Meaningful Inspections before a Sheriff's Sale, and almost never on the mechanical systems. Post-Sale "Surprises" in these often long-neglected properties, which may still be occupied by former-owners-in-possession, can prove costly. Heating, electrical, plumbing, and air conditioning systems. Boilers. Roofs. Doors. Wet basements. Broken pipes and broken walls. Kitchens stripped of their appliances. Cosmetics. Without Access and Inspections, and with others sometimes remaining in possession and control through and post-Sale, Who Ever Knows What To Expect And How To Figure Costs, and thus potential Profit?

Then there is that thorny problem of Dealing With Former Owners Or Tenants-In-Possession in an often unfriendly post-Sale environment. Although a former owner can be evicted or "bribed" for the keys, there are the interim continuing Delays, Carrying Costs and Legal Fees. There is the possibility of Further Damage being done to the property, and the chance that a former owner might also Prolong his Stay and impede eviction through a Chapter 13. More Delay and Expenses, and then still probably an expense to move the former owner out and perhaps even pay for his initial storage.

Post-Sale Tenants create similar Problems, but here the successful bidder may encounter still further costs and delays which complicate his original plans, due to a tenant's leasehold rights which must be recognized. As noted earlier, a written lease which does not have a subordination clause and predates the foreclosed mortgage, or a lease which was not otherwise subordinated to the mortgage, may have to be honored or bought out by a new owner. And in some jurisdictions even a subordinated lease or a verbal month-to-month tenancy (more likely in residential properties) will entitle a tenant to certain protections, i.e., perhaps a new six to nine-month term at market rental.

There may indeed be a Lot of Costly Foreseen and Unforeseen Matters for the successful bidder, all superimposed on those basic expenses which face any spec. buyer, and the Threshold Question of "How Good A Buy Did I Get?" in the first place.

Time, Delay, Expenses, and Repairs. The post-Sale variables require a terrific Buy at Sale. (Note – often some of the best opportunities at Sheriff's Sale are commercial parcels.)

A somewhat more "exotic" Specialized Way of "Buying" into Foreclosures is by "Buying The Paper" from either the original lender or some intermediate assignee: Buying, that is, the Actual Mortgage in foreclosure, along with its

ROBERT METZ

Note. A mortgage is a security instrument, a commodity, a right, an asset. It can be bought and sold on whatever mutual terms parties may agree to. As discussed earlier, depending on various factors, including their status (performing or non-performing), interest rate, other terms and market conditions, mortgages are sold at a premium over their remaining balance, at par or at a discount. The lender's Rationale to sell mortgages in foreclosure parallels (earlier discussion) its Rationale to deal with owners and/or buyers in any foreclosure context – be it a Short Sale or other form of loan workout whose goal is to enable the owner to Hold Onto His Property or Sell it.

In Buying non-performing Paper, at first blush it may be tempting to adopt a strategy of "buying only at a sizeable discount". And that is the accepted protocol. Especially when the selling mortgagee is a second or third assignee of the original lender, particularly when a part of the business of the selling mortgagee is dealing in "bad and marginal" Paper. Such mortgagees typically buy their Paper at very sizeable discounts. They are often willing to take a bigger hit on the "bad" loans because the essence of their business is, in buying at a discount, weeding out the Paper, keeping and servicing some of it, and selling some at a profit and taking "hits" on the balance – but their "hits" are simply part of their business.

Whether the Paper you purchase is Performing or not, always "look behind the Paper to the property", to the present loan to value ratio, and to the "Potential Better or Best Uses of the Property". Indeed, buying a mortgage in foreclosure at a less than significant discount may sometimes be quite an attractive proposition depending on the value of the property, the existence or status of any other liens, and what you might be able to "learn" from your initial discussions with the property owner or secondary lienholders.

Consider the following scenario, which is not merely an academic puzzle: A property is worth $210,000.00, the First mortgage in foreclosure has a remaining balance of $130,000.00, and there is a Second for $80,000.00. And the First wants $110,000.00 to sell its position – which does not seem to be such a huge discount. On the surface it looks like an overall negative equity situation – but look again; a bit closer – it is a Possible Gold Mine!

You contact the Second, who already knows or who you will tell, about the numbers, including fair market value of the property. The Second will realize, if he does not already, that by the time he gets to any Sheriff's Sale your First will be well over $130,000.00 plus accruing taxes, costs, and interest; at

126

Sale the property should go for less than fair value, or it might be foreclosed with you (your First) taking it back.

If the Second does not go to the Sale and bid out your First (unlikely for many Seconds to do this), and you thus take the property back, the Second's lien will be wiped out to zero. If a third party buys at Sale, the Second does not get paid anything unless and until you, through your First, with its accruing interest and costs of foreclosure, have been fully satisfied, together with accruing real estate taxes, which occupy the most senior primary position. In either case, the Second should not have great expectations.

The Second should jump at a sizeable discount, up-front, knowing he will thus fare far better than he will at Sale. And if the First has not been getting paid by the mortgagor, in all certainty the Second is also in arrears, and probably more months in arrears than your First.

So, let's say the prior owner of the First sells its $130,000.00 mortgage for $110,000.00 (hardly a terrific discount), but the Second takes $40,000.00 for its tenuous $80,000.00 Paper. Now, as the buyer of the First and the Second, you control $210,000.00 of debt for $150,000.00; if you go to Sale and take the property back, you have a Good Deal; and if some third party bids the full face (or upset) balance on your First at Sale, the third-party bidder would not be required to pay anything towards the Second, since your First is foreclosing and the bidder therefore need not satisfy the Second in order to get the property.

But as you are foreclosing the First, which Paper you just bought, you also have the right to bid higher than the amount of your debt being foreclosed (the First), and thereby force any other bidder who wants the property to bid higher than any "initial bidding" which would have been sufficient to satisfy your First, in which case that Surplus will go towards the Second and thus, in our example, into your pocket, since you are the owner of the Second, also! You, the buyer of the Paper actually become a participant in the bidding in order to force up the Sale price, in order to satisfy all or part of your Second Paper, also!

Since the Second position is not the one foreclosing, a third party bidder cannot, on the face of it, be forced to also satisfy the Second in order to win the property; but as a way around this reality, the First can always intervene and outbid any third party to either "compel" it to satisfy both his First and Second (as the result of a bidding war); or he can take the property back, which would be a far superior Deal to just having had his $130,000.00 First, or both the First and part of the Second, paid off!

Buying The Property, Buying The Paper, Making Deals at the Right Time with other lienholders, Discounting, Going to Sale with or without the Paper; it's all a bit of a Chess Game. But Get Some Knowledge, Buy Something (Buy Low, Buy Right), Find Some Paper, Get the Comps, Think, Do, Maneuver, Add in Some Creativity, and You Will Be Able To Turn Many Seemingly Marginal Situations or Dead End Deals, into Windfalls that the Other Guy Could Never See; Profitable Deals may jump out and hit you in the face, or they may be hidden puzzle(s) waiting to be thought through by the Right Buyer with the Right Knowledge and Savvy.

In Buying Paper the speculator is a mini-mimic of Wall Street and the Federal Government. (Like the Seller who Takes Back Financing and later sells his own Paper – call him the "originating lender" – the context is different, but the Game is quite Similar.)

Clearly, the Purchase of a Mortgage In Foreclosure has the speculator stepping into the shoes of the foreclosing lender from whom he bought the Paper. He buys both the rights and the liabilities which go with the mortgage and note. If he wants to try to Take Title or Cash Out at Sheriff's Sale, he will pursue the Foreclosure (in which case it often makes sense to retain the prior lender's attorney, both for the sake of continuity and a more reasonable fee to complete the action). Or he may put a hold on the proceedings and try to make some sort of Deal with the owner / borrower.

Should he prefer to Hold onto the Mortgage, any (attempted) Workout with the property owner can of course take a variety of forms – Modification, Reinstatement, etc. Or he can try to negotiate a Deed In Lieu, or work with the owner to do a Short Sale and Cash Out in this manner. Or he may approach any number of Hybrid Arrangements. There are many Paths to Profit in Buying Paper, with or without going to Sheriff's Sale or otherwise Taking Title to the Property.

A few years back an associate and I purchased a small Second Mortgage-In-Foreclosure from a local mortgage banker at a good discount. The collateral property was solid, the borrower had good income but poor credit, prevailing criteria in the mortgage market were relatively loose, and the borrower wanted to hold onto her house.

We directed her to a willing institutional lender and she was able to Refinance her First (which was also in foreclosure), together with our Second. Even after discounting our payoff to help bring her Refinance to fruition (our original payoff figure was magnified by the high interest rate on the mortgage), our Profit, $45,000.00, funded through her Refinance, more than doubled our five-month-old $40,000.00 investment – the purchase price of our Paper!

Most often mortgages are sold and resold in bulk, packaged and securitized. It may involve minimal or greater effort to locate Good Buys on individual mortgages, performing or in foreclosure, from either institutional or small private lenders (i.e. a seller who Took Back). But the Deals are always out there. And Remember: You do not need the consent of the owner / borrower to buy the mortgage; This Is A Good Way To Bypass An Owner Who Is Unwilling To Deal With You, And You Still Gain "Control" Over The Property! There are financial firms and consultants, attorneys and real estate people among others, who broker, for a commission or for a flat fee; Deals between buyers and sellers of individual and small lots of mortgages.

Scouring Foreclosure Lists (see if the plaintiff is an individual or a large or small entity), and Searching Recorded Mortgages and Lis Pendens in the County Courthouse or Recording Office for similar information will also produce solid Leads. You can find out which "little guys", your most likely Sources, own "good" and "bad" mortgages in your desired geographic or Farm Area. Write to these "lenders". Call them, Follow-up. You can find that one mortgage or handful to buy.

And based on the status and terms of the mortgages which you select, the value of the underlying property, local market conditions, and the motivation (or lack thereof) of the particular lender to unload its Paper for Cash, Make Offers, Negotiate, Make Multiple Offers on Different Mortgages; Do Not Be Shy! The Buying Process should include speaking with ("your") borrower and analyzing potential Profit Margins for the Different Avenues you might pursue once you own the Paper. Weigh your Options, and Act. Even the mini-investor can Make It Big by Dealing in "Bad" Paper. There are always Good Deals to be had in Buying Mortgages. It is a big pond out there.

As for Financing your Purchase, since it is not actually real estate, it cannot be funded by using the underlying property as collateral. Purchase money must come out of pocket or from other equities or credit lines. It can be most efficient for several or more investors to pool their cash and credit in a partnership arrangement in order to be best equipped to handle significant and multiple transactions in a timely manner.

When Then Is The "Best" Time To Go After A Foreclosure? Notwithstanding earlier discussions, considering the reality that Markets are huge and typically in a state of constant flux, and the fact that there are many issues and variables in every debtor's situation, the truth is that Anytime In Any Case Can Be A Good Time Or A Bad Time, and this fact itself can and will change in each matter from time to time. This may sound like a lawyer's "answer", but it really is the only truthful assessment.

In a strictly textbook sense though, there are Certain Times when it Typically "Can Be" Most Opportune to try to Negotiate a Deal. As a rule you can best maneuver, you can best Deal, when the owner and/or lender have an incentive, an active interest; preferably when there is still "sufficient equity" in the property; or when there is a "sufficient" negative equity in the property; or when the lender's losses are still very "modest"; or when the owner and/or lender are looking to cut their accrued losses and potential future exposures.

Today, however, is a different kind of time, a different kind of market. As previously noted the lender's traditional Rationale to Deal has been accentuated; and, in fact, current and emerging Government intervention and Pumps are on the one hand serving as an impetus / catalyst for lenders to make certain Deals, yet at the same time they are periodically curbing lenders' appetites to Deal, as the lenders wait, so to speak, for the other shoe to drop, to see if future Government initiatives will make it still more sensible and cost-effective for them to do their Deals at some later date.

But as a rule in more stable times the Best Time To Buy Distressed Real Estate, to Negotiate with Lenders (especially in a Judicial State), is when the default is either about four months old or, further down the road, two to three months before Sheriff's Sale. Depending on the preceding course of the action and the Court's Volume, or Docket, this two to three-month window may occur less than a year or so after the case is filed or even years after the initial default.

During this time the foreclosing lender will have been steadily losing its cash flow from the mortgage, paying property taxes and other carrying charges, incurring legal fees, and having its balance sheets and day-to-day lending abilities burdened with the non-performing debt. The next Big Hit and Exposure could come through the Sheriff's Sale, or from the costs and delays incident to Chapter 13 filings.

This Is Prime Time; but again, with all the variables and in such a fluid context, Whenever a Potential Deal may present itself, any time can become

Prime Time. And remember, despite any rules of thumb, when something Looks Good, at whatever time, Give it a Shot – the rewards of Success can be Huge, and the worst that can come from an inopportune inquiry or effort is that you are told "No". And get used to being told "No" – one "Yes" makes up for a lot of "No's".

Aside from the technical Legal Documents which are used by the appropriate professionals at closing, and which are not our concern here, and the Purchase Contract (which should be drawn by either an attorney, real estate broker with input from the investor, or experienced investor himself), the Core Documents and Forms which are most commonly needed in Making Deals On "Foreclosures" include: (a) A basic form of Adjournment Letter to delay Sheriff's Sales in those States where permitted; (b) Borrower's Authorization for a third party (you) to negotiate with the lender on its behalf; (c) Broker's Price Opinion, Comps, and Repair Estimate; (d) Financial Worksheet and other Forms (which are included in Packages submitted by lenders to Negotiate Mortgage Modifications and Short Sales and Lender Discounts Generally); (e) Proofs / Letter Forms to verify income and expenses and Hardship Letter Forms, to be included as Exhibits when submitting these completed Packages; (f) Generic Forms for Financial Statements, Profit and Loss Statements, Conditional Mortgage Commitments, and Credit Lines; and (g) Binder Forms, to act as interim agreements pending signing of more complete Purchase Contract.

Caveat – while some of these Forms may also be useful in Buying Mortgage Paper, the operative documents in Buying Paper are a Binder Agreement and Assignment of Mortgage and Note Forms, and only the experienced investor should attempt to prepare or review such documents and their ancillary paperwork – Good Deals should have more than enough Money in them such that you can retain decent Counsel when you need it!

A Potentially Good Deal On A Foreclosure Property Having Been Pinpointed, You Must Be Able To Close It In A Financially Prudent Manner; Financing the Purchase – as basic as anything, a matter which of course should be thought-out in advance, yet a matter which is always subject to change as circumstances warrant. It is absolutely critical for any investor or speculator to fully Understand the Methods which are generally available, and in order to act in an efficient and profitable manner, to also understand which among them may be the best to use in any particular Purchase. Part of the idea of

<u>Buying Foreclosures is to Maximize the Potential of the Transaction in any number of ways, from the purchase price on down, and this of course includes its Financing (Chapters V & VIII).</u>

<u>The Availability Of Financing Is Paramount. And You Must Understand The Methods And Their Application</u> in order to best select which Method may be available in a particular case, and where there is a choice which Method is best suited in a given Deal. Accordingly, the investor's ability and resources to raise Cash or Credit, in conjunction with Market Impact on Available Financing, must similarly be considered.

With regard to <u>Forms Of Financing</u>, there will always be the pros and cons of each, the considerations and issues in deciding to proceed with one Plan or another – assuming, obviously, there is in fact a menu of Financing Vehicles to choose from in the first place.

<u>Leveraging</u> – If Financing will be used to Close a Deal, whatever its scope, you should initially determine how <u>to "Control" the property with the Least Amount Of Cash Out Of Pocket</u>. This notion should frame the context for going forward with any Plan. The "Amount Down" affects many things – for starters, the extent of your present and future Purchasing Power; and with regard to the particular investment at hand, it affects a multitude of key functions, including Cash Flow, Amortization, Depreciation Impact, Appreciation Percentage, And Various Risk Factors.

Such criteria may be more or less relevant in different situations. There is no magical formula in any of this. Each case is unique. We must make our decisions and act on our individual preferences in accordance with our own abilities and personal comfort zones. But in order to make <u>Intelligent Financing Choices from whatever the available menu may be</u>, One needs a Full Understanding of the Objectives of Making A Deal in the first place.

<u>The Various Forms Of Seller And Seller-Assisted Financing, Including The Installment Contract Method Of Buying And Holding Real Estate (Certain Forms Of "Holding" Can Be "Equated" With Forms Of Financing)</u>, were discussed in Chapter V. By their own terms these Methods will prove to be of limited use in Financing the Purchase of Foreclosures. (Never, however, underestimate their value to both buyers and sellers in the Bad Market Scenario.)

By way of quick overview, one should understand the seemingly inherent contradiction in thinking we can have a seller-in-foreclosure act as Co-Signer on a mortgage for his buyer in order to "lend his credit" to the cause. <u>Yet</u>

<u>There Are Limited Applications Where Other Forms Of Seller-Assisted Financing Can Help Facilitate The Sale Of A Property In Foreclosure.</u>

<u>Adding The Buyer's Name To The Deed</u> with the seller remaining in title to some negligible extent, in order to retain the existing mortgage (which we can presume is in foreclosure and also Non-Assumable), can work when combined with a prior Modification, Reinstatement or Forbearance of the mortgage. The remaining debt can (depending on the numbers) stay in place, and thus cover all or part of the balance necessary to Finance the Deal.

<u>Assumption Of An Assumable Mortgage-In-Foreclosure</u>, again pursuant to prior Modification, Reinstatement or Forbearance, can similarly Finance or help Finance a Deal.

<u>Assumption Of A Non-Assumable Mortgage-In-Foreclosure</u>, pursuant to obtaining lender approval (with the seller / debtor staying on the Paper), and again pursuant to prior Modification, Reinstatement or Forbearance, can also be a smart choice in the appropriate situations, and thus Finance or help Finance a Deal.

With all such Means of Financing the same issues and pros and cons as noted in Chapter VI will apply. Key, however, to viability in <u>Financing "Foreclosures"</u>, is the amount of Equity in the property and the amount of Cash Down Payment which will be required. <u>These Forms of "Assuming" A Modified Mortgage</u> which was in active foreclosure <u>can obviate the need to do a Short Sale and/or obtain New Financing</u>, (and a Short Sale is often more difficult to accomplish than a Modification).

Depending on the equity in a property, the balance on the mortgage in foreclosure, and the amount of cash needed (and available) to bridge any remaining gap in the purchase price, the seller himself might also be able to <u>Take Back A First Or Second Mortgage</u>. In any such scenario the foreclosure action must first be "resolved" or cured, and the issues involve not only how much has to be paid off, but also what the seller can actually do, whether the seller has to come out of pocket to satisfy the foreclosure action, and how much the buyer must commit to closing the Deal. Again, it is all a product of the numbers in the property, the parties, and the status of the existing problem mortgage.

In still another possible scenario, provided the foreclosure action is first "cured", essentially through either Modification or Reinstatement, the "Cured" Mortgage can then be left in place and the <u>Installment Contract</u>

Method Of Financing (as between Contract buyer and seller), can be utilized as a viable Plan to flesh out the Financing Arrangement.

As mentioned in our earlier discussion of Installment Contracts, it is irrelevant whether the now-"Cured" existing mortgage is or is not Assumable. Pending the conclusion of the longer term Installment Contract relationship, the old mortgage can simply be left in place, with the seller / borrower remaining in title, subject to and in accordance with his rights *vis-à-vis* his buyer, as set forth in the Installment Contract, with the eventual merging of this Contract into a deed at closing.

And again, as previously noted, in certain Forms of Seller-Financing or Seller-Assisted Financing (including the Installment Contract), and particularly in the foreclosure as opposed to the non-foreclosure situation, a paramount issue (and risk) is in the (sometimes) continuing relationship in title with a "financially unstable" seller who might be vulnerable to other liens which could attach to the property at some future date, as long as he remains in title. The shrewd attorney must protect his client, the buyer – either by "over collateralizing" the property in the buyer's favor through a "straw" mortgage of a grossly inflated amount far surpassing the value of the property itself, or through other recorded Agreements which can similarly protect the buyer's equity interests from possible future liens against the seller which might attach during the Contract period.

A second issue goes to the question of whether there is enough cash available to enable the seller to enter into the Installment Contract and (along with subsequent payments) satisfy his needs before the future closing, or merging of the Contract into the transfer of title.

In Addition to The Above Singular Category Of Seller And Seller-Assisted Forms Of Financing (Coupled With "Cures" Of The Mortgage-In-Foreclosure), There Are A Host Of Other Ways In Which To Fund The Purchase Of "Foreclosure" Properties.

The All-Cash offer and closing is always an attractive option to a seller, and where negotiations with a foreclosing lender are necessary it is similarly appealing to the lender, and such a strong offer creates an excellent bargaining position for any buyer. The All-Cash buyer will invariably gain more credibility and be better able to negotiate a more favorable price and other terms with a seller and certainly with a foreclosing lender. (Though sometimes a seller's retort to a buyer's boost of "all cash at closing" is simply: "It has to be all cash anyway, regardless of where it comes from.")

But A No-Financing-Contingency Offer assures both the seller and the foreclosing lender of a quicker, more certain closing by a strong buyer who is putting his contract deposit at risk if he does not perform. And this translates into Strength. In Funding a closing entirely out-of-pocket, unless it is to be an immediate Flip or the buyer has unlimited liquidity, the buyer will lose part of the Traditional Yield Benefits which are inherent in Leveraged Speculating And Investing (Chapter II).

Leveraging The Purchase Price Is Important. The Smart Buyer Who Does An All-Cash Deal Will Maximize His Position By Closing All-Cash (Either Entirely His Own Cash, Or Partly His Own Cash And Partly Proceeds From A New Mortgage Which He Is Free To Obtain And Use At Closing Even Absent A Contract Contingency Or Mention Of A Mortgage), And Shortly After The Purchase Closing Pull As Much Of His Own Cash Out Of The Deal As Possible, Through A "Refinance" Closing.

The Most "Standard" Methods Of Financing Are The Various Forms Of Conventional Mortgages. For all intents and purposes, Closing a Purchase Agreement which contains No Mortgage Contingency by using one or another Form of Purchase Money Mortgage is, in a way, the best of both worlds; "Financing after having just Negotiated your Deal as an All-Cash Buyer". But if the buyer thus has no "out", no legal means by which to cancel his contract upon legitimate (or non-legitimate) failure to obtain a mortgage, while the lack of the contractual contingency will have presented a stronger offer, absent other means to close, failure to secure a mortgage can land him in default and risk his deposit and make him vulnerable to the seller for other claims resulting from breach.

Most Conventional Mortgage purchases do in fact close pursuant to a sales contract which contains a Mortgage Contingency Clause.

The wording of any such contingency may be slanted more or less in favor of either buyer or seller, or be more balanced. A buyer, for example, may be able to legitimately back out of a given Deal if the Contingency is worded one way, while under an identical set of facts he might be in breach if the Contingency is worded differently. And depending on the context, overly loose or overly stringent terms in a Contingency Clause can drastically change the meaning and very validity of a contract for either party; again, in favor of one or the other.

A "standard" Mortgage Contingency should state, in essence, "That if the buyer does not obtain a purchase money mortgage in the principal amount of

$_____, at _____% (or prevailing) interest rate, with _____ points, on a _____year direct reduction plan (or interest only, or with stipulated balloons), from a licensed lending institution, by_____(date), using bona fide good faith efforts to obtain same, then, if this Contingency is not waived, the buyer (or seller) may declare this contract null and void with the deposit returned to the buyer."

If the Clause has an unrealistically low or possibly unobtainable interest rate, even where the buyer might actually obtain a mortgage commitment, but perhaps at a slightly higher rate than he is "obligated" to accept under the Contract, the Contract can then become a virtual Buyer's Option – he can legally void it due to "failure of the Mortgage Contingency" and proceed to either walk away or try to Renegotiate a Better Deal; or he can settle for the mortgage which he obtained.

Similarly, terms in a Contingency Clause which compel the buyer to perform provided he receives almost any kind of mortgage, will work to the benefit of the seller and obviously make for a more certain binding Contract. So then, "What principal amount should be stipulated in the Clause? Should the Contingency dictate a low, high, or simply prevailing interest rate? Zero or two points, one or three points? A 20 or 30-year term?" Never be too casual in your review of Mortgage Contingency terms in a Contract which has been drafted by the other side. As the buyer you should understand that its terms should be governed by your own abilities and qualifications and market realities.

The matter of How Much Or How Little Cash To Put Into The Down Payment On The Purchase Price goes both to Perceptions and Reality. Perceptions in the sense that the All-Cash Buyer, or at least an All-Cash Buyer On Paper, as a rule, is seen as a stronger buyer and his offer is seen as a better offer, and he thus gains a superior Negotiating Posture. Reality in the sense that Leveraging is a vital element in Maximizing One's Potential Yields from a given Investment (or Deal), and in Maximizing One's Ability to do Additional Deals. The best of both worlds is the presentation of an All-Cash or Strong Down Payment Buyer who can either close All-Cash and then Refinance out, or who can close with a minimum of cash regardless of his presentation (assuming he can Finance the balance at closing).

The prevailing terms of Conventional Mortgages vary with the times and markets. Rates and points, like the qualifying process, run the gamut, as does the relative availability and diversity of Forms of mortgages at any given time:

Direct Reduction, Balloon, Adjustable Rate Mortgages, No Doc. And No Verification Loans, Full Doc. Loans, Etc.

FHA Mortgages, and for those eligible would-be owner-occupants Veterans, or VA Loans, are not, strictly speaking, Forms of Conventional Mortgages, but they certainly are Standard Purchase Money Mortgages. Since they are assumable and have become easier to process in recent years, FHA Purchase Money Mortgages have become more appropriate Financing Vehicles For Buying "Foreclosures" than they were in the past. Yet with the time they take to close and their other real estate-related conditions (i.e., inspections, property repairs) not to mention general FHA limitations on investor funding, they are not a first choice of Methods to Finance a "Foreclosure Purchase" (though they are a very good choice for doing a Refinance).

VA Mortgages are narrowly restricted to owner-occupant Veterans, and considering their processing time and other conditions, they can be a stretch in Financing a Foreclosure. However, a strong applicant who has a firm VA or FHA Conditional Approval in hand can posture himself in a good Negotiating Position.

Third Party Secondary Financing can also prove useful in raising capital. By virtue of their enhanced risk (behind the First in priority), Seconds command higher interest rates, as alluded to earlier, and are usually written for shorter terms. They will also require a sufficient equity cushion in the property, and are thus more difficult to originate in Bad Markets (which of course are characterized by depressed Values).

A buyer is in position to Best Negotiate if he can secure his own Financing. Having An Equity Line Or A Line Of Credit on some other real estate, or unsecured, which can be drawn down to Fund new Deals, is a natural edge. The rewards are self-evident.

A Bridge Mortgage, which simultaneously encumbers a property that is being sold and a new purchase, requires a showing of sufficient income by the buyer and adequate equity in both properties for qualifying purposes. Most lenders will also require an executed, and preferably firmed up (Contingencies satisfied) sales contract on the property which is being sold. The Bridge Mortgage Technique offers a lifeline when a buyer is temporarily caught between two Deals and needs cash out of the first to help Fund the second. Bridge Money is a bit more expensive than Conventional Financing, but when available can be arranged very quickly for the qualified buyer.

Hard Money (expensive short-term Financing, in its most sensible context) is typically originated by smaller niche or individual lenders / investors, and as noted earlier, is more plentiful in times of Easy Money and stable or rising real estate Values. Depending on the Potential Upside of a given purchase (Flip, as is often the case), expensive Hard Money can be the ticket to a Profitable Deal. It is a Source born of necessity, but at times a convenient and valuable Source.

Typical Hard Money terms range from one to five years; the rates and point structures vary with the collateral, credit, and market; and are usually interest-only and carry strict default clauses and penalties. Some Hard Money lenders require that an executed deed together with an escrow agreement be deposited in escrow so that in the event of default, the deed can be released from escrow and the lender will *ipso facto* own the property and not have to go through any foreclosure process (and this is a Hard Money lender that you want to stay away from).

Standard loan to value ratios are 50 to 75%, and many times these loans are offered only to corporate borrowers. Lenders can charge higher rates and points to corporations, and with a corporate borrower the lender is also better insulated from other consumer-oriented mortgage regulations and oversight – which, considering the terms of some of these loans, is sometimes a concern to the lender.

Hard Money lenders usually present their product as strictly business, "buyer-beware" arrangements. They want to deal with business people, with investors and speculators. Their borrowers are sometimes required to sign disclaimers at closing acknowledging they are in business and they know what they are getting into. Nevertheless, Never, Never, depending on your overall Financial Position or Strength, your Knowledge and Sophistication, and the Potential Upside of a particular Deal, look at Hard Money Financing with a jaundiced eye.

This brings us to a general umbrella heading best described as a potpourri of Venture Capital / Creative Financing Avenues. While there is some overlap between this area and certain Methods discussed previously, this general label essentially summarizes the process of piecing together Equity Participation Deals As An Art Of Raising Capital.

More particularly, Third Party Partnership Financing, wherein a property is Held in the name of the Third Party or an Entity which has been formed for such purpose, has its drawbacks, but in a properly structured transaction certainly also has a role. Such ventures should be accompanied by recorded agreements between the primary buyer and his "investor partners" (Chapter III), which address respective rights, interests and obligations. If a Deal is good enough, and maybe too large to handle going solo, and this is the most available (or only) Method for Funding, using Investor Partners, the same or different partners in different Deals, can give an active primary buyer a great deal of Leverage and traction going forward. But the Deal must be sufficiently profitable to make everybody happy.

Capital And Credit – today more Credit with a bit less Capital – are at the heart of doing anything. Deals, Ideas, Are Fine. But Then What? You Must Be Able To Pull The Trigger. And very often getting a piece of the action, part of this Deal and part of that one, is the price of Financing and Building Equities and Income. Absent sufficient Capital and Credit of your own, and assuming you want to do a volume of Flip and Hold (longer-term) Deals, you must look at all reasonable possibilities and variations of Financing – use some ingenuity and hustle.

Putting property In The Name Of A Spouse Or Other Family Member in a non-businesslike arrangement in order to use their "better" Credit to qualify for Financing, can at once be the best and sometimes the worst of ideas. Often one or the other Spouse may have poor credit and/or judgments which restrict his or her ability to Finance, and which in any case would also jeopardize the property if it were Held in their name, since judgments automatically attach to the realty. Many spec. and personal properties close only because of the superior qualifications of a Spouse.

As previously discussed in a different context, using a Friend or Associate, for a Price or as a Favor to Co-Sign the Mortgage Note, without joining on the deed and becoming "a partner", is another viable Method of Financing. It assumes adequate, but not quite good enough, qualifications on the part of the investor himself. Unless the Price for a signature is just exorbitant, this Method probably has more potential downside for the Co-Signer than for the Investor. However, as noted earlier, if the mortgage payments are made timely the credit of both parties will benefit.

Sale-Leaseback Financing is an additional Means to Finance the purchase of "Foreclosure" Properties (discussed earlier in a different context). In a variety of ways, this Method can simultaneously serve the differing needs of both buyer and seller and benefit both. All Deals need not be characterized by a windfall for one and a disaster for the other. Sometimes even a small gain, or what some may see as a "non-benefit", can be a lifesaver for the seller in distress.

A Sale-Leaseback may yield a small or larger cash net to the seller. But the value of the Leaseback aspect of the Deal may prove immense, in terms of future dollar value, in possibly sustaining a seller's going business concern at the subject location, or for a variety of other family or personal considerations. Take the case of a business owner – retail, wholesale, manufacturing or service – who is in foreclosure on the premises which house his operations. He may very well have a large capital investment in fixtures and amenities. The location might hold substantial good will for his business, and this good will may in fact be the primary value of the entire business.

The physical assets or personalty of an income-producing convenience store with a busy lottery machine in an established location may carry little more than salvage value if the business were forced to move quickly and there was no better or affordable spot to jump right into. How about the retail store which is a viable business and has been in the same location for 20 years? The future revenues and value of a going concern (a different issue from the real estate in foreclosure), will often hinge on its ability to remain in the foreclosed premises. Many times the diminishing or destruction of the value of the business and its income stream can be avoided only if it can remain "as is, where is".

In the case of a personal residence, it goes without saying that family tensions and trauma may be ameliorated if the owner-in-foreclosure can remain in the premises for a longer or a shorter transition period, or even as a tenant.

The Leaseback provision in the purchase contract for a property in foreclosure can be a very valuable benefit to the seller. In the commercial scenario, the future dollar value of such a provision for a seller's going business concern may far outweigh the value of any remaining equity in the real estate itself. Offering a Leaseback can be a huge bargaining chip. And in those cases where the investor will want a tenant anyway, much of any potential downside in offering a Leaseback will be eliminated.

Please Note – "Sale-Leaseback" discussions for our purposes should not be equated with the flim-flam "version" where hucksters "take" title to a property in foreclosure, collect rent from the former owner, and do not pay anything on the existing mortgage-in-foreclosure, "in exchange" for an empty promise that the former owner may later "buy the property back".

The needs of both investor and seller must be meshed; the seller must be able to afford the rent and the investor should be made comfortable in now having a tenant who was just in foreclosure. Any concerns that the rent will not be paid in a timely manner or not be paid at all can be somewhat ameliorated by requiring an extra security deposit or even some pre-paid rent, which might be partially funded from any sale proceeds in the transaction which were going to the seller / tenant. A UCC (Uniform Commercial Code) collateralized filing with the County Clerk of a chattel (non-real estate) lien on the business or its assets, can also offer the investor / landlord added assurances under any lease between the parties.

Use of the Sale-Leaseback mode is often the result of off-handed conversation in the course of negotiating the original deal on the real estate. The astute investor should make inquiry in negotiations where this might seem to be a secure and productive concept, and particularly where a seller hints at his longevity in the premises or what might sweeten the pot for him. (Many times it is an intangible or inexpensive concession from the investor that goes a long way in helping to make a Deal.) The investor should always be attentive, and thinking, "What can I do? What can I throw in to make it work?"

Buying As A Purchaser Under Contract (PUC), especially when doing quick Flip foreclosures, can be a most effective Means of "Buying" or getting Control of a property. And sometimes when we say "Buy", what we are actually referring to is a more intense process designed to "Get Control", which may be all that we want for the moment, anyway. And when we say "Buying" as a PUC, we mean much more than the simple notion that there is a buyer who is under contract to buy, to close later. We mean a Technique, a separate and distinct ability to do something more, which is subsumed within the Contract.

Provided the purchase agreement is properly drafted to ensure that the investor has the Option, or privilege, to Assign or sell his interest in the Contract to a third party (who would thus step into his shoes and become the buyer who actually closes on the property), the investor can enter into Contract with a seller-in-foreclosure, tender a minimal deposit in escrow (or to the seller personally, at the investor's risk), and then Assign his Contract to a third party for a Profit, in cash or other consideration (or actually close himself and later Flip the property).

This Deposit-Money Method Of "Financing" As PUC may mean that any Assignment Profit will be only part of the proverbial loaf, but for the investor who is looking for the quick Flip, who may be looking to minimize transaction costs, who may not be very credit-worthy or flush with his own cash to perform under a Contract, "Buying" and Flipping as a PUC can be a terrific Technique. There is always the risk of being unable to Flip the Contract in time, and being unable to close on the property as a back-up position, and thus losing the deposit. And this circumstance may lead to a larger problem or negotiations with the seller, for a consideration of course. But the Rewards, especially for the less-than-qualified cash or credit-strapped investor, can be enormous.

Basic to success as a PUC is Moving quickly on the Flip (of either the Contract or the Property); Looking for Deals which have adequate margins; Negotiating the smallest deposit possible; and Trying to throw some potential Delay Clauses into the Contract (which may prove valuable down the road). The PUC investor should always be seeking and cultivating his own second-tier "Flippee" / retail buyers and investors. The smart, under-capitalized investor should always have his own investors and retail buyers on call waiting for his Deals.

Such Secondary investors can be found through local real estate professionals (attorneys, brokers); contacts made through memberships in real estate trade groups and property owners associations; "want ads" in newspapers and real estate publications; the Internet; signs; and in the course of everyday life. The Core Strategy to Buying and Flipping with only Deposits? To aggressively search for Deals, and to constantly search for your own Investors / Buyers.

Some years ago, in a much different price era, I went into contract to buy a small burned-out one family home on a 35 by 100 foot lot in a semi-middle class town in Central New Jersey. The property was referred to me by a painter with whom I did some business. The house had been in foreclosure at the time of the fire; the insurance proceeds paid off the mortgage and put a small balance in the owner's pocket and left him with the land, a shell of a structure, and the Town breathing down his neck over what was truly a dangerous site wrought with property Code violations. The owner had relocated and had neither the drive, means, nor knowledge to do anything with the charred shell except to try to dump it and net a few more dollars.

This small Deal would epitomize the beauty and validity of the PUC Flip – be it on a property in foreclosure, or any property. My purchase price was $10,000.00, with a $1,000.00 deposit going directly to the seller; the property was to be conveyed in strictly "as is" condition; I was to assume all responsibility for Code violations; and closing was to take place within 30 days of the date of contract.

Because at the time I lacked sufficient experience to handle a multi-faceted rehab by myself, after I notified the Code Officials that based on an engineering study (cost $750.00), the property could and would be rebuilt by "somebody" (subject to submission of architectural drawings to the municipal Building Department), I called a few investors and quickly found a builder who was happy to take the Contract off my hands, and at a nice Profit.

I had made sure that my Purchase Contract stated that it could be Assigned "to any third-party individual or entity" (LLC, Corporation, etc.) of my choosing, with no consent required from my seller. I Assigned the Contract, my $1,000.00 Deposit remained with my seller, my buyer paid him the balance of the purchase price, they closed, my buyer rebuilt the house, and he made a lot of money which in retrospect I wished I had made on the Project instead. But you cannot always do or know everything, and Smaller Profits do add up, and they are sometimes the best and only Profits to be had in a given situation, depending on your wherewithal. In any case, my $1,750.00 total investment brought a gross from my buyer of $13,750.00 in a two-week turnaround. And at the time that was a pretty good Profit on a quick little-down minimal exposure Deal.

Never under-estimate the Value of a Deal that can be Structured based on your Knowledge, Right Numbers, and a Smartly-Worded (and thus very Valuable) Contract – even where you cannot handle the actual Transaction by yourself.

A final Means of "Financing" a purchase is through the Option Purchase, Or A Right Of First Refusal, a form of Option. "Either" can be used to "tie up" real estate in a variety of ways. Options and First Refusal Agreements can be Negotiated for nominal or other agreed consideration. They may be independent contracts, standing on their own two feet, or they may be provisions in a general lease agreement. At first glance it might seem incongruous that A Form Of Holding, Or A Method Of Obtaining A Proprietary Interest In Real Estate, Can Also Be A Method To "Finance" A Purchase, Or To Control, A Piece Of Real Estate.

But both the overlap and the distinction are clear. Simply having an Option To Purchase, which is a contractual right containing specific terms, or a Right Of First Refusal, which means you can match (upon specified terms and procedures), an Offer of some other party to buy a particular piece of real estate and you can thus buy it, if you so desire, are in fact <u>Ways to "Finance", to Control, to tie up</u>, to have your foot at least part of the way in the front door, (for a certain period of time, anyway).

An Option or Right Of First Refusal ties the property up. These are Contractual Rights of Value. They are Assets. They can be Worth a lot of money. They are Tangible. They can be the subject of dispute, litigation, Resale, Assignment (specify this in your document), or bequest.

And to the extent that one possesses a <u>legal right, (of Value or Profit)</u>, to something, the Power to do something with that Right, the Power to Get a piece of property and Sell that piece of property based on the <u>Entitlement</u>, or to Sell the Entitlement itself – he is in fact <u>Facilitating a "Purchase", a Deal, via a Contractual Right which we call an "Option" or a "First Refusal"</u>. You may not have taken a mortgage or closed. You may have spent something, or very little, to get this Entitlement to the property. But however you want to look at it, you have Obtained Certain Rights, Control, Potential, Inherent Profit or Value. Through <u>Financing Vehicles called Options and First Refusals</u>, through the initial cost, if any, of that Option or First Refusal, you are <u>"Moving Forward" on a real estate Deal</u>.

CHAPTER VII

BUY OTHER-THAN FORECLOSURE / UNDER-VALUED / BARGAIN-PRICED REAL ESTATE, & OTHER ASSETS, TO HOLD OR TO FLIP

Again: <u>BUY LOW, BUY RIGHT (& SELL HIGH); WHEN BUYING & SPECULATING IN REALTY AND OTHER ASSETS, A CERTAIN PROFIT MUST BE BUILT-IN UP-FRONT AT THE TIME OF PURCHASE – BE YOUR PLANS TO HOLD OR TO FLIP, FOR THE SHORT OR THE LONG TERM, FOR PERSONAL USE OR FOR BUSINESS GAIN</u>.

Everything discussed at the outset of Chapter VI concerning the Ends, the Rewards, the Potential and the Pitfalls of Buying "Foreclosures" also applies to the Purchase of Any Type of "Good Real Estate Deal". And there are any number of <u>Varied Sources In Addition To Properties In Foreclosure Where You Can Find Excellent Real Estate Deals – And Along The Way, Other Types Of Assets To Go With Them.</u>

<u>Bank-Owned Properties</u>, often referred to as (Bank) Real Estate Owned <u>(REO's)</u>, represent the proverbial "second chance" to buy a property which was "in foreclosure;" these properties are "post-foreclosures". Years ago they were commonly called "foreclosed properties", which of course is what they are. Some people refer to them incorrectly as "repossessed properties" – "repossessed" is the proper terminology where lenders take back non-realty items, i.e., autos, boats, furniture, chattels, business and personal assets.

In the REO Arena the seller is the former lender who took title at Sheriff's Sale or through a Deed In Lieu Of Foreclosure. This is the flip-side of the "pre-foreclosures", or "properties in foreclosure".

Looking at the sequence chronologically, generally speaking, as noted earlier, the best Deals on Foreclosures are usually to be had by Negotiating with the owner and/or lender either as a property goes into and through the earliest stages of foreclosure, or skipping months ahead, by negotiating in the months immediately before the Sheriff's Sale is to be held. Should the process go the whole route past Sheriff's Sale, and the lender Takes the property Back, then you are Negotiating with the former lender / new owner. And it is a new game, different rules and procedures. Yet the investor's goal of getting that Good Deal remains the same.

The former lender is typically motivated to sell. Everything which we have already said about a lender's not wanting to be in the real estate business, wanting to cut its losses and carrying costs during foreclosure proceedings, wanting to be in compliance with regulatory requirements and shareholder demands (relative to ratios), and wanting to return its non-performing assets (lending capital) back to working capital, applies similarly when the former lender has in fact become the owner. And such Motivation is especially strong in a poor or declining market.

In a hot market those lenders with a strong regulatory and business posture tend to be more independent when pricing their "better" REO's, which are usually in high-demand areas. But as a rule, and particularly when talking about urban area REO's needing rehab, in anything but a stellar market REO's present excellent opportunities for the qualified Buyer; if you Look and you are Persistent, there are almost always Good Buys in virtually every REO category.

Remember – as I wrote 19 years ago – this is the bottom line: "The lender is stuck with what is usually a vacant or a non-performing property. A commercial building, a house, or raw land, which costs money to carry, to insure, to manage, to maintain, and to market. These are their headaches. There are the drains on their revenues, the liabilities on their balance sheets."

While many of the Financing Methods outlined earlier are also appropriate for Funding REO's, and occasionally a former lender may Finance its own REO sales (really not "Owner Take-Back Financing" per se), a key point for any investor who is Negotiating an REO purchase is to prove his Strength, Stability, and Seriousness, to the seller. The bank will value a Firm Deal which seems certain to close, and they usually want to close As Soon As Possible.

A Quick Closing Date in the Contract (Offer); Minimal Pre-Closing Inspections; Few (and many times the bank will accept No) other Contract Contingencies; An "As Is" Clause as to the property's condition; A Substantial (10% or so) Deposit at signing of the Contract; And either a Short-Term Seller-Friendly Mortgage Contingency or No Mortgage Contingency at all, are among the most important Components of a Successful REO Purchase Offer.

Depending on how long an REO has been on the market, whether the bank has previously reduced its asking price, the number of prior or pending bids, and market conditions, an Offer At or Close To Asking Price may or may not be wise. And even where the bank does not require a Conditional Mortgage Commitment or other evidence of availability of closing funds with the offer, by presenting a Conditional Commitment or a sufficient Bank Statement or other Proof of Funds / Equity Lines, the buyer adds a Powerful "Addendum" to any REO Offer.

Bank-Owned Properties are available directly from the bank (or other mortgage lender / owner), through real estate brokers, and increasingly, through bank-retained asset management companies at (often deep) discounts.

REO's are marketed through brokers' multiple listings and real estate websites; and are available in lists published by banks and asset management firms (hard copy or on the Internet). Fresh REO leads, so fresh you can start monitoring the lead even before the bank has processed and priced the listing, can be generated by the investor himself in tracking post-Sheriff's Sale Bank Take-Backs, and following up immediately with the bank's REO Department. Through a variety of means, depending on procedures in the particular jurisdiction, an investor can obtain complete Sheriff's Sale lists, together with Sale results, from the local Sheriff's office.

Municipal (Or County) Tax Liens – in many States, particularly those where a mainstay for local and regional Government to raise revenue is through real estate taxes – there have traditionally been great opportunities in the purchase of Tax Liens. An investor's purchase and any ultimate foreclosure on a real estate Tax Lien will result in ownership of the property, with clear title, for sometimes literally pennies on the dollar. And during the time that he owns the Tax Lien, through the date the foreclosure of the Lien has been completed (if in fact he does foreclose), or through the time the Lien is paid off (where there is no foreclosure), the investor earns a solid per diem interest on his original investment (purchase of the Lien), and on subsequent monies invested to keep accruing taxes current and thus maintain the "priority" of the Lien.

By far one of the best and safest vehicles for the speculator, and the cautious investor alike who wants to hold out for that potential windfall while accumulating a guaranteed return on his "virtually" 100% secure investment, the purchase of Tax Lien Certificates – representing unpaid real estate taxes and municipal utilities, sewerage fees and local assessments – is a form of smart "passive" real estate speculation with a storied past.

The Liens (not the real estate) are sold at advertised Sales typically conducted by the municipal or other local tax collector. The bidder knows in advance the amount of overdue taxes and other charges (face amount of the Lien to be purchased), the property in question (PIQ), and the interest rate which will accrue on his investment (i.e., the face amount of the Lien plus any subsequent additional payments to keep the taxes current during the time he holds the Lien).

Regardless of any other liens which may be on the property, the Tax Lien almost always comes First. In order for the property owner, a successful bidder at Sheriff's Sale, a lender who Takes Back at Sheriff's Sale, anybody at any time, to sell the property or otherwise clear title, this Lien has to be dealt with First. Even a prior pre-existing first mortgagee must satisfy a subsequent Municipal Tax Lien, together with its accrued interest and recording and other permitted legal fees. The mortgage may be dated and recorded in 1998, the Lien dated and recorded in 2005, but the result is just the same; the Lien comes First.

A Foreclosure by the Lienholder / investor pursuant to a Tax Lien, which is initiated per statutory rules in the event the entire Lien is not paid off (Redeemed) from the Lienholder within the requisite period of time (unless an extension is granted by the Lienholder), will typically wipe out any rights and liens of other third parties in the property.

The Tax Certificate (Lien) holder can thus reap a huge windfall – truly buying a parcel of real estate for just the back taxes! In a small percentage of cases Lienholders do actually get the property; and in an even larger number of cases the well-financed Lienholder, should he so desire and have the real estate Smarts and Knowledge to so Maneuver, may also seek to Negotiate any Variety of Equity, Purchase or Financing Deals, with the property owner.

Where a Lienholder commences Foreclosure and is subsequently paid off, or if there is otherwise a Redemption of the Lien by the property owner prior to the Lienholder completing his foreclosure action, again the Lienholder receives his original investment plus reimbursement of any subsequent advances made for accruing tax payments, plus costs and fees, together with the applicable rates of accrued interest on the original investment, costs, and various advances, through the payoff date.

In most jurisdictions a Tax Lien Foreclosure is a different process from a Mortgage Foreclosure. Tax foreclosures are not necessarily open bid auctions; they are typically a paperwork procedure, not a live or public event; the Lien-holder having made sufficient statutory proof of his right to foreclose, a Judge may grant the foreclosure with, so to speak, the stroke of a pen, in Chambers. However, the process of initially buying a Tax Lien Sale Certificate, which of course represents the right to the Lien on the property and the right to maintain it by paying subsequent taxes for a stipulated period after which the Lien-holder may foreclose, is a public Sale.

There was a time when Tax Liens, in most jurisdictions, accrued interest from Day One at very high rates across the board, often a standard 18%. That translates to 18% guaranteed, and compounded, plus a shot at a piece of property. Over the last fifteen or so years, an increasing number of institutional investors – banks, brokerage houses, hedge funds, and the like – have become the largest buyers of Tax Liens in most of the country.

They started buying in large quantities, often sight unseen, usually never even riding by the property (the collateral behind the Liens). They started attending the local auctions, urban, suburban, anyplace, as long as there were enough Liens being sold to make the trip worthwhile, bidding on blocks of Liens, and sometimes everything the local Collector might have for sale. In certain areas the practice started working to the detriment of the average investor, with the "Big Boys" wanting as much as they could get their hands on, often "bidding down" the initial interest rates on the Liens, with the Collector awarding the Liens to the lowest bidder.

"Bidding down" means different things in different jurisdictions. Usually it will involve a lower interest rate, even 0% (or a premium might even be bid) on the initial face amount of the Lien, for a certain period of time. The successful bidder must subsequently keep the accruing taxes current in order to maintain the priority position of his Lien. These payments augment the amount of the Lien. And the interest rate on these additional sums typically bounces back up to the higher statutory rate, regardless of any lower rate bid on the initial Lien purchase. All in all, with a safe priority position in title, the interest invariably works out to a terrific return, and all the more so during those Cycles when banks are paying next to nothing to depositors.

Tax Lien statutes set forth the mechanics which enable local tax collectors to bring in cash from investors in exchange for their receivables (the Tax

Liens). The tax collector needs liquidity to pay municipal bills. The property owner remains in title (and in arrears), with taxes and costs accruing, but still retaining his chance to Redeem. The investor steps into the shoes of the "previous Lienholder" (the tax collector); Tax Liens can be Bought and Sold, Assigned from one investor to another – at par, at a discount, or at a premium – just as Mortgage Paper can be Resold and Assigned.

Where the Big Boys bid rates down on large blocks of Liens, smaller investors are squeezed out of the bidding or otherwise forced to compete more aggressively and thus compromised on their rates of return.

But there are still many opportunities for the small investor. For one thing, "bidding down" may take a bit of the luster off of a particular purchase, but even a staggered, marginally less than 18% return is quite attractive, especially when coupled with the possibility of "getting" the property, and in the context of Cycles where prevailing rates of return on other forms of passive investments are dismal. Moreover, institutional investors often ignore the "smaller" Sales – too much work, too much overhead for them to show up and bid on "only" a small number of Liens. Tax Liens remain a fantastic Deal.

With the fallout from the recent Real Estate Bust and other changes in the financial landscape, the institutions' once-coordinated invasion of the Lien markets has subsided in certain areas. And one of the realities which has sobered their assault and led to a more reasoned appetite is the fact that they have sustained some big losses – in Liens and elsewhere.

Buying so many Liens with initial zero or low interest rates, combined with the overhead costs of the institutional versus the individual buyer, and on top of this, buying basically sight unseen, they have either foreclosed on or otherwise been stuck with a number of Bad Deals. A "Bad Deal" in buying a Tax Lien and then foreclosing? Normally unheard of, but in certain cases, Yes!

Paying years of tax and corporate overhead to maintain a Lien and then looking at a property which may be totally depleted (or tainted with environmental problems or be but a sliver of unsaleable land), where the owner will never pay or Redeem the Lien, can be a "Bad Deal". What if the investor initially paid $8,000.00, then another $12,000.00 in "subsequents", and the property turns out to be worth say, only $5,000.00, or maybe $20,000.00, or perhaps $60,000.00 (after $40,000.00 worth of rehab or environmental remediation)? What has the investor bought? What is the Value of such a Tax Lien?

If the owner does not Redeem, the Lienholder can stop paying the current taxes and leave his existing Lien in limbo, probably to then lose its priority to a third party who will pick up a subsequent Lien on accruing taxes.

Or of course the Lienholder can continue to pay subsequent taxes and foreclose, and then perhaps be stuck with a property that might be worth even less than his actual investment. He must also deal with the carrying and marketing costs, expensive casualty and liability insurance on a property possibly in poor condition, and the possibility that the parcel may not be insurable at all and the investor or his holding company can potentially be individually responsible for losses or third party injuries. So too once he owns the property can he become responsible as a civil matter for fines and regulatory penalties, and even become criminally liable for things like uncured Code violations, fire hazards and environmental problems.

The Moral? Ride By, or otherwise have some Knowledge about the property on which you are buying a Lien. It is true – as a function of condition and other relevant factors, no matter how small the Lien may be or seem, each and every piece of real estate does not just have to be worth more than the amount of its Tax Lien plus accruing taxes and costs.

The Second Moral? Institutional buyers have been backing off and are no longer leaping at every entire Sale docket, and the Lien markets have been reopening for the individual investor.

The purchase of Liens can be fantastic; but verify there is enough behind them. You may wait a year or two or more to recoup your investment and interest (Redemption), but you get a good return. Or you may "have to" foreclose, and perhaps reap a windfall. And again, you can also Buy and Sell Tax Liens – for a premium or at a discount from your investment or anticipated profits, or at par – either before or after you have begun a foreclosure action.

Note – most Government entities which offer Tax Liens advertise them in local newspapers; and a telephone inquiry to a Tax Collector will usually get you the lists and information on upcoming Sale dates. Local Collectors will typically hold from one to three Lien Sales a year. Unless the Lienholder forecloses and takes title his payoff, be it through Redemption by the owner or third party proceeds, flows to him from the payor through the Tax Collector.

VA Foreclosed Properties are sold by the Veterans Administration. Mortgages on these properties are originated by lending institutions (banks, mortgage bankers), authorized by the VA and are Guaranteed by the VA for

151

designated categories of Veterans. VA offerings often constitute good buys. Due to strict VA underwriting standards which must be followed at the time of mortgage origination, most VA properties are typically in good condition when closed, and where they are subsequently neglected by their (former) owners or otherwise damaged post-Sheriff's Sale, the VA is liberal in building rehab allowances into its Resale prices. And VA policy has historically been to quickly divest itself of its foreclosed properties.

The cumbersome newspaper-advertised bidding process of a few years back has been replaced by a more efficient system whereby third-party vendors handle marketing for the VA. They oversee property management and overall sales efforts, while local brokers participate in showings. As this written, the Website VA.REOPRANS.COM directs investors to regional offerings and terms of current sales. The VA as a Source of Deals is akin to a Bank selling REO's, with the caveat being the VA can be among the most motivated of sellers for the qualified investor (who may also benefit from VA Financing Programs on certain Resales).

Another Federal Agency Whose Acquired Properties Offer Good Buys Is The FHA (Federal Housing Administration), operating under the auspices of HUD (Department of Housing & Urban Development). FHA Insured mortgages were originally the backbone of the mortgage origination business in urban and other lower income areas, focusing on those properties which most Conventional lenders would avoid, and those more marginally qualified (income and credit) buyers who were also typically left out or on the fringe of the Conventional markets.

By the 1980's, "the urban FHA loan" also became "the suburban FHA loan" – a different geography, usually a higher mortgage amount, and a different socio-economic borrower. In either case however, the FHA offers a constant flow of foreclosed properties, often underpriced, and unlike the VA, FHA offerings include mixed-use and multi-family (sometimes even large high-rise) apartment buildings as well. The FHA offers attractive Financing on its multi-family Deals.

Outside contractors handle the sale (not auction) of FHA / HUD assets, and at the Website HUD.GOV, investors are directed to a State by State listing of properties. HUD is always willing, and more so in a Down Market, to entertain (through its agents) sensible offers and reasonable applications for FHA Financing to close a Deal.

Still another Federal Agency which offers Good Buys on realty and personalty is the FDIC (Federal Deposit Insurance Corporation). The seasoned investor, and the layman alike, "know" all about the large number of banks which have been taken over and liquidated by the FDIC – failed, barely liquid, and unsafe thrifts – an extremely high number in the early 1990's – and a mounting number during the recent Bust. (Though today it is often said that certain banks are "too big to fail", meaning the Feds. tend to intervene earlier, using their own tools or Pumps to infuse, to orchestrate mergers and buyouts or to do their own bailouts, and try to "nip" the problem and avoid bank failures which would otherwise lead to FDIC control and probable liquidation.)

Few investors are truly aware of the depth of Government-owned real estate and other assets which are available on attractive terms from the FDIC. The lists run the gamut from residential to commercial, motels, multi-family dwellings, and land. Some Deals are "all cash" (or the investor's own Financing), and others offer Government-sponsored Financing.

In the early 1990's the number of failed thrifts, not to mention the array of assets being sold, became so overwhelming that the RTC (Resolution Trust Corporation) was formed by Congress to assist the inundated FDIC. Until matters subsided and the RTC was dismantled and its remnants merged back into the FDIC in 1995, the RTC published its own sales lists and conducted broker-run sales and auctions. The RTC sold assets individually, by portfolio, by auction and by sealed bid. There was land, buildings, golf courses, loan packages, furniture, and every form of real estate and fixtures and other personalty in between. The physical assets of failed thrifts and their loan collateral were often liquidated at pennies on the dollar.

While today many banks are "too big" for the Government to let fail, there are still plenty of "smaller" ones which have failed in recent years and which will continue to fail. Among its other functions, at present the FDIC's Division of Resolution and Receivership handles the liquidation of failed institutions and their assets. Real estate (former bank branches), foreclosed real estate, mortgages-in-foreclosure, performing mortgages, unsecured loans both performing and in default, repossessed assets, and the computers and paintings of the institutions themselves, are offered individually or in lots at set asking prices or by auction. The Website FDIC.GOV, "Assets Sales", is updated continuously with many listings which can be parlayed by the shrewd buyer.

In a certain sense the thought of buying Government-seized assets or contraband, especially when tinged with intrigue and stories of smuggling and border patrol, carries an aura of the exotic. What until recently was known as the Customs Service has taken on the more expansive moniker of U.S. Customs & Border Protection. Now including all of those Agencies which are supported by the Treasury Department – The IRS, Customs, Immigration, The ATF And The Secret Service – The Office Of Fines, Penalties, & Forfeitures is part of the Department of Homeland Security.

Like its less complex predecessor the Customs Service, this Agency is a treasure trove of Buys and Steals on everything from basic real estate to beachfront villas, Rolex watches to gold coins to shipments of leather coats to exotic cars and junk cars, to lots of computers and warehouse quantities of socks and shirts.

Customs, and now the expanded Division, has long been an overlooked arena of Potential which has been leveraged mostly in bargain Deals at privately-administered auctions and sales. Good Buys, and unique pieces of realty and personalty. I have seen jewelry, aircraft, pleasure boats, and even businesses go for a fraction of their value. The quantity of offerings is at times limited, but they are usually Good Buys.

Basic auction information is available at the Treasury's Website, TREAS.GOV> AUCTION> TREASURY. Customs' own Website is CBA.GOV. The Treasury vendors who handle the consignment, storage, and disposition of real and personal assets, by auction and by direct sale, are indicated by asset categories and geographic regions. Most of these national vendors post their listings of general property and motor vehicles to the Treasury Website. Realty sales and auctions are usually handled nationally by one contractor and these listings and their bid dates are on the Websites.

The U.S. Marshal's Service National Asset Seizure & Forfeiture Program Disposes Of Seized Assets On Behalf Of The FBI, DEA, And U.S. Postal Service. As a rule their Website is the best starting point for navigating their many outlets. The vendors and disposition methods vary from time to time. Their Website breaks the States down into Districts, and indicates which vendor is handling what type of asset in each region. Go to USDOJ.GOV>MARSHAL'S, or google U.S. Marshal's Service – Assets, and also check out BID4ASSETS.COM.

Marshal's asset categories include real estate, jewelry, general merchandise, motor vehicles, airplanes, helicopters, and boats, with some unique and exotic realty and personalty interspersed. Some assets are listed on a national basis, others by region. Motor vehicles are sold by Districts within each State– see USDOJ.GOV>MARSHAL'S. Jewelry is handled by auction on a national basis – either online or by live auction with a webcast for bidders. At this writing Lone Star Auctioneers in Texas – see LONESTAR AUCTIONEERS.COM for offerings – has the jewelry contract.

Real estate is available through two primary venues. As of this writing a private vendor, Lender Processing Services, whose Website FNAMS.COM also carries foreclosed and other depressed properties for private institutional sellers, lists most of the Marshal's Service inventory. Lender Processing retains local brokers to list and sell (not auction), and the properties are all posted to their Website.

The Marshal's official Website, BID4ASSETS.COM, also offers some real estate directly. A few years back, when Marshal's dispositions were by local public auctions handled through smaller auctioneers, attendance and bidding interest was invariably slim, in no small part the result of the scant public notice accorded to Marshals, like some other Government dispositions.

An expansive network of State, County, Municipal, And Regional Law Enforcement And Other Agencies hold periodic auctions in virtually every part of the country, with rules and scheduling set locally, to dispose of seizures and their own surplus. Sale and auction information is available through official (.GOV) websites of the various entities and their departments (i.e., Highways, Taxation, etc.)

These auctions and sales mirror the type of assets which are available on the Federal level. Many regional auctions are attractive because they are Absolute Auctions, meaning the items are to be sold, period, at the best qualified bid, regardless of true value or anticipated sales price.

Bankruptcy Assets, in different contexts and venues, have always been a Source of under-valued opportunities in real estate and every other asset category imaginable. On the one hand Bankruptcy is a Vehicle for the debtor; but it is also often a Source for the bargain-hunter.

A convoluted yet comprehensive way of describing "Bankruptcy": The legal process by which a debtor (individual, business entity, charity, or Government body), can obtain immediate and/or long term relief from creditors by Staying creditors' legal remedies already implemented or about to be exercised and ultimately by dealing with creditors through either reorganization, compromise, payment or elimination of debts, and then going forward with or without some or all of those obligations (or in the case of an entity, by possibly dissolving and ceasing operations). The United States Bankruptcy Code, 11 U.S. Code Sections 101-1380, is the operative body of Federal Law which governs the process called Bankruptcy and the operation of the Bankruptcy Courts.

Every State (District) is divided into regions for purposes of geographically distributing the jurisdiction of each of its Bankruptcy Courts. New Jersey, for example, has three Bankruptcy Courts (Trenton, Newark, and Camden), which handle the caseload for the entire State.

There are three Chapters, or provisions, of the Bankruptcy Code which address the procedures and substance of those forms of Bankruptcy which are relevant for our purposes.

Chapter 7 is a Petition For Liquidation which can be filed by an individual debtor, by husband and wife, by otherwise related co-debtors, or by a non-corporate business entity. With the exception of certain exempt assets, under a Chapter 7 the debtor's assets are surrendered to the Bankruptcy Court for sale or other liquidation or distribution, with any net proceeds, to the extent available, to be used to pay associated Court, Trustee and transaction costs first, and then creditors. This assumes, of course, there are available assets of net value not already fully encumbered by secured liens (i.e., a mortgage), or which for other reasons are not being abandoned (disregarded) by the Trustee. Trustees will often abandon assets if they are of such negligible Net value that it seems senseless to liquidate them.

Chapter 11 is the Corporate Filing, designed to either liquidate or to try to carry on and stay alive as a going entity, through any of a variety of Reorganization Plans (relative to income, assets and creditors), which Plans are administered under the auspices and protection of the Bankruptcy Court. (In complete liquidation or dissolution cases, the Chapter 11 is converted to a Chapter 7.) Plans will usually involve the grouping of creditors into Classes (secured, unsecured, priority and non-priority), and setting terms to govern the sale, auction, leasing and/or retention of assets, in order to fund (along with any current income), whatever payments may ultimately be made to the various classes of creditors. All Plans must be approved by the Court.

Chapter 13, discussed earlier in the context of Foreclosure Delay And Reorganization (Workouts), is an alternative to Chapter 7. In its purest non-Delay applications it is a remedy, primarily for individuals ("wage earners") who typically have positive net assets over liabilities (debt), or who have primarily secured debt (a mortgage), and want to retain all or some of their assets (house, etc.), and in some fashion Reorganize their debt into a manageable repayment schedule. Chapter 13 is the most common vehicle through which debtors can actually effectuate a Cure. Through a Chapter 13 Plan the debtor is given the option to repay his debts over a stipulated period of time, often three to five years, and upon completion of payment of the arrears under the Plan (in addition to maintaining current obligations), the debtor will be discharged from Bankruptcy.

Note – as discussed in Chapters I and III, the Court's authority in formulating a Chapter 13 Plan may soon permit Judges, in specified circumstances, to rewrite the terms (principal, interest, length, etc.) of residential mortgages in foreclosure, and to thus formulate in such cases Plans which are based on a "new debt". The particulars of such Plans may play out over a period of time as a debtor remains in bankruptcy, or the "cramdown" may result in the debtor's more immediate discharge from bankruptcy, with a "new mortgage" as part of the "Cure" or Reorganization.

The essential point in our immediate discussion, however, is: "Are you looking for Good Buys in Bankruptcy Assets?" When looking for bargain-priced Assets in Bankruptcies remember that most assets which are disposed of pursuant to a bankruptcy filing sell for a fraction of their true value.

Historically the public has been in the dark, knowing next to nothing about what assets are for sale, and when, where, or how to obtain information about them. In most cases labeled "Asset Cases" real estate and personal (or business) property of the debtor is either summarily sold (or auctioned); abandoned; retained by the debtor; or otherwise made available by the Trustee for distribution in the course of the debtor's liquidation or attempt to work through a Plan, in order to satisfy debts and emerge from bankruptcy as a functioning individual or entity.

Where the debtor's Case is dismissed by the Court or, for reason, the debtor himself moves to have it voluntarily dismissed, Assets are not disposed of by the Trustee. Yet the fact that the debtor even filed for bankruptcy to begin with can often help identify an anxious seller who is now outside of the Bankruptcy Court's purview, but nevertheless might have some "bargains" for sale.

Case Information as to status, types of assets for sale, prices, sale dates and manner of bidding, was traditionally obtained by contacting the debtor, his attorney or the Trustee.

Today such substantive and procedural information is available at the Court's Website (State prefix first; so, for example, in accessing a New Jersey case: "NJ>B.USCOURTS.GOV" and go to the "Cases" category). And you must be persistent. Dead ends and delays are the norm. You should diary interesting Cases and Assets and Follow-Up. There Is Money To Be Made In Bankruptcy Assets, For Future Investment; For Short-Term Speculation; For Resale, For Business Inventory; and For Personal Or Business Use.

In Chapter 7 Cases there is a Standing Trustee (a Court Agent who handles a huge docket of cases), and asset disposition is handled through the Court. In Chapter 11's – often rich in asset sales – there may or may not be an Independent Trustee appointed to oversee asset disposition, or a sale may be conducted by the debtor or its attorney or by the debtor and its creditors jointly, all in accordance with directives of the Court. Chapter 13 Cases employ Standing Trustees and asset sales are handled through the Trustee's Office.

As a rule, in tracking the status of Assets it is important to stay in contact with both the Standing and Independent Trustees Offices, whether you are following a specific case or cultivating a relationship and inquiring about classes of assets generally (i.e., real estate or jewelry), in the hopes that the Trustee will point you to upcoming sales or pending cases. And again, today your Bible is the Court's Website.

All Cases are different. The Trustee may do the marketing or the Trustee or the Court may order private sales, with the auctioneer sometimes handling the marketing and (e)-mailing sale notices to his own lists of potential bidders. But the Trustee is the one who runs the Case. And when in the discretion of the Trustee Assets are not sold but are instead abandoned they might revert back to a landlord, go back to their owner (the debtor), or go to a lender or other secured creditor. And here again, the "recipients" of such Assets may themselves become motivated sellers, outside of the Bankruptcy.

It might seem paradoxical, but regardless of their motivations, bargain hunters who seize upon Assets which are being sold or abandoned should not be categorized as "vultures". For even when they get a Good Buy, they are often helping the Bankruptcy Estate (the reservoir of Asset proceeds) bring in more dollars than it might have otherwise through the historically unpublicized arena of Bankruptcy Auctions – an old insider's club known for quick deals at fire sale prices.

In a different vein it should be noted that <u>Private Auctions Of Realty And Personalty (Auctions by Foreclosure, Bankruptcy, and Government Agencies)</u> discussed previously, are both an effective means for sellers to generate interest and a rich Source of underpriced realty and other assets. Good Deals can definitely be had at Private Auctions, particularly in Down Markets, particularly when bidding frenzies do not dominate. When bankruptcies and foreclosures are high and survival might mean downsizing or liquidating fixed assets or inventory, many business and real estate owners – individuals, developers, builders, professional landlords – are forced to dump solid equities, partially completed projects and raw land. Liquidation by Private Auction is common in Down Markets.

The sharp buyer can Leverage this phenomenon. Equity Accumulation, Generating Income, Flipping, Buying a personal residence or a home for a business, it's all there. The investor should keep tabs on the Websites of local auctioneers who work independently for owners and secured creditors. Search their Sites and the Legal Notices and Auction Advertising categories of local newspapers; speak to local auctioneers and get on their (e)-Mail Lists. Know your Market Areas and your own Abilities to handle and quickly close on a given purchase; Ignore the Mob Psychology at Auctions (Foreclosure, Private, Etc.); Bid Sensibly and Good Auction Buys will come your way.

What we might call <u>Everyday Common-Sense Sources</u> for finding opportunities should never be downplayed as being "too simplistic". Personal Contacts and Connections made at all sorts of functions, Chance Meetings, and Observations and Leads which you develop or which fall into your lap in the course of your daily routines, can all result in Good Buys. Keep Your Eyes Open.

Form and Cultivate personal, business and professional <u>Relationships</u>. Form your own Networks, "Farm" your Territory, Hustle, Solicit, Talk to people, Tell them what you're doing, Be out there, Know what's going on – all with a Focus on your Goal of Finding Deals.

Be Observant, be Aware of problems and positive situations of every sort. Look for the Sleepers, the Rundown and "Beat" Properties, the Vacant and Overgrown Properties, those which have been on the Market (with or without a broker) for a long time; Look for that "Worst House In The Neighborhood".

<u>Check out that Fire-Damaged Property</u> which is sitting neglected (perhaps the owner already collected his insurance and will sell cheap). Take a second look at <u>properties of Environmental Concern</u> – you might find a Steal;

maybe you can partner with an environmental clean-up firm which can save you a fortune in turning some of these properties around, and by giving such a firm "a piece of the action" you may profit greatly with little downside risk.

Cultivate Relationships with local residential and commercial Brokers. Have them scour the multiple listing or permit you to, looking for whatever may be of interest, a Potential Deal or a Good Value. Maintain a Standing Offer – for example, on a good find the broker gets his commission "plus" a piece of the Deal or a percentage of your Profit.

Establish a Relationship with local Attorneys, especially those who specialize in real estate, business, matrimonial and estate law. Within the parameters of ethical guidelines, an attorney may refer a Good Deal while at the same time promoting the best interests of his client. Or an attorney may often be in a position to point you to other Deals where he may not even have a client involved.

Follow the "For Sale By Owner" Ads in the newspapers and on the Internet, "FSBO's" lawn signs, and word of mouth Tips. Some FSBO's tend to be overpriced and wither. Many ultimately sell at below market. Pay attention to the Visuals – anything on or around a property which might give the slightest hint of something amiss, a Deal. Join some clubs and professional, civic, religious, fraternal or political organizations. Talk to People, let them know what you do. Maintain your Network of Contacts – Family, Friends, Associates and Referrers.

And as an investor you can also "Target" specific owners (addresses), "Farm" geographic areas, Form a Mailing List of your own Contacts and Referrers, and send your own "Principal Real Estate Buyer Solicitation Letter" on a regular basis to your lists and to targeted geographic areas.

Send a Targeted Letter to attorneys, to local fire insurance adjusters, to fellow club members, to local brokers, to commercial property owners in the older section of town just down the street from that brand-new strip mall!

If you are Determined to Make Money in Buying, Selling, Renting, Rehabbing, or otherwise Speculating in any Form of Real Estate, or even Non-Realty Assets, it's up to you to Get A Handle On What You Can Afford Financially And Mentally; and To Decide How Much Effort You Want To Devote To Learning The Business And Your Market Area, and To Actually Finding Potential Deals.

Decide Which Way(s) You Want To Go – REO's, Foreclosures, Multiple Listing, Bankruptcies, Government Agency Dispositions, or Any Combination.

The Sources are there. The Methods can be perfected. The Question – "Do You Want To Do It?" If so, "Which Ways, What Price Range?" seem best suited for you. In Any Market And Certainly In A Down Market, Prudent Choices Founded In Knowledge And Business Maturity Will Go A Long Way In Accumulating Wealth And Producing Income Through Real Estate Speculation And Investment.

CHAPTER VIII

STRUCTURING THE (BUYER'S) DEAL

The process of <u>Negotiating Price And Other Terms</u> of a Contract, regardless of the type of Purchase or Transaction of Real Estate or Proprietary Rights, is obviously a key step <u>in Making the Deal</u>. <u>Combing Your Sources, Doing Your Due Diligence, Finding A Motivated Seller And The Right Property, Finding That Potential Deal, Are All Crucial Enough Matters In Their Own Right, But These Are Just The First Steps</u>.

 <u>There Is So Much More Involved In Making A Deal Happen</u> (with the exception of those Chance Buys which occasionally just somehow come together). If the investor keeps his eye on the ultimate rewards and can grow to appreciate real estate speculation and investment as the Business and Art that it truly is, the Work and the Steps can become the proverbial Labor of Love. Sure, it helps to have a knack, but it also helps to become Immersed in the Process.

 Enjoying the Work, the Challenges, the Game, with its many diverse issues and range of personalities, should help instill a certain ease into your Negotiating. Having a handle on the Business Aspects; feeling Comfortable (not cocky or over-confident); having an Interest not only in the particular parcel of realty and its Potential but also in the Process and its inherent Dynamics and life stories; going in with a Confidence and a Positive Attitude; these are the <u>Starting Points Of Success</u>.

 There is no need to know every last detail of every step and every document which may be involved <u>From Locating A Prospective Deal Through Closing. What Is Important Is That You Have A Conceptual Understanding And A Functional Knowledge Of The Game. Know Your Ends</u> – And Know

Enough about what your attorney, inspectors, real estate and mortgage people, and contractors do so that you can Ask Questions, Oversee, Compare, Direct, Decide, and Keep them Honest and Focused, as you Proceed with your Deal and you Continue Learning. No need to be that walking encyclopedia of values of every type of property in the areas where you are working – if you are, if you memorize numbers with ease, fine. But the point is to acquire an Overall Feel for values and trends in a given market area and era, and to Know Who To Call and When To Look Or Inquire should you need up-to-the-minute information or details to assist with a particular Negotiation.

"Cash Is King" (in today's world we should add "Credit Is Co-King"), and "Knowledge Is Power". Provided, however, that by Knowledge we mean primarily An Intelligent And A Perceptive Knowledge. Similar to the theory behind law school teachings – an Ability to Think a problem or situation through, an Ability to Focus on what is Important and Relevant, an Ability to Ask Questions, an Ability to Guide and an Ability to Know when it is time to Hire (Buy) Brains and Expertise. All coupled with a certain Recall of Relevant Facts and Necessary Learned Statistics.

Incorporated within the true meaning of the wider term "Knowledge" is a thing called "Understanding" – Understanding of the Market and the Real Estate Business, of the individual Potential Deal itself. Your sense of the Market (buyer's? seller's? trends? values? regional?), must impact your Perceptions and your Fiscal and Physical Analysis of a Property. Commencement of the Negotiating process should be premised on a Gut Feeling that this could be a Deal. A Deal, however, that is Right. A Gut Feeling should come from Knowledge of everything involved, from an Understanding, from Asking Questions, from your own Business Acumen, from your General Perceptions, and from your personal Experience. You Negotiate for a Purpose – because there is something of Potential, and thus Value, to talk about – to achieve your ultimate Goal(s).

Boil it all down. Go back to the Basics. That is the starting point. What are you After? The Overall Goal(s) – Buy Low, Buy Right. The Built-In Up-Front Profit. The Yields And The Possible Additional Cyclical Appreciation. The Goal Is To Get This Thing, To Get Into A (Right) Contract, To Control It, To Use It, To Grow It, To Benefit And To Profit From It.

Caveat – In Doing The Initial Assessment, In Order To Get That Gut Feeling As To Whether This Is A Potential "Buy", To Determine If There Really Is Something To Negotiate Towards, you must do more than run your numbers and know the comps. You must be able to see the True Value and the Forms of Profit or Yield. You must also Look Inside and Look Behind and Beyond in your own Analysis, any documents and paperwork which may be presented to you to "assist" in your evaluation.

You Must Ask Questions: "Are the entries and the bottom line of the seller's tax returns accurate? What do they really mean for me? Do they show a true picture of the property in question? Are the income and expense figures real, or are they made-for-buyer consumption?" And importantly, "Are the seller's Financial Statements, prepared by a CPA or otherwise, accurate?" (Whoever said that Numbers Don't Lie was Dead Wrong!) You must ask, "How strong is that lease? Do its seemingly lucrative terms and option really mean anything? How strong is the tenant? His track-record? Are the handwritten or other seller-generated rent receipts real or accurate? What is the true condition of the tenant's business? Are there grounds to terminate or buy-out a poor lease?" Look Inside and Beyond any leases and financials which may be presented to you.

"Are the seller's termite and environmental reports or roof guarantee verifiable and/or meaningful? Is there a great deal of deferred maintenance on the property? Are the broker's comps really on point and reflective of true Value? Are they the most appropriate ones from which to extrapolate Value?" (Chapter IX discusses tangible and non-tangible market and other specific factors which may affect the possible future Use, Rehab, and other Conversion of a property, and which should thus also impact a Buyer's Valuation And Gut Feel On Day One.)

So, Now That You Have An Empirical And Gut Feeling That This May Be Something To Go After, Your Negotiations Should Proceed With A Foundation Of Adequate Knowledge Of The Relevant Facts, A Knowledge Of The Business, And A Knowledge Of Real Estate And Mortgage Terminology. No need to be overly professorial. Those Latin legal terms and that out-of-everyday context overly-technical language does not accomplish anything and at best can be scary and resented by your average seller. Just be Conversant, be able to Express Yourself, and Know what the other person is Talking about.

(And through Experience and Exposure, by Asking Questions, by Listening, by Reading about your Business, your real estate Vocabulary will grow and your education and real life situations will better tie together and make you a more Skilled Deal-Maker.)

Demeanor is an important factor in Negotiations. Particularly when dealing with sellers-in-distress, as a prudent business person and indeed as a decent person you, the buyer, should present yourself not only as a Knowledgeable individual operating from a position of Strength and Confidence, but also as a "Gentleman". You must appear Credible, Understanding, and Respectful. Your seller should be treated as a business person and a member of the community. Nothing overdone or artificial, and nothing of a condescending nature.

Your articulated concern for your seller's situation should come across as Real and Heartfelt. The seller should walk away feeling he is dealing with a decent person, a businessman who is out to make a Profit, who is Strong, Capable and Down to Earth. Avoid bravado. Do not be overly flashy. The Right Attitude – which one would hope comes naturally, anyway – will go a long way in gaining an Inside Track and your seller's ear.

Always bear in mind that virtually every seller-in-foreclosure is being bombarded by all types of would-be buyers, advisers, real estate and mortgage brokers, attorneys and scam artists, many promising dollars, hope and remedies which do not exist. So many of these sellers are being fed unrealistic "truths" by so-called experts, things they may want to hear, things they would want to believe are true. They are being lied to left and right. Impress upon your seller that you are not there to mislead him, to exaggerate, or to promise him the impossible. And your corporate and business sellers, the banks selling REO's, the attorneys and the brokers – on a somewhat different level they also want to deal with a reliable straight-shooter, someone they can depend on, someone who once he makes a Deal will perform.

Negotiating Strategy can take many different forms – some more or less appropriate for different situations and types of sellers. Strategy must often be reassessed or adjusted as matters evolve, as a situation or seller may present new issues or positions or responses to the buyer's proposals. But there is a basic rule of thumb and parameter in all Negotiating Strategy: As law school "Contracts I" professors drill into their first-year students, "There Is No Such Thing As A Free Lunch."

Most business and personal relationships and interactions involve a certain give and take. The essence of any definition of the word Contract – and what in life is not "a Contract?" – lies in the fact there is something of "value" – money, goods, services, emotions, personal satisfaction, or I.O.U.'s – flowing both ways, to and from, between the parties.

That is what lawyers call "mutual consideration". Without "a meeting of the minds" and "mutual consideration", there is no Contract, there is nothing. This goes to the core of the most basic of human motivations – "What's In It For Me?"

In an arms-length voluntary agreement each party looks to walk away with something. Save for those situations which amount to capitulation and are not truly Negotiations anyway, or where one party just does not care about the outcome, it is rarely productive to try to corner your counterpart, to leave him nothing and no room, to try to get the last dollar or benefit in the Deal for yourself. Everything is relative. But Mutuality, even where the Buyer is in Control and the Seller is Vulnerable, or even desperate, is still typically a vital trade-off in any "meeting of the minds".

Bear in mind that even the vulnerable Seller is not always totally without Options, and with or without other options he can always be capable of just saying "forget it" and walking. You may not be the only Buyer who has his ear. He can get disgusted and shy away, feeling he is being "had" or "pummeled". There are times to Compromise and times to be Firm and apply Pressure. Be Businesslike, go for the Best or the Almost Best Deal. And try to make a Friend of your Seller – many times it helps!

Understand his Position, his Strengths, his Weaknesses, his Needs, his Desires, and his Goals. Assess your own Points, and his Points and Trade-Offs in the Negotiating Process. Be Straight-Forward, yet Know when you should Weave or Stall. Remember that small Trade-Offs or Refusals to Compromise often Make or Break Deals. Know when to Draw Back and when to try to Close the Deal. Know how to critique your competition without seeming small or petty. Always show that you are "Ready, Willing, And Able" to Perform in the Right Deal. And try to inject a bit of Humility and some down to earth Likeability where called for.

Who, in a given situation, is your Best Lead Negotiator? You, the Buyer? The Brokers (assuming one is involved)? Your Attorney? A Partner? In certain types of Negotiations, i.e., multiple-listed properties, rules dictate that the Broker take the Lead, though the parties may be brought in later in the process to try and resolve outstanding issues.

"Contract Negotiations Post-Execution," during the "Attorney Review Period" are handled primarily through respective counsel. Certain institutional sellers – i.e., banks disposing of REO's – often require that Negotiations be handled through their Brokers. Negotiations in commercial transactions are typically through counsel. To the extent that legal and ethical considerations relative to the role of Broker / Professional permit, a sensible experienced buyer who Knows the Business should be directly involved and take the Lead in his own Negotiations. With or without professional involvement, the savvy buyer should Control, Guide and try to Deal One On One with his seller. And so, too, should the buyer solicit and consider Input from his broker and attorney.

The desired net result is to secure a Contract or other form of Legal Instrument containing such terms and conditions, including price and contingencies (financing or otherwise), such that a particular Potentially Money-Making Property Falls Under The Ownership Or Control Of The Buyer In A Desired Manner.

What then should be the Role Of The Professionals and Third-Party Contractors in the Sequence from Locating a Potential Purchase to Negotiating it to Contract Execution through Contract Review, to Closing – including the handling or satisfaction of Contractual Terms And Contingencies? The answer will vary with the type of transaction – residential; commercial (retail, offices); industrial; land; problem or promising properties presenting rehab, zoning or other legal issues; and the more complex Deals. So too should the Role of the Professional and Third Party Contractor vary in importance depending on the experience and sophistication of the buyer, the type of seller, the context of the transaction, and the attendant business issues.

Even market conditions come into play: "Is it a buyer's or seller's market? Is the property a steal in the present market?" The answers to such questions should "help" determine how much "assistance" the buyer needs, and when. Additionally in some States the law itself or the norms and regulations of the State Bar or Real Estate Commission / Multiple Listing Systems will govern in certain matters – i.e., the extent of the Broker's role in contract preparation, whether an attorney must conduct a closing or if it can be done by a title company.

In the final analysis, at every step Decisions must be made as to whether or not to use a certain Professional, and if so what the scope of his role should be. You must balance the extent of the individual professional's experience, his expertise in specialized types of transactions, his fees relative to prevailing norms, other necessary costs and the Profit Potential of the Deal, and what you, the buyer, can and should do by yourself and what you cannot and should not do by yourself. Buyer Knowledge and Savvy imply an Understanding of

When to Buy Brains and When to Ask Questions and Seek Third Party Input. They also infer Having a Feel for When to Overlook the advice of others and to not let the Smaller Issues get in the way of the Larger Goal, the Larger Picture, the Good Deal, Your Vision and Ingenuity.

So it is a fine line with no fixed answers. There are times when you should be directed by your attorney or inspector and defer to their guidance as to your legal or business position. And there are times when you should look past it. There are times when you should take to heart the structural report which shows the roof's life expectancy is just about up and a big repair bill may be in the offing. And there are other times when you should jump at a Deal no matter how bad that roof is leaking. Should you upset things and possibly kill the Contract because the termite inspector has sounded an alarm, albeit one which in the final analysis a decent carpenter might cure for the cost of several days' wages? But maybe you should apply the brakes when the environmental people alert you to a subsurface condition which might be a catastrophe down the road.

The Context, the Potential in a Deal, the Market, the Second Opinion and the Third Assessment, your Own Abilities and Wherewithal and Experience, your Gut Feeling on the Upside and Downside, are all part of the Mix in deciding who to bring in, when, what to do with their reports and advice, and how to boil it all down. Academic or technically correct or observant advice can sometimes "Protect" you right out of a Good Deal!

As a rule and of course with certain overlap, there are Categories of Professionals and Contractors whose services are more or less relevant at Different Stages of the Process. In Locating a Property obviously the Real Estate Broker may be an integral participant (though you can do just fine going solo with foreclosures and in other distressed venues). Input from the Mortgage Broker is often vital in determining a price range and what liquid assets and documents are needed to secure Financing. A Prospective Lender can also provide a Conditional Commitment which may prove a valuable lever in Negotiations. An Independent Appraiser (or broker) can counsel a buyer on comps and value – perhaps to second guess a procuring broker.

Additionally, Property Inspectors and Contractors, or so-called "contractor inspectors", might be engaged to get a better handle on expected costs of future repairs and improvements, or to provide written ammunition for Negotiating purposes. Generally speaking, the label "inspector" includes Termite, Environmental, Structural, Engineering, and other Specialty Categories – i.e., for more involved matters Experts on complicated mechanical systems, sub-surface conditions and the like.

In <u>Negotiating</u> a Contract or other legal instrument, as stated earlier the use of either Broker or Attorney to assist or in place of the buyer may or may not be required or indeed prudent in any given situation.

<u>Execution of the Purchase Contract</u> is facilitated by either the Broker, the parties themselves or Counsel. This process is basically a function of the mode of the Negotiations.

<u>Contract (Attorney) Review</u>, which is required in most jurisdictions in res-idential (and for certain non-real estate consumer) transactions, is presented as a Contract Contingency. Unlike the purely buyer's prerogative which such "waiting / cancellation periods" amount to in the consumer sector, in real es-tate transactions it is a means whereby either buyer or seller may void the Con-tract and walk away with no liability to the other. This Contingency (usually three to five business days) is tantamount to turning the initial signed agree-ment into a three to five day "Option" going both ways. (Albeit not our literal "Option" wherein one of the parties will always remain obligated to perform.)

Standard Review provisions do not typically require that either actual cause or substantive issues be in dispute as a condition or reason for either party to kill the Deal. A letter voiding the Contract can be as simple as: "Coun-sel for (buyer / seller) disapproves of the Contract" – either in its "as is" form, or period, in its entirety, no further discussion required (or invited). In those situations where Attorney Review is not mandated, customized review clauses may still be inserted into the draft and provide for cancellation within a given Review Period for any number of stipulated reasons or again, for no particular reason, cause, event, inaction, revelation or disclosure at all. It can say whatever the parties agree it should say.

Whatever the substance of the Attorney Review Clause, if the parties want to try and compromise and hold a Deal together, Disapproval by either may obviously be converted back into a Meeting of the Minds and thus a final bind-ing Contract. Attorneys and Brokers are the main participants in this Process, as in any subsequent Renegotiations. When resolving issues, input from In-spectors and Contractors may also prove useful. As part of an <u>Attorney Review</u> period, any number of clauses and contingencies (i.e., mortgage, structural, termite, tenancy, etc.) may be inserted, deleted, or changed from the original Contract draft.

Once a Contract has been solidified, the Process to and through <u>Closing</u>, including satisfaction and resolution of issues related to <u>Contract Contingencies</u> and other matters which may arise, must be attended to by the buyer and, where appropriate, his "Experts".

Obtaining a <u>Mortgage Commitment</u> obviously requires the interaction of the Mortgage Broker, Appraiser and other Agents. More commonly in a commercial purchase and particularly in the case of the self-employed individual, retaining an Accountant to prepare financial statements is also advisable. The Real Estate Broker should help facilitate the mortgage application process. The Attorney should be involved in any Mortgage Contingency / Contract changes – i.e., price, amount of mortgage, anticipated closing date, etc., which are occasioned by delay or problems incident to obtaining a commitment – assuming the parties want to avoid killing the Deal based on failure of the contingency.

Inspectors are usually required to complete their own specific assignments within contractually-stipulated periods of 10 to 45 days from signing. (In order to make a Deal tighter and narrow the Contract Contingencies, parties may agree to pay for and conduct <u>Inspections</u> prior to signing the Contract – most notably where "The Deal Is Right" to the buyer.)

Again, Contractors will often become involved after the <u>Locating Process</u>, either to inspect so as to price or plan future repairs and improvements; or to do pre-closing repairs which may be required of either party (a risk, mostly for a buyer, but often an invaluable time-saver and profitable gamble, if indeed not required by a mortgage commitment or Code Official in order to close). <u>Insurance</u> must also be secured prior to Closing. And the various roles of Attorney, Title Company, Surveyor and other ancillary third parties in the actual <u>Closing</u> are self-evident.

<u>A major consideration in Structuring A Deal is the Method, or Form, of initially and subsequently Holding the real estate or, sometimes, more precisely put, of Facilitating a buyer's Interest in a piece of real estate. The Form of Holding Property Rights (ownership, etc.), Interests, or Proprietary Rights in real estate, be those Rights purchased or otherwise acquired, carries strong implications *vis-à-vis* the most basic matters which go to the very heart of a Deal and the Future Use and Benefits of the Property.</u>

<u>A Host of Matters are impacted by the Form of Holding, including Both Speculative and Investment Aspects; Expectations; Goals or Plans; and Structuring.</u>

The Anticipated Benefits, the Underpinning of a Venture Itself, can be magnified or dissipated based on the Form of Holding. And the ease or difficulty of Dealing, Managing, and Other Matters, are similarly affected.

There are essentially Eight Categories of Concern, or Facets of Real Estate Investment, which are impacted by the particular Form of Holding in a given transaction:

1. Matters involving Federal Taxes, including: (a) Ordinary Income (brackets); (b) Write-Offs during the period of ownership; (c) Methods of Depreciation and its maximization, advantages or lack thereof, during the period of ownership; (d) Resale issues (Corporate Double Tax, Capital Gains treatment where qualified); and (e) Gift and Estate Tax Considerations.

2. The "Visibility" of an Individual Buyer's Interest in a property – i.e., if the individual does or does not want to be, or "can" or "cannot" be, identified on legal documents as an owner of record.

3. The Cost Effectiveness and Potential Profitability, or Gain, from Capital Improvements made during ownership.

4. The available Methods and Potential Financial Gains associated with initial and subsequent Leveraging (Refinancing) of the property.

5. The Methods (and ease or difficulty) of Decision-Making; Dispute Resolution; and Formulating Buy-Sell Agreements relative to death and disability among ownership and management.

6. The ease or difficulty of procedurally (mechanically) Dividing or Selling Individual Interests where more than one principal is involved; either to bring in more owners or to divide and dispose of existing Interests.

7. The Resolution of Situations Occasioned By The Death of a Principal – Disposition of the property or Devise, (where Death is not specifically addressed by Agreement).

8. Matters of Individual Personal Liability – mortgage; taxes (realty, withholding, franchise) which can lien the property or the owner; other financial obligations; casualty / liability claims; and overall property operations and management – (maintenance, Fire and Building Codes, tenant issues, environmental matters).

<u>Again, The Actual Forms Of Holding Real Estate, Or Interests In Real Estate – i.e., Rights, Entitlements, Scope Of Ownership, Proprietary Interests – Are Diverse, And Each Of These Forms Has Its Own Unique Relationship To The Aforementioned Eight Facets Of Real Estate Investment. (Caveat – It Is Vital To Understand That Certain Methods Of Financing Are Defined By, And By Their Very Terms Are In Fact Sometimes Actually Forms Of, Holding.)</u>

<u>The First And Most Common Form Of Holding An Interest In Real Estate Is Through Individual, Or Personal, Sole Ownership.</u> In this scenario, ordinary net income, or profit from the property such as rent, becomes part of the owner's personal gross income and is taxed accordingly. Tax write-offs during the period of ownership – mortgage interest and real estate taxes, certain other expenses on investment property, and any actual losses incurred in carrying investment property where expenses exceed income on an annual basis – become deductions from otherwise-taxable personal income of the Individual Owner.

Depreciation – that artificial tax shelter on investment property (not owner-occupied residential units), where the Tax Code says the value of your improvements (everything except the land), is decreasing as its utility is wearing out (while in reality of course it is typically increasing), and therefore you should receive a tax deduction for this (make believe) "loss", directly affects the Individual Owner. Owners in higher income brackets can best maximize the benefits of any Depreciation Method in offsetting net operating profits (rental, etc.) from the real estate, and perhaps in also sheltering additional unrelated income. This all depends on the amount which can be deducted for Depreciation in any particular case, as compared to the actual net profit generated from the property.

A resale of property which qualifies as a Capital Gain (again, stipulated period of ownership prior to resale), allows the Individual a preferential tax treatment by virtue of its lower tax rate on net profit.

For the Individual who due to either personal or creditor considerations (i.e., having or anticipating personal liens), would find it imprudent to be legally named as an Owner, this Form of Holding is not the way to go.

On the other hand in this Form the Individual Owner will usually benefit from having a wider choice of methods and more favorable terms in obtaining a purchase money mortgage or in later Refinancing. Additionally, the non-taxable proceeds from any Refinance will go directly into the Individual's pockets. But compared to Holding in the name of an Entity, it is usually more involved for an Individual Owner to bring in a partner or grant others co-interests in real estate. And to the extent that any Form of Holding can bring with it Personal Liability, this is the one.

The Individual Owner will be signing personally on any mortgage note. He will also be responsible for other financial obligations, routine bills and debts relative to his property, and he will have exposure to uninsured or underinsured losses. Governmental levies on account of fines or remediation costs for Fire or Property Code violations, environmental clean-up, and the like, will all be lodged against the real estate in the form of an assessment, and in certain cases also become a personal liability for the Owner.

Holding Real Estate "Individually" But In The Name Of A Sole Proprietorship Or Trade-Name is not a smart choice. These entities are usually loosely documented forms of a company, shells in which to do business. In most jurisdictions such names are "registered" in the County Courthouse, usually with the County Clerk. They are sometimes referred to as the "doing business" route – "John Smith, DBA Acme Painting," for example. Or simply "Acme Painting". The "Individual Owner's" name is listed along with the name of his business at the Courthouse.

In such a loose entity Ownership is not evidenced by shares, and the name itself is not usually protected on a Statewide basis against others who may decide to do business under an identical or similar name in the future. Indeed, even where such a name has been registered, others may already or later be operating under the same name in other Counties within the same State. This lack of certainty, this vagueness, is certainly not a defining characteristic of any legal entity which should be a shell to house a valuable asset. All sorts of potential title, lien, resale and other complications are invited when using a loose, nebulous entity to Hold real estate.

Moreover, the personal liability issues and exposures, incident to the Individual Owner, will follow in the Sole Proprietorship or Trade Name Forms. In these Forms you cannot be an "invisible owner" either, inasmuch as your Individual name can be traced to the property through a quick record check in the Courthouse. But the financial and tax advantages which inure personally under the Individual Ownership Form will similarly benefit the Individual in the Sole Proprietorship scenario.

There is basically no point in Holding as a Sole Proprietor. Just more paperwork, potential confusion and complications down the road. Operating a small informal business which has no real tangible assets as a Sole Proprietorship is one thing – and even here, the advantages, albeit with some "name protection", are very limited. (The mom and pop "Acme Painting" can easily do business as other than a Sole Proprietorship, and in the process achieve more name protection and better limit its owner's liability.) And as foolish a Form of Holding that such DBA Forms are, many real estate owners do actually rely on them.

Holding Through A Registered Partnership which in actuality may be nothing more than a sparse legal entity, is not a wise Form either – there are superior ways in which partners may band together in a real estate venture and better organize, control, and define their concerns and interests.

A Partnership is simply two or more individuals (or entities) linked together in a joint endeavor or interest. Oftentimes investors actually Hold in the name of a more organized legal entity, yet casually in a conversational, but not a legal sense, refer to themselves as "partners" or as being "in a Partnership". Be that as it may, if a Holding is in fact through a legal Partnership, the group may or may not have an Agreement which addresses issues such as respective percentage ownership interests, decision-making, dispute resolution, Buy-Sell, death and disability matters, and the myriad other concerns incident to ownership, rehab, management, and resale.

In all other respects the personal links to tax and other financial benefits (income, Depreciation) which inure to the Individual Owner similarly pass to the Individual Partners in accordance with their pro-rata interests in the property (or Partnership). Liability issues will also impact them; and liability premised on a joint personal guarantee or by operation of law, can conceivably leave one Partner responsible for not only his own portion, but for everybody's – unless the creditor or lienholder agreed otherwise in advance. For example, a 10% Partner might get stuck for 100% of a judgment, municipal fine, mortgage deficiency or roofer's bill. In many business situations, by his signature alone one Partner can bind the others "Just like that". There are ways far superior to the Partnership Form by which "Partners" can join together and Hold real estate.

With one notable exception everything discussed above will also apply to that Form Of Holding Known As The Limited Partnership: In a Limited Partnership each Partner will have "limited liability" with respect to obligations which must be guaranteed by a personal signature, except for the partner(s) whose personal signature(s), on a mortgage note, for example, will suffice. Thus, in such an important matter where one or more of the Partners assumes all personal liability such that the other, or all of the other Partners, need not sign the mortgage note personally, personal liability is Limited, eliminated, capped, for all but the signing Partner(s).

While those within a Limited Partnership may generally operate with or without an Agreement as to their rights and other matters, the Unlimited Partner(s) must always be identified by a signed writing.

In order to limit liability to only one or some of the Partners in a given matter, the party on the other side, the lender for example, must of course be satisfied with the given signature or signatures. Typically there will be a certain Consideration flowing from the Limited Partner(s) to the Unlimited Partner(s) – in dollars or in extra shares or profits from the property. Such a (solo) signature must be strong – backed by sufficient credit, personal assets and income. Particularly in more speculative situations, such as major rehabs or new construction, there can be significant risks for the Unlimited Partner(s), often endearingly referred to as the "patsy" in a Limited Partnership Arrangement. Again, in a Limited entity, there may be any number of Limited Partners, but you need only one Unlimited Partner.

Some years ago I was privy to a Limited Partnership in which some eleven local doctors, lawyers and business people, along with one builder / developer, had formed a group to buy a large tract of land for industrial development. The purchase agreement was signed (subject to a mortgage contingency), they had the ability to obtain construction financing, the architect drew a tentative layout, and everybody was set to go – except the builder, the designated Unlimited Partner, who had last minute reservations. He was semi-retired and living off the rental income of his personal Holdings. And in this new venture he would be guaranteeing a sum which far exceeded his net worth, and it was a speculative Deal.

If he went for it and the Project was successful in time his net worth and income would multiply many times over. Failure could wipe him out. And he backed off at the last minute. None of his other Partners were willing to step into his shoes. The Deal was off. (As it turns out, had the Deal proceeded, in time each Partner could have comfortably retired just on their income from this single investment; Hindsight is always 20/20.)

Whether we are talking about Partners or an Individual, the increasingly Popular Form Of Holding (and format for doing most any type of business), through formation of <u>A Limited Liability Company (LLC)</u>, is the way to go. This Form of Holding enables its members to benefit from most of the advantages available in any of the optimal Forms of real estate Ownership.

It also narrows those areas which have historically been the rough spots in organized Forms of Holding. Where an LLC is formed and an Agreement executed by its Members, most issues can be addressed in advance, making for a smoother run. The LLC is a solid, tightly organized legal entity formed in accordance with specific State Statutes.

It affords name protection within the State – in New Jersey, for example, if a name which is identical or too similar is already being used by either a chartered LLC or a Corporation, a new LLC cannot register under that name. An LLC may be comprised of one (or more) Member(s) – Individual(s) and/or legally constituted entities such as other LLC's, Corporations or Limited Partnerships. This is a real framework within which to do business or Hold realty.

With regard to tax issues, Members declare their respective shares of ordinary income on their Individual Returns, as they do with their shares of any "write-offs", including actual losses, to the extent of their interest in the LLC. Depreciation is also taken as a personal tax shelter meaning, of course, that if the amount of income which a Member can Depreciate, or make tax-free in a given year, exceeds his Cash Yield from the LLC, the differential will apply to unrelated income and also make a portion of that income tax-free. Provided the property has been owned for the requisite time period, a Member's share of any profit upon resale will also filter back to him personally as a Capital Gain.

If due to a personal reason (liens or other creditor issues), an Individual wishes to remain anonymous to the rest of the world with regard to his real estate interests; if he does not want or cannot have his name appear on a deed or other recorded legal document; the LLC will afford such "cover". The name of the LLC, not that of any Member, appears on the deed. Only one Member or even non-Member needs to sign the State paperwork to form an LLC, and neither Agreements among Members nor their names have to be made public or recorded. A Member can thus Own real estate equities, he can be doing Deals, and "nobody" has to know.

To the extent an LLC is comprised of one Member or ten, each will benefit from its initial Financing and any Refinancing according to the Member's pro-rata interest, just as he would if he were an Individual Owner. In multi-Member LLC's, issues concerning decision-making, dispute resolution,

Buy-Sells, management, and death and disability matters can all be handled through the Operating Agreement. And so too can there be relative ease (at least as easy as things can ever be when Partners are involved in anything), in any division, resale or other disposition of individual interests.

In the event of the death of a Member, unless the Operating Agreement specifies otherwise the decedent's interest will go as a simple devise in accordance with State inheritance laws and any Will of the decedent.

Absent any actual guarantee on the mortgage note or other obligations, individual personal liability in an LLC is limited – be it a one or a ten Member LLC. The LLC itself is the responsible party. It, not its Members, is the legal entity which is doing business.

With the exception of some narrow and special circumstances, Holding Real Estate Through A Corporation is simply foolish. It does not matter what type of Corporation – and the States and IRS vary as to forms – be it a basic Corporation, a Sub-Chapter S, a non-profit or one formed in a corporate-friendly State like Delaware. A Corporation may consist of one or more Shareholders (Stockholders), a Shareholder being either a person or a legal entity, and it may or may not have a Shareholder's Agreement respecting salient issues and operating procedures.

Where real estate Held in a Corporation generates ordinary income, unless a Shareholder can justify to the IRS that he does sufficient actual work relative to the real estate (or Corporation) such that he can call his draws "earned income" and thus take his Yields in the form of a corporate expense (ordinary taxable income to the Shareholder, an expense in the form of salary, commission or the like to the Corporation), the income is subject first to the corporate income tax as corporate income, and then, in order for the Shareholder to get his money out and into his own pocket, it must be drawn as a Dividend and the Shareholder must also pay personal income tax on the same money.

This has been dubbed the corporate "double tax". Net after-tax Yield on income (profit) is thus significantly lower where property is Held in a corporate shell. Few situations justify classifying corporate rental income or profit as a corporate expense in the form of Shareholder salary or as payment for "services performed". It is typically deemed passive income and labeled a Dividend and thus whacked by the double tax when drawn from the Corporation.

Write-offs incurred during the period of ownership inure to the benefit of the Corporation, not the Individual Shareholder(s); thus, all or part of the tax benefits are typically "lost" (assuming the Corporation is in a lower tax bracket than its Shareholder(s), which is usually the case). Depreciation benefits also go to the Corporation – another potentially huge loss for the Shareholder who is unable to shelter his Dividend (which has been hit by the corporate and personal income taxes), or other unrelated personal income.

Upon its resale of qualifying property the Individual or LLC seller will pay a Capital Gains (15%) tax rate on net profits. The Corporate seller, on the other hand, and thus its Shareholder(s), get penalized even when qualifying for Capital Gains treatment. It is the typically lower tax bracket Corporation which "benefits" from the lower Capital Gains tax; thus even that benefit is diluted. So upon a resale profit is first hit by the corporate Capital Gains income tax, and further diminished as the Shareholder pays personal income tax at his own (usually higher) rate on any profit drawn off as a Dividend. Similarly, in the case of death, any bequest (devise is a legacy of real estate, and Corporate Stocks are not actually real estate, they are personalty), of a Shareholder's stake in the Corporation is also hit twice – profit (Dividend) as the bequest is drawn from the Corporation (subject to Personal Income Tax), and then the net is subject to any applicable Inheritance Tax – before the inheritance reaches the decedent's beneficiary.

As with the LLC, a lien or credit-conscious Shareholder or one who is concerned with hiding assets, perhaps because of matrimonial reasons, can utilize the Corporate veil (shell) to maintain a certain anonymity as an Owner. With regard to Refinancing, a valuable means for an Individual or LLC Member to pull out tax-free dollars, there are fewer advantages and more complications in the Corporate context.

The Corporation can certainly refinance and pull money out. But it belongs to the Corporation. In neither a single nor a multi-Shareholder Corporation can a Shareholder just take money out. In order to get his hands on any Leveraged proceeds and avoid turning them into taxable income; he must sign a detailed Loan Agreement with the Corporation. The Agreement must be "sensible", contain a fair market interest rate and maturity date, and stipulate regular "repayments" to the Corporation, which over the course of time must be made so as to justify pulling refinance proceeds out as a "loan" and not having them considered income.

The principal thus drawn out will be smaller, more costly, and more cumbersome to arrange than draws in the non-Corporate context. In the non-Corporate setting you just refinance and put your tax free dollars in your pocket, and quite legally so. The rigid Corporate "loan" repayment obligation of principal and interest will still further diminish the funds available from any Corporate refinances.

Decision-making, dispute resolution, management, death and disability issues and Buy-Sells, should all be addressed within the Shareholders Agreement. The concept and utility of having Shares of Stock does facilitate divisions and conveyances of Corporate ownership, including buy-outs and buy-ins.

Obviously a 100% Shareholder can sell or otherwise convey Corporate-owned property by deeding it from the Corporation to a buyer, or he may sell his actual Shares to a buyer and leave title to the property in the name of the Corporation. While the latter course will pose its own subset of tax and legal issues along the way, it is a viable means to convey "property" where other objectives may be in play, such as the earlier-noted maneuver of wanting to leave desired Non-Assumable Financing in place.

As alluded to in our earlier tax discussion, absent other Agreement as to its disposition upon the death of a Shareholder, a decendant's Shares will go in accordance with his Will, the Shares being a bequest as they are personalty, "merely" evidence of one's ownership in an entity which itself owns real estate.

And as with the LLC, personal liability is also generally limited in the Corporate context, unless a Shareholder has executed a personal guarantee.

The Condominium Form Of Holding, Or Ownership, referred to earlier, and I cannot over-stress the Uses and the Potentials of this Vehicle, has proven to be an ingenious method for creating wealth, and a brilliant technique for facilitating Individual Ownership Of Portions Of A Larger Parcel. Indeed, otherwise possibly indivisible parcels can be split up, "Condominiumized", with the resultant newly-formed individual pieces or Units possessing those advantages normally incident to Individual Ownership of any real estate together with other benefits which are unique to the Condominium regime. What is a Condominium? It is a Form Of Individual Ownership of a piece of real estate; the Condo Owner owns his Portion of the entire Condominium complex in Fee Simple, or 100% Ownership; he is vested in title to his own Unit; and as an ancillary he also owns a pro-rata Share of the Common Elements.

The individually-owned Condo Unit may consist of an entire building (100% of the complex, along with 100% interest in its Common Elements), if the Master Deed so defines the "Unit" as being the entire complex. The Master Deed describes, identifies, and defines each Unit – when a Unit is on the ground its description is by metes and bounds (survey boundary); when it is in the air it will have a Unit Number which is tied into an engineering and physical schematic of the entire complex. The Master Deed also defines the Common Elements – whose actual Ownership is vested in the Condo Association. The Association maintains and governs the use of such Common Elements, which are an ancillary Proprietary Interest of each Individual Unit Owner in the same pro-rata Share that the actual Unit bears to the entire complex, unless the Master Deed attributes more or less than a strictly pro-rata share to a given Unit.

A Condo Owner may own Unit #104 on the tenth floor, meaning he owns that Unit (residential, office, whatever), from its (sheetrock, plaster) walls in; from the (sheetrock, plaster) on its ceiling in; and from its under flooring in. This is his piece of real estate. Or he might own #10 Main Street, a self-contained or adjacent / joined residential, office, retail, industrial or other type of property, from either its exterior walls and roof in, or from the interior of any common walls which may be contiguous to an adjoining property, in. Or the Condo Unit might be known as Parking Spot #45 in a certain lot comprised of 150 Spots. Or the Unit might be called Cabana #6A, designated on a survey location for some private beach bordering the Biscayne Bay in Miami, Florida.

Again, the extent of a Unit's pro-rata Share in the Common Elements is typically fixed at the same percentage that the Unit itself bears to the totality (100%) of all the Units in the complex. One Unit out of 100 equally sized Units usually entitles its Owner to a 1% Proprietary Share in the Association's Common Elements. Should those 100 Units differ in size, value or otherwise, any one Unit may be stipulated to represent more or less than a 1% Interest in the Common Elements.

The bottom line is, up in the sky or on the ground, on the beach or in the back of a parking lot, this Unit, this Condo, is a piece of real estate owned in Fee Simple; and its pro-rata Share in the appurtenant Common Elements does not represent ownership of such realty (or personalty) per se, but instead represents a Proprietary Interest of economic value and functional utility which is part of the overall Asset which we call a Condo Unit.

Common Elements consist of everything that is not physically a part of or otherwise stipulated by the Master Deed to "accompany" (such as a designated parking spot), an Individual Unit. Heating and other mechanical systems which service more than one Unit, common driveways and foyers, shared roofs and common sidewalks, the community swimming pool, the elevator, the lobby in an office building whose suites have been converted to Condo Status, are among the countless examples of standard Common Elements.

Condos may be created through new construction or by the conversion of existing structures or parcels. In both cases their creation is partly physical (though arguably certain conversions may be effectuated literally without "touching" or "changing" the actual real estate), and mostly paperwork. The engineering / architectural / survey schematics which are incorporated into the descriptions in the Master Deed govern. The Unit Deed conveys title to a Unit pursuant to its delineations in the Master Deed, all in accordance with the Provisions of the Rules and By-Laws of the Condo Association.

The genius and ingenuity of the Condominium concept takes many forms. It can create wealth and value. It can create individual properties where none, or only one, would have otherwise existed. It can create a diversity of properties. It can uniquely make certain Assets and Rights subjects of Individual Ownership. Units created through new construction or conversion will invariably have a much greater aggregate value than the "non-Condo" Value of the undivided whole.

The diversity and divisibility which is gained by whacking up an existing property can also enable a developer (speculator) to circumvent existing zoning and other land use regulations which might otherwise prove costly impediments, if not outright immovable obstacles, to the creation and conveyance of new and smaller (or converted or constructed) Units (Chapter IX).

Throughout virtually the entire country, Condo Ownership has evolved from a novelty to a common Form Of Ownership for all types of real estate. The speculator and investor who is hunting down any type of Good Buy, from any Source, will run across Condos on a regular basis.

Since Condo Ownership is tantamount to Individual Ownership of a Unit, albeit with unique defining legal and physical characteristics as to the Unit and its Common Elements, the benefits and advantages of "Individual Holding" also apply to Condo Ownership. From taxes to personal liability, from management to Leveraging, the upsides and the downsides of Individual Ownership, it is all here.

"Holding" real estate in the <u>Cooperative (Coop) Form</u>, however, is a far different matter. Condominium Ownership is owning a piece of real estate acquired by deed. Cooperative Ownership, on the other hand, is owning Shares of Stock in a Corporation which Shares, together with a "Proprietary Lease", represent the individual's Interest in the Cooperative Corporation, and thus his stake in his "Unit". The Lease evidences the Owner's Rights to exclusive use and occupancy of the designated Coop Unit, and it delineates various other parameters of Rights and obligations which may be associated with the Shares of Stock and occupancy of the Unit.

The Coop Association has the one and Only Deed. It owns all of the real estate, both the Individual Units and the Common Elements. The Association may have a mortgage on the entire property (Units included), and the Individual Units are thus "encumbered", quite opposite to the Condo Scheme of things. The Association itself, as an entity, and not the Unit Owners in any way, is the mortgagor. The Unit Owners contribute their share of overall carrying costs in the form of monthly Association Fees. Any loans which they may have on their own Units are just that, "loans" which are securitized by their Stock and Proprietary Lease. The Coop Unit Owner has no real estate on which to place a "mortgage".

While decades ago many "Big City" apartment house conversions were made in the Coop Form, and while many of the most exclusive apartments in the most upscale (and not so upscale) sections of cities like New York still Hold in the Coop Form, this Method of Holding (an interest in real estate) has never been universally embraced, especially when compared to the later evolving more popular and desirable Condo Form.

Unlike the Condo (Individual) Form of Ownership, Coop Ownership is the ownership of personalty, and thus most of the benefits (and a few of the liabilities) which are incident to realty ownership are absent in this scenario. Forget about most of those tax angles, (except a non-real estate Capital Gain), forget about any notion of sheltering visibility of ownership or maximizing any Leveraging to equity value in a future refinance.

The transfer or resale of a Coop Unit is not necessarily a routine matter, as an Association's Membership and Screening Committee have considerable power to block any kind of disposition. The Committee can reject the application of a prospective new owner for Membership, and thus for Ownership. Be they articulated as such or not, grounds for rejection may range from the most legitimate to socio-economic and downright discriminatory reasons – some of the same grounds which can no longer block the leasing or transfer of real estate, including Condos.

Thus, the most basic decision-making relative to the Use and Utility of one's Unit may be fettered by restrictive and discriminatory Board policies.

So, too, many aspects of daily life in a Coop complex are impacted by an Association's "norms" – which, legally, can be more restrictive and stifling than any possible regulations of a Condo or Homeowner's Association.

General liability concerns inure primarily to the Association. Borrowing on the equity of an Individual Unit, again, either in buying or refinancing, is in the form of a loan, a note, and not a mortgage. The LTV (Loan to Value) ratios used by lenders are typically much tighter than they are in real estate financing, and obviously there is also a personal liability for the debt in Coop borrowing. Absent developer or Association-sponsored pre-packaged financing, loans which are backed by Coop Shares as collateral have historically been more difficult and costly to arrange than a mortgage.

Caveat – you will never find a Good Deal on a Coop in any foreclosure list. With loan collateral that is non-real estate personalty, by definition a Coop is never subject to foreclosure. As with most non-mortgage chattel loans – i.e., autos, furniture, business inventory – per terms of typical loan documents upon default by the borrower the lender may seek forfeiture here, of the securitized Shares, through other legal means and, subject to the Coop Board's approval of any new buyer, in trying to recoup the lender-in-possession can later resell its Rights to the Unit.

In another context for Holding, an investor, particularly an independent business person who may have unrelated and ongoing exposure to possible liens, or who may already be subject to liens (judgments being a form of lien) or other personal liabilities, may seek to shelter his assets, and thus find it prudent to <u>Hold Real Estate Solely In The Name Of A Spouse</u>. Additionally, in cases where credit and liens are not an issue, but rather where one Spouse may have a much higher net worth than the other, and the parties wish to better equalize or balance their assets in an effort to minimize future estate tax liabilities, the transfer of real estate from one Name to the other can constitute a most effective cost-efficient solution. At this writing, inter-spousal transfers have no gift or other tax implications.

At the time of acquisition or subsequent transfer, when the real estate is placed solely in the Name of one Spouse, the Individual advantages and potential liabilities of Ownership will inure solely to that one Spouse.

While it may be an unplanned or unintended <u>Form Of Marital "Partnership"</u>, where over the course of time a Spouse attains a <u>Spousal Interest</u>, the end result is another <u>Method By Which To Hold An Interest In Real Estate</u>. In most States, if ownership of a married couple's principal residence is in the name of only one or the other, by operation of law the non-owner-of-record Spouse will automatically obtain an Inchoate Right (Dower or Curtsey), in and to a "Share" of that property, by virtue of the marital relationship and common occupancy of the premises.

The operative common law Rationale, having evolved as it did in an older more agrarian and early industrialized Society where women were neither bread-winners nor equals nor "very important" in the "man's world" of business, is self-evident. By operation of law the Rights thus acquired will require the future signature of the "Non-Owner Spouse", should the "Owner Spouse" (who could be the Wife) sell or refinance.

In a somewhat different vein, one of the most common and widely recognized Forms in which real estate can be <u>Held Is In The Names Of Both Husband And Wife, Jointly</u>. Where the principal residence or marital domicile is so Held a few words on the Granting Deed, next to their respective names (i.e., "his wife" or "her husband"), will establish <u>Spousal Co-Ownership With Its Automatic Right Of Survivorship (Tenancy By The Entirety)</u>. Similarly, the same relationship is established if their names are followed by language stating "As Tenants By The Entirety".

Here both parties, individually and jointly, will reap the benefits incident to home ownership, including mortgage interest and real estate tax deductions. (Depreciation of course does not apply to one's home.) Upon resale net profits are not sheltered by a Capital Gains tax (not applicable to owner-occupied residences), but in varying and changing respects the current Tax Code provides shelter incentives based on the owners' ages and intention to purchase another home. Usually there will be no Federal tax liability on profits. And there are also favorable inheritance tax considerations for such Co-Owners.

Assuming harmony within the family and absent impending credit issues for either Spouse, basic decision-making and refinancing should be routine matters. And indeed, as we should all understand, home equity loans (lines) or refinancing have long been a primary sustenance of our Economy. Both Spouses will have personal liability exposures (which again, in the event of foreclosure will most likely be more of a credit problem than a deficiency claim).

And just as they are tied, legally and otherwise, in the marital relationship, in most States the law also imposes some very strict "protective restrictions" on the parties in their Joint Ownership of a marital domicile. Neither can uni-laterally convey clear title to "his" or "her" Share by Deed or Will without the other's signature. Each owns an Undivided Interest in and to 100% of the home. Neither Interest is divisible in the ordinary sense – meaning neither Spouse can sell or devise an undivided 50% Interest in the whole.

Even a recorded deed or probated will wherein one or the other Spouse has purportedly "conveyed" or "devised" his or her Interest without the other's signature will be deemed void and of no effect. Assuming no prior Joint Con-veyance, upon the death of a Spouse the decedent's Interest will, by operation of law, automatically vest in the surviving Spouse. The Surviving Spouse will thus become vested with complete and unfettered title, and he or she may sub-sequently convey or devise the entirety of the property as he or she sees fit.

Multiple Owners Other Than Husband And Wife May Also Hold As Joint Tenants With The Right Of Survivorship (Tenants By The Entirety). The Husband-Wife version is a special unique relationship; it is really a sub-cate-gory of the general Tenancy By The Entirety Form Of Holding. In any case, Holding as Tenants By The Entirety is a relationship with binding ties between two or more owners.

The binding reciprocity becomes set in stone simply through language in the granting deed immediately after the names of these "Partners" which de-scribes them as "Joint Tenants With The Right Of Survivorship" or "Tenants By The Entirety". Here, as in the Husband-Wife context, neither Co-Owner can devise or sell on his own; and in the event of death the survivor(s) takes it all. Yet contrary to the clear public policy and familial considerations inherent in the Spousal context, here there is no public policy which can make any sense of the permanently binding and irreversible bond established when "mere" Business Partners, friends, or other family engage as Tenants By The Entirety.

While Holding by the Entirety is a legal relationship, founded in initial business or personal motivations, regardless of how willingly it may have been entered into, for a variety of reasons over the course of time many such Joint Tenants (or their family or heirs) come to regret such pre-ordained suffocating terms – especially as changes in their lives and the lives of their family and fi-nancial fortunes may occur. In most cases this will prove to be a foolish Form Of Ownership.

Which brings us to the more generally recognized Tenants In Common Form Of Holding. "Tenants In Common" Is A Legal Characterization For

More Than One Specific Method Of Holding An Interest In Real Estate – i.e., where Held by two or more related or unrelated individuals, as in a Partnership format; or where just simply Held in two or more names on a deed. Absent other terms of a Buy-Sell or operating or restrictive agreement among multiple owners, a Tenant In Common may sell or devise his or her Undivided Interest in a parcel on his or her own volition, without need for the other's signature.

The purchase of a part of a total realty Interest in such situation, absent an agreement to the Deal by all other Owners, and when the Deal is not consummated in accordance with either a new or a pre-existing inclusive Buy-Sell or Management Agreement (which would give full credence and a definitive future value and marketability to a Partial Ownership Interest), can be tantamount more to the purchase of a Problem rather than a Valuable Interest. True, a Tenant In Common may sell his 50%, or his 30%, or whatever his Interest may be absent a writing to the contrary, on just his own signature.

But where there is a hostile or difficult business situation and/or the remaining "Partner(s)" do not want to play ball, they can make life impossible for any new "Partner". An investor buying in, particularly where he is not getting a majority interest, will usually want no part of the Deal unless the price is vastly diluted from what the "true value" should be in a more guaranteed amicable relationship. Without a fair and attractive Buy-Sell or Management Agreement, a Tenant In Common may find a buyer for his Partial Interest, but he may also wind up selling cheap. (Buy-Sell Agreements themselves may preclude a Tenant In Common from selling on the open market in the first place. A Tenant's own legal rights will be superseded by any Agreement among Co-Tenants, and Agreements are usually the best way to handle issues relating to the sale and devise of Partial Interests.)

The Installment Contract, previously discussed as A Means Of Financing (Chapter V) Is Also Inherently A Form Of Holding. Prior to the ultimate closing on an Installment Contract (which may be years after its execution), and its merging into a deed conveyance to the "Purchaser Under Contract" (PUC) (again, a PUC may also be other than an Installment buyer), the purchaser is not (yet) actually the owner of record of the property, but he does have some real Rights and Interests. Their Value and certainty, saleability and assignability prior to his obtaining title will be affected by the terms of the Contract. But they are Rights of Value. The Contract functions as a vessel in which to Hold An Interest In Real Estate.

While the Installment Contract buyer maintains the legal status of PUC, and is not yet the Legal Owner, tax benefits of Ownership do not inure to him. Assuming the Contract is recorded, which of course it should be, his Interest will be visible to the entire world. And in the event a judgment, a lien is levied against the PUC prior to the closing of the Contract, it will not *ipso facto* become a cloud on title, or an encumbrance, since he does not (yet) Own the property. However, as the Contract is an Interest, an Asset of Value, and is traceable to the PUC, a judgment creditor may execute on the Contract. Its current or future Potential Profits, Income or Net Value may be seized, partially or totally as the case may be, in an attempt to satisfy the lien. And should any type of lien against the PUC remain open on the official records at the time of closing, it will immediately become a lien against the real estate, also.

An Installment Contract cannot usually be further collateralized (unlike purchase borrowing or refinancing), without the seller's consent. Again, decision-making and management topics should be delineated in the Contract. Not being owner of record, the PUC is not in any *prima facie* sense subject to any personal liability which might occur during the life of the Contract and, as noted earlier, those unique liabilities and exposures of both parties to an Installment Contract which are inherent in the relationship itself must be allocated in the Contract.

In the appropriate circumstances the Installment Contract can operate as a beneficial bridge to Ownership for the long-term, or it can be a bridge to a Quick Flip.

Purchaser Under Contract (PUC) is a broad umbrella term describing A Form Of Holding An Interest in real estate by way of a Present Contractual Right morphing into an Anticipatory Contractual Right Coming to Fruition (the Installment Contract being a sub-category, with particularly detailed and enhanced Rights, of the PUC Form). Most of the implications for the Installment Contract buyer discussed above will also apply to PUC's generally. But unlike the more specific Installment Contract variety, the typical generic PUC Arrangement stipulates a much shorter term, a few weeks or months being a "standard" Contract to Closing Period.

The Contract may be drafted as a basic purchase agreement designed to lead to a quick closing. It may or may not be Assignable, which obviously affects its Value and the Potential for a PUC to engage in (hopefully) Profitable Transactions as PUC prior to the scheduled closing date.

Where a PUC has specific Rights which make his purchase contract amenable to a Quick Flip or which otherwise confer Value on the PUC (i.e., the Right to collect rents prior to closing, the Right to apply for a Variance prior to closing, the Right to work on the premises prior to closing, the Right to list the property for rent or resale prior to closing, the Right to Assign the Contract itself prior to closing), the Value of the Contract is significantly enhanced above any inherent basic Good Buy Aspect of the property itself.

So while the Contract does not confer actual Ownership, a short or a longer-term Contract, by chance or by design, can be Structured to be more than a mere conduit to closing. In its most basic functional sense, the status of PUC equates with a Form Of Holding. Add in some Specific Rights, some Wiggle Room, the Right to Assign, and a Good Deal, and PUC means "Holding Valuable Interests", whether the Contract is Flipped prior to closing or the Good Buy is Flipped or Retained after closing.

A Right Of First Refusal, which may be bargained for or otherwise conferred on a Potential Buyer (or Tenant) through an Independent Agreement or pursuant to a Lease, essentially means that the party Holding such Right has the Privilege to match the purchase (or rental) offer of any third party. If he does so he will have Exercised his Right Of First Refusal and thus preempt the "other" offer and may proceed to consummate his purchase or rental accordingly. The stipulated standard terms of any third party offer which may be "matched", and they should all be itemized in the First Refusal Grant itself, must include at least the essentials: Deposit; Price; Contingencies; Closing Date; Description; Boilerplate Legalities; Proposed Form of Legal Documents to be used in connection with any transaction; and The Method of Exercising this Right (Time, Content and Form of Delivery of Notice). A Right of First Refusal is not Ownership. But depending on its business terms and specificity, the Right may be very Valuable. It may or may not be Assignable or Saleable. Most frequently used as a "Hedge", it can be a great Means for Holding An "Interest".

Likewise, a Related Means Of Holding, The Option To Purchase, should, in its most viable form, be specific as to legal and business terms and be Assignable. This Form of Holding is an outright Privilege to decide to buy or not to buy something, on specified terms, in a certain manner, by a given date. Consideration for an Option can be nominal or considerable, and the Option can be pursuant to a lease or other Agreement.

Options can be a cheap or expensive way to play the market. They can be a Great Hedge, a Potential Lifeline for the financially strapped would-be speculator, and a Smart Tool for any investor. Prior to closing or tendering full payment through an Option, a Potential Buyer may "develop, reshape or maneuver" a property. But vague terms will render an Option empty, as in: "Buyer A may buy #10 Main Street from Seller B by January 1, 2000, at a price and terms to be agreed upon by the parties." Again, where properly drawn as to legal and business terms, the Option itself does not convey title, but it will often convey something that can be even better and cheaper than actual Ownership, particularly for the aggressive or strapped investor or the tenant who hopes to someday own his leased premises.

A Lease which contains an Option to Buy and allocates all or part of rent payments to the down payment on any future purchase pursuant to Exercise of the Option, is but one variation of the <u>Leasehold Option Form Of Holding</u>. At first blush, one might ask, "Why give a tenant such a free ride? Rent is rent, purchase price is purchase price". A poorly drawn Option, from the landlord's vantage point (as to price, scope of rental allocation, closing date, and faulty market adjusters), can prove a windfall for the tenant. But an Option might also be worded unfairly in favor of the landlord. And obviously it can be drafted in a variety of ways to ensure a fair and balanced future sales price and to avoid diluting the Deal with an unreasonably high allocation of rent proceeds to the future purchase price.

But only the landlord and tenant may understand what each sees in the Deal. For example, an otherwise hard-to-move gritty dilapidated industrial structure in a depressed area might be an interesting permanent home to a tenant whose heavy smokestack operation complies with local zoning but who is unwelcome most everyplace else. And the landlord concerned with insurance issues and vandalism may be quite happy to keep his beat facility occupied, indeed at a low Yield as his tenant works to put together a down payment, and he could very well consider the Deal a stroke of luck even if some of the down payment will come from current rent.

But the parties must bear in mind that depending on the amount of rental payments, how much is to be allocated to any future purchase down payment, the ability of the tenant to come up with additional cash and the tenant's overall strength, down the road a third-party lender may frown on a down payment funded "largely" out of accrued rent payments. Reasonably drafted, though, this type of <u>Option Interest</u> can be an excellent solution for many landlords and tenants.

<u>Holding An Interest In Real Estate With Title In Trust</u> may not afford the Trust Beneficiary, personally, all of the tax and other advantages of Ownership (or the personal liabilities, either), as the property is In Trust, and it is The Trust, not the Individual, who is the "Owner".

A Trust is a legal entity established in accordance with State Laws. It can sue and be sued, it can execute deeds (through signature of the Trustee), it can collect rents, it can own and operate any type of business, it pays taxes, it may declare a Capital Gain on a resale, it can take Depreciation on its own accord, it can manage real estate in accordance with its Trust Agreement, and the assets of the Trust and sometimes even the assets of the Trustee himself will have personal exposure incident to its Ownership of real estate and its general operations. The Trust can essentially fill the shoes of an Individual Owner.

And there are often compelling reasons to have, to Hold, real estate using a Trust as the Custodial Owner on behalf of a person or entity, and thus making that person or entity the Trust Beneficiary in lieu of being an Owner in an Individual capacity. Among them; estate tax considerations for the devisee / grantee; tax considerations for future heirs of the property; political / ethical necessity for a public figure to insulate himself from knowledge, decision-making and management with respect to his assets; and protection of a Beneficiary's assets from liens, a possible myriad of other financial and marital entanglements, and even from himself.

In the <u>Blind Trust</u>, often mentioned in a political context, the Trustee manages the assets and, during the period that the Trust Beneficiary's property is so "Held", the Beneficial Owner is in the dark as to income and management details.

Property may be voluntarily surrendered to a Trust or transferred into Trust by Court Order, as in the case of an Individual adjudicated unable to manage his own affairs. An example of a Voluntary Surrender is where property is Held in a Trust capacity through devise (real estate), again possibly to protect assets from lien creditors of the Beneficiary; to protect them from the Beneficiary himself; or to shelter them for tax considerations.

Property devised and <u>Held in a Generation Skipping Trust</u> can provide Income and certain Corpus to its Beneficiaries, and <u>This Form Of Holding</u> is designed to achieve tax savings in larger estates where property is being handed down in two "separate stages".

For example: Husband leaves real estate to Wife In Trust, she draws income and, if needed, Corpus, and upon her death the remaining Corpus passes to the next generation and thus escapes being hit with a second inheritance tax. The premise is that the Wife never owned the real estate. The Trust did. She was just the Beneficiary. So when she dies, this (Trust) Asset is not a part of her estate, it is not subject to estate tax. The Trust had Owned it, and now the Trust shall either continue to own it, or disgorge by deed to the next generation (or other devisee) in accordance with the formative terms of the Trust from the Husband's Will.

Property acquired via a <u>Living Trust</u> is so conveyed, at least in part, for estate planning purposes (minimizing taxes), outside of, or prior to, a testamentary (by will), devise.

An investor may engage in advance estate planning by buying a property and immediately putting in into Trust for a third party, perhaps a child or grandchild. The Trust is Holding it.

A drawback, of course, is that the investor thus makes himself ineligible for certain benefits of Ownership which will now inure to the Trust; but "losing something" is frequently the trade-off in seeking a different or greater Gain, in some other area (here, his estate-planning angle). With even a modest down payment on a piece of property, an investor can immediately remove from his estate (and thus from a variety of future tax liabilities), an asset which based on Appreciation and Amortization, should be worth a great deal more at some future date.

Lien and marital concerns may be further addressed by putting assets, even for a short period of time, <u>In Trust In The Name Of A Child Or Other Third Party</u>. The underlying Rationale – the "broader good" trumps the Individual's loss of standard Ownership advantages, which themselves are not "totally lost" but may instead be diminished in scope as they will inure only to the Trust.

<u>Easements</u>, which in and of themselves constitute an entire area of study in land use law, are an intriguing <u>Form Of Holding An Interest, Or Property</u>. To the layman, the most identifiable symbol of the Easement is the old "joint driveway" or "common driveway". Generally speaking, an Easement is permission, a Form of Right, to use, for (typically) stated purposes or reasons, (usually) in a designated fashion, under certain conditions and at certain times, or for a stated duration, property (land or otherwise), which belongs to another

or to others, for Consideration paid or to be paid. The most common Easements are for ingress and egress over a common right of way.

The Owner of "Easement Property" Is The Legal Owner of Record; Whereas The Owner Or Recipient Of An "Easement" Is The Owner Of A Certain Beneficial Right Or Interest Of Use In And To That Piece Of Property. Both Forms Of Ownership imply a pecuniary or proprietary Interest in and to something of Value. The Easement Property Owner of Record reaps (Potential) Benefits and bears Liabilities of Ownership, as discussed earlier (with certain of these liability issues, perhaps casualty, related to Use of the Easement probably being shifted by the language of the Easement Grant to the User).

For the Owner of Record an Easement can bear "Use" Income; it is Depreciable; it can be Refinanced; it may qualify for Capital Gains treatment; and it can be Partnered.

As for the Owner of the Right to Use the Easement, besides more esoteric connotations of Value or Use, his Interest may also generate income or profit, directly or indirectly, by virtue of its enhancing other real estate or business or personal activities. Not Owning realty, he has no Depreciation. The bottom line is that Both Types Of Owners Hold Interests in different ways with respect to the Easement.

An Easement Right, then, may be conveyed out by deed or devise, by covenants in a development subdivision or master plan, by the by-laws or deed covenants (see below) of a property owners / neighborhood association, or by any other variety of instruments of conveyance and Right.

Easements may "run with the land" (those of a more permanent nature), or they may be valid for stipulated periods of time. They may be conveyed out or retained (held back), by specific language in a conveyance. They can be limited or unlimited; general or detailed; and they may contain any number of financial, maintenance, liability, and other Rights and Obligations flowing to and from both parties to the Easement Agreement.

An important subject, akin to the genre of Easements and one which will become more relevant in our ever-smaller and more interactive world, is that of Restrictions, Limitations, on the scope, use and enjoyment of real estate Ownership. In a *prima facie* sense virtually any partnering, leasing, granting of an Easement Right, granting of an Option to Purchase, or even execution of a Sales Contract, imposes certain Restrictions or Limitations on the existing and/or future use of the affected property. This is basic and goes to the essence of business.

The concept of Restriction / Limitation is made relevant through both contemporary and long-forgotten <u>Restrictive Covenants</u>. These are basically prohibitions and conditions, contained in deeds and other recorded instruments, "covenants running with the land" for the most part, which may impede or promote commerce and development, or which may seek to impose another's personal, political, religious or socio-economic views and objectives on future generations of property owners.

Many of them "speak from the grave", as it were. And indeed, both the architects of restrictions and conditions, whether or not they are here today to see the results of their handiwork, and the Owners who may thus reap benefits or bear burdens due to the existence of such restrictions and conditions, do actually <u>Hold Interests By Virtue Of The Stipulations</u>.

Those who are affected <u>Hold Rights And Interests</u> of a positive or negative nature or both. Restrictions may provide them with a financial benefit. They may enhance the value of their property. By their terms they may also diminish values. Or they may do a bit of both in different ways. And they may give one Owner a power over the property of another.

For example: A 1958 deed covenant concerning the 1940 "development" cape cod which was built in the-then "new subdivision" requires all future owners of every house in the locale to maintain neat white picket fences and paint the exterior of their houses every four years. Or: the Condo Unit deed prohibits future owners from placing pre-fabricated structures or storage containers (which may be permitted under local zoning laws), on their 10 by 15 foot plots of land in the rear of their townhouse style Units (which land in this case is not part of the Common Elements but is instead part of the Condo Unit, per deed). Or: the deed conveying a 200 acre farm for future development contains a Restrictive Covenant requiring a ten acre set-aside for parkland (regardless of whether the municipality would require this or some future developer would volunteer it).

While it is usually the developer or the Property Association which inserts "beneficial" or "benign" Restrictions and Conditions, over time property conveyances have been wrought with an endless array of stipulations, many of which have been ruled invalid by the Courts for being unconstitutional / discriminatory (mostly in regard to race and religion), or contrary to the "public good" or "public policy". There are, and there have been, clauses which seek to restrict ownership, use and occupancy based on race, creed, and religion; and others which seek to prohibit "saloons", doctors, or even educational institutions which might teach Darwin from particular premises.

Holding Rights Or Interests Can Also Include Holding Narrow And Specific Property / Proprietary Rights Which Represent But A "Divisible" Portion Of A Piece Of Real Estate. Subject to applicable Federal, State and local regulations (zoning, etc.), and those of regulatory bodies (i.e., environmental, waterway), and subject further to the legal Rights of contiguous or other affected local Owners, a Property Owner may divide various Rights or Components of his Ownership which are literally inherent in the Parcel, into diverse Categories of Interest and Value. We know that certain Rights may be expanded or diminished by transactions which involve Leases, Easements, Partnering, Options, the creation of Condo Units and so forth. Here, however, we are addressing more of the lateral or innate traditional "business aspects" of a piece of real estate.

Certain Categories of Rights can be "chopped off" and made Divisible for others to Hold, in a more physical, utilitarian, albeit legal sense. Subsurface Rights (minerals, gas, oil, precious metals, mining, drilling); Logging Rights (cutting down trees, removing timber); Air Rights (building out and over the structures of others); Aesthetic Rights (building and perhaps obstructing / interfering with another's million dollar view); and Riparian Rights (using a body of water, building a dock or recreational facilities); all constitute Forms of Specific Property Rights which are "literally" a part of the totality of a Property Interest.

Conveyed by deed or other sufficient instrument, granting such Rights does transfer Valuable Interests. While this Specific, or Subset "Rights Notion", overlays an analysis of traditional benefits and liabilities of Ownership generally, it also has its own unique set of profit producing, tax, and liability issues.

Additionally, The Concept Of Holding An Interest, An Ownership, can in and of itself inherently be more or less expansive, more or less limited, by Defining or Qualifying Language in a given Conveyance. And here we are not talking about Restrictions, Conditions, Divisible Components, or other Forms of Parceling.

Holding Title In Fee Simple, for example, constitutes a Complete and Unfettered Ownership (Rights which can be conveyed out and/or diluted by a new Owner). By way of further illustration, an Individual Owner, an LLC, a Corporation, a Limited Partnership, each having its own indicia of Owner-ship implications, may nevertheless all Hold In Fee Simple.

Holding through a conveyance which grants a <u>Life Estate</u> means all Rights of Ownership terminate upon the death of the "Owner" of such Life Estate and, consequently, the Owner of a Life Estate (in and to a piece of Property), cannot sell or make use or other conveyance of his Rights which would be greater than his own Finite Life Estate Rights. Should any such Owner sell or lease to another, the Interest of the grantee or lessee in and to any Purchase or Leasehold will cease upon the death of the grantor or lessor. Holding A Life Estate Interest means just what it says: your Interest and Rights die with you. And again, the LLC, just like the Individual, can possess a Life Estate in a piece of Property.

<u>Holding An Interest With A Right Of Reversion,</u> stipulated in the Grant-ing Instrument to trigger upon the happening or non-happening of a specified event or the tolling of a specified date, means the Property Interest will auto-matically terminate and transfer, revert back, to either the original grantor or lessor or to some other designated third party recipient, as stated in the Grant.

By way of <u>Overview</u>, earlier we addressed the basics in <u>Financing The Deal</u>, be it with good or bad credit, with more or fewer Choices. Leveraging options must be selected with an eye on what should be the best means for a particular Deal and the Times. "What does the Market offer? What does the buyer qualify for? What seems to be the most Profitable Method in terms of Yield, Depreciation and other factors? And, in light of any other obligations and opportunities which the buyer may have, what type or amount of Financ-ing seems most sensible?"

Key – "How much Cash should (and can) be tied up in a Deal like this? Should the buyer seek maximum or minimum Leveraging? Is any significant amount of Cash or Financing (including Assumptions or other Seller-Financ-ing) necessary? Would it be wise to try and tie this particular Deal up as a PUC or through an Option?"

<u>Closing Or Otherwise Controlling The Deal</u> where an investor has poor <u>Credit</u> makes for a more narrow window of Financing Alternatives and more Challenges. Phrases and words like "Credit Clean-Up, Credit Jail, New Credit Life, TRW, Equifax, and Credit Score" have become basic jargon in today's world. Dealing with one's Credit Report is often more important than having a lot of Cash to work with. Speculating (and Life) is a lot easier when you can

just go out and borrow what you need at sensible rates. <u>Creative Financing And Other Avenues Go A Long Way; But Knowledge Plus Ambition, And Smart Hard Work And Just Enough Cash And Good Credit Open Doors Much Easier.</u>

Some years ago an investor or businessman with some Smarts and Where-withal could simply go see his local banker and lending decisions would often be made on the spot, with some subjective personal criteria and familiarity being key determining factors (which for the most part are out the window today). Now most banks and mortgage companies will e-mail your clinically-presented objective data to some processing center (precisely where and to which underwriter the locals often have no idea), and wait for a Decision.

So today's concern with Credit Scores, again more often a bigger issue than "extra Cash", focuses on the realities of our financial world: a credit-oriented environment which has become increasingly objective (though less so during Boom and Free And Easy Money Cycles). And periodically examine your Credit Reports – by some accounts over 80% contain errors.

Aside from the rip-off artists who promise miracle credit cures, there are viable, if longer-range ways to climb out of the proverbial Credit Jail and start Rehabilitating for the future. For those with minimal assets and large unse-cured debt or judgments, a Chapter 7 Bankruptcy can wipe out virtually all li-abilities (save for fines and related levies, support obligations and secured debt like mortgages), and thus clean the slate and permit the debtor to start over.

The blemish of a discharged (completed) Chapter 7 on one's Credit Re-port, which of course shows obligations were wiped out, will "linger". But if there is no other ability, or if it is just too overwhelming to otherwise settle one's debts, Chapter 7 does provide a way to clean-up and go forward. With a debtor's timely performance in other credit-related areas, subsequently obtain-ing secured credit cards and merchant credit cards and more general unsecured credit cards starting with small credit limits and working up, and paying any-thing that is reported to credit bureaus in a timely manner, the Credit Score will slowly but steadily start turning around from a Bankruptcy Discharge.

Assuming adequate resources and liquidity to do so, curing defaults and other credit problems through late payoffs and partial settlements will show as a better resolution on the Credit Report and make for a quicker Credit Re-habilitation than Bankruptcy. And of course future timely payments are always a prerequisite to re-establishing good credit. No fake Social Security numbers;

no fraudulent letters to credit bureaus contesting legitimate entries to try and "remove" them for a short window of time; such charades are illegal, they are fraud, and they do not truly "work" and have no place in the Real Business World. (And what do the hucksters say when they may temporarily "clear" a lien or judgment from a Credit Report and allow the buyer to possibly obtain credit, and the same lien or judgment shows up later on the title search and kills the closing anyway?)

Pending Resurrection of a sufficient Credit Profile which will eventually Re-Open the doors to more Favorable Financing, the poor credit investor must work with whatever other means of Financing may be at his disposal, as aforesaid, including: Use of a Co-Signer (with extremely poor credit or liens, the investor himself will not want to be on title, and/or the lender will not want him on title – it being preferable or necessary that the Co-Signer become the Sole Signer); a Purchase Money Mortgage or Refinancing solely in the name of a Third Party (and putting a huge protective secondary mortgage on in favor of the investor, this being the ultimate backup whenever title must be held in the name of a Third Party).

And again, the deed and Financing can be put in the Name of a Qualifying Spouse, or secured by some form of Partnering through an LLC or other Entity or Arrangement. There are viable ways to Play the Game even where one must deal with his bad credit and perhaps keep his name off, and away from, title. The Installment Contract (name not on title, at least prior to any closing), and other PUC Techniques can also facilitate a Quick Flip with no need to take title, or even Finance; and they can also act as a Bridge to a subsequently Reshaped Deal which might bring in another credit-worthy associate. Other Methods of Seller-Financing, or Seller-Assisted Financing (i.e., Assumptions), are also viable approaches by which lien or debt-ridden buyers who must, can stay off title. Hard Money can be a boom or a bust. And provided a Deal warrants the outlay, if it is available, putting up a larger Cash down payment will at times better qualify the poor credit applicant for (more favorable) Financing.

Buy Low, Buy Right; Knowledge Is Power, Cash Is King, (And Credit Is Co-King); Find That Good Deal; Understand the Potentials of Real Estate; Learn The Business; Learn How To Structure The Deal; Remember – If You Cannot Put It All Together "What Is The Sense Of Hunting Down A Deal In The First Place?"

CHAPTER IX

REHAB, RENOVATION, OR DEVELOPMENT – A HIGHER & BETTER USE, LEGALLY & / OR PHYSICALLY?

"Is This For You?" The Real Potential of that Good Buy may Lie in taking a property a step or two further, and not in just going to closing and simply Flipping or Holding "as is". The Progression of Locating and Getting the Good Deal should involve a certain Analysis going forward. Buy Low, Buy Right – the Underpinning of it all. And depending on the investor's Goals with respect to any particular property, depending on the angles and circumstances of the Purchase, at some point an Initial Essential Decision must be made – "To Flip Or To Hold".

And In Either Approach The Questions Ring: "Should The Real Estate Be Left Essentially In Its 'As Is' Condition? Should Something More Be Done With It – Legally & / Or Physically – To Enhance Its Potential Or Utility, To Best Maximize Its Profitability, To Follow Through On Any Original Vision, To Convert It To That Thing Of Extra Special Value Or Utility (Which Transformation Will Really Make The Deal A GOOD DEAL?")

Not every Purchase lends itself, optimally, to an "as is" post-closing afterlife. Sure, some can be Flipped or Rented out "as is", but others may require a bit more Work and Ingenuity to help reach the grade of a Good, or Better Deal.

Any Form of Physical Rehab Or Renovation, And Any Tinkering Of A Legal Nature, can carry Great Promise, along with certain pitfalls, and (sometimes) require a Persistence, a Time Commitment and Focus, and an additional level of Knowledge and Savvy.

Once the decision is made to proceed with some Form of Physical Improvement or change to the property, whatever the scope, you must decide on which of the Four Primary Methods for Executing the Project you will use.

The most basic way to approach the work is by doing it yourself. Often referred to as "Sweat Equity", this Method obviously poses limits as to what and how much an investor can do – physically, timewise, and in terms of know-how. In trying to do extensive manual labor and perhaps some skilled work, for a variety of personal, financial, and career-related reasons an investor may be acting "penny wise and pound foolish". The scope or complexity of the work and budget constraints (or the lack thereof), are among the determining factors.

But indeed, while Sweat Equity or do-it-yourself jobs have been grossly glorified and exaggerated on "reality" TV shows, there are situations where investors, including those who might choose to live in a property as they rehab it or those with a construction or trade background, do often make Good Deals come to fruition by using their own hands (and brains), where otherwise their Deal or its Best Potential may be unobtainable.

The Second Method Will Have The Investor Act As His Own General Contractor (GC), contract with Sub-Contractors (Subs) for specified work areas such as plumbing, electrical, HVAC and masonry, and perhaps do segments of the work himself or with the help of day workers – thus saving on costs for less-skilled labor. And where left unchecked, whether through a sub or an employee, labor costs always have a tendency to balloon. The GC investor must comply with Municipal Building Permit and Code and Inspection ordinances and carry adequate general liability and contractor's and workmen's compensation insurance covering his subs. and his own workers who are not otherwise covered.

Thirdly, at a higher overall cost a Method most appropriate for larger, more involved projects, is to use the services of a General Contractor who will essentially take charge of the entire construction end of the Deal. This will typically include obtaining permits and arranging for Municipal Construction and Code Inspections, carrying necessary insurances, contracting with subcontractors, ordering materials, and ultimately applying for and securing any Final Certificate of Occupancy required for the work by local Codes.

In major projects an investor might consider hiring a Construction Manager (Fourth Method), whose role is to oversee the GC and all aspects of construction. This is not for the ordinary job. A Construction Manager usually earns a flat fee plus expenses and a percentage of the Project cost, including overruns and costs of extras (add-ons, change orders to the original contract).

A common complaint is that Managers often encourage cost overruns as they bloat the total price and thus increase their own compensation in the process.

As alluded to earlier, there are always issues, pitfalls, and concerns in employing any of these Methods. In all cases, including those where a GC or Subs are used, the investor should have at least a basic understanding of the trades, materials and ways of the business. He should also know or quickly get a handle on which materials are more or less popular and appropriate for a particular type of property, what the options are for given aspects of the work, and how to figure rudimentary prices and mark-ups for labor and materials.

The investor should have, or gain, at least a functional background Knowledge of the local Permit Process; he should know something about local and State building and maintenance Codes; he should understand the nature of a Construction Agreement and Insurance Terminology and requirements; and he should be familiar with Time Parameters involved in various segments of his Project, including scheduling sequences, the effects of local seasonal weather patterns on scheduling, and the practicality of even doing certain work at certain times of the year.

A crucial point when employing a GC or Subs is that the investor have an Understanding of Fiscal, Quality, and Quantity Control, with respect to Payments (Draws), disbursed on account or for work completed. First there is the matter of a Down Payment – Investor to GC, Investor to Subs, or GC to Subs (in accordance with terms of the contract between investor and GC). He must grapple with the fact that a Down Payment may be a financial necessity for the GC or Sub to literally get in a position to start work. They may need the money to purchase materials, labor, permits or insurance. Then there are the issues of mutual trust, credibility and motivation on the part of both payor and payee. (The attorney usually wants a retainer up front, the travel agent wants a deposit, the ball player a signing bonus, and the baker may want a deposit on a special order.)

The payee wants money in order to proceed and as a hedge against breach by the payor. A Down Payment shows good faith and helps motivate the payee. But again, we have a construction contract with some money down and the issue: "Who trusts who, who makes the first commitment?" The payee wants or needs his hedge, and the payor does not want to get duped. There will be a natural tension, but if there is to be mutual performance there must also be mutual trust and respect as evidenced by the written contract, and also on a

201

personal level. The arguments can be made on both sides, but the norm is that a Down Payment is standard. On a "small" job, perhaps 20 or more percent; on a "larger" contract, sometimes to the chagrin of the GC, as low as 7 to 15%.

The overriding concern for the investor is (or should be) to "stay ahead" of his GC and Subs (who themselves also want to stay ahead, or at least not be too far behind), as the work proceeds. Payments made subsequent to the Down Payment are referred to as "Draws". The contract between investor and GC (or Subs) should contain a barebones or detailed "Schedule of Values" – a table which correlates percentages of completion of specific areas of work to the payment of stipulated amounts representing portions of the total contract price.

Both GC's and Subs will typically resist an Investor's proposal to peg dollar amounts to broken-down or detailed aspects of the work (i.e., "kitchen cabinets" versus "kitchen", "concrete in the foundation" versus "foundation"), lest the GC or Subs be second-guessed or "discovered" in broader categories of work where they may like to disguise the extent of their costs and profits and any padding of the contract.

Moreover, too detailed a description of "work areas" to specified prices (values) will better enable an Investor to pick his GC's or Sub's brains, as it were, and gain an upper hand in negotiating down or shopping their prices, on the present project or in the future. GC's and Subs will push for a very general schedule of values / completion which correlates broad subject areas of work to individual draws.

The subjects of "Draws" and "Percentage of Completion" are often ongoing issues through the life of most projects. Both sides have their points. Where they are acting out of legitimate concerns with no ulterior agenda, neither wants to "be had;" the GC and Subs want to make sure they get paid (preferably a bit ahead of the work being performed), and the Investor does not like the risks involved in making pre-payments. As the investor, you want that edge – to the extent it can all be quantified and measured, you want to be a step ahead, you want to be "into" your contractors.

It is smart to insert a clause in your construction contracts requiring both GC and Subs. to provide you with Periodic Proofs of Payment to their own Subs. and third-party workers and material suppliers. You do not want the GC's unpaid plumber to walk off the job because he is angry. Especially at a crucial point, and particularly when the plumbing permit was issued in his name; he can hold up progress, complicate a variety of matters, and make the job more expensive. You do not want the unpaid roofer to file a Mechanic's Lien on your property (especially where you have already paid the roofer's money to your GC), which might have you paying the roofer ("again") and perhaps also paying an attorney to get the lien removed in order to clear title for resale or financing purposes.

And neither do you want a material supplier engaged by your GC to halt deliveries of brick, for example, with the total job order perhaps only 70% fulfilled. A delay in deliveries or a switch to a different supplier can lead to a number of problems, not the least of which might be that subsequent deliveries include brick that are mismatched from the initial orders; the new brick veneer (façade) on the front of the newly renovated house or storefront will not look very good as a two-tone hodge podge.

Caveat – your construction contract should require the GC to have his Subs. and Suppliers execute a form agreement in advance waiving their right to file mechanics liens regardless of any payment disputes they may have with the GC in the course of the project. Where such an agreement is signed and the property is later liened, in most States the investor can cause the lien to be removed as almost an automatic matter and also collect costs and damages from the Sub. or Supplier who placed the lien.

Where an Investor is operating as his own GC and dealing directly with Subs. and Suppliers, the above-mentioned <u>Payment, Completion, Proof of Payment and Lien issues</u> will all come into play in a similar fashion.

The contract with the GC or Subs. should also specify the Method and Standards of Inspection which will be used to confirm performance, or <u>Completion Compliance, a pre-condition to the Disbursement of Draws.</u> Actual field inspections, as may or may not be appropriate for the particular work, can be conducted by an agreed-upon third party independent inspector, by the Municipal Building Inspector, by the engineer or most commonly, by the architect. The investor will prefer that "his man" do this job, but in any case the contract should specify who the inspector shall be.

The matters of <u>Change-Orders and Add-Ons (Extras)</u>, which constitute deviations from the original contract, should be addressed in the contract. For mutual protection (more or less), it should be stipulated that any changes or extra work be detailed in a signed writing and payment for same be incorporated into the schedule of payments at the appropriate point.

Barring an emergency situation, change orders and authorizations for extras should be signed before the work is done. A common source of disputes and costly litigation is the practice of making changes and doing extras on a handshake, or less. GC's and Subs. might pad a job where there are alleged or verbal change orders; conversely, the same GC's and Subs. can be duped when a knowing investor accepts the extra work, claims he had not signed off on it, and just refuses to pay.

Some years ago I represented a GC who would sprinkle his larger jobs with scores of "extras" and "changes", many aesthetic, which cost him very little if anything to do, on the premise they were verbally agreed to or "understood", only to submit excessive invoices down the road, expecting to make a "second profit".

At the conclusion of the project the investor should want to see at least 10% of the total contract price held back, in his pocket or with the lender who is funding the construction (a 10% Retainage); satisfactory Certificates of Completion for previously disbursed draws; Municipal Approvals (where mandated) for Building Code Inspections; and adequate Proofs of Payment from the GC and Subs. The last payment is called the Final Draw, and the contract should further condition this payment on (1) issuance of a clear Certificate of Occupancy (CO), if so required by the nature of the work completed; and (2) the GC's and Subs.' completion, or correction, of any items on the Final Punchlist (and concurrent compliance with the Final Contract Inspection).

The Final Punchlist is a written summary which ideally should be formulated during a joint final walk-through of the work site by the investor and contractor(s) and architect (or other arbiter). It is designed to insure complete or substantially complete performance under the construction contract prior to disbursement of the Final Draw and Retainage. The items on the List should be cleared before disbursement. The items can run the gamut; from completing the carpet to doing plantings to painting touch-ups, from removing debris to installing kitchen cabinet hardware, from completing the rear deck to painting the front railings to paving the driveway.

Your Choice of GC and Subs. is an important decision. References should be obtained from others in the industry, and payment and performance histories checked with material suppliers and other subs. and owners. The State Division which licenses contractors, the local Chamber of Commerce, Consumer Affairs, the Better Business Bureau and the Internet are also good sources to check.

Choosing your GC or Sub. based purely on price comparisons is not always smart. Price is a factor, but far from the whole story. Many of us have seen the picture of the contractor wearing a tattered hat and shirt leaning on his shovel, with the caption "I was the low bidder".

GCs or Subs. may bid very low, get the job and quickly fall behind in their work schedule and labor and material payments, and ultimately limp out of the site (fully or more likely only partially completed), on their own volition or having been fired, leaving a costly mess for the investor to clean up. "Cheap" can indeed sometimes be "Expensive."

Some contractors intentionally underbid jobs, knowing there is no way for them to fully perform at the agreed price. They may pull money out of the down payment or from progress draws to clear up unrelated personal obligations or to satisfy unpaid bills from previous jobs. Or they may just squander the money. If a bid is too close or too low for the contemplated work, even where the contractor seems (is) sincere and may truly hope to comply with the contract, unforeseen complications – i.e., weather, strikes affecting material availability, subsurface conditions, delays, change orders, rising material costs, an overly demanding Building Inspector – can tilt the balance and not only cause the contractor to lose, but in the process also raise havoc for the investor with resultant delays and cost overruns.

If you receive four bids from reputable local GC's or Subs. of comparable size, and one is substantially lower than the other three, Beware. In a similar vein, engaging a GC or Sub. whose business operation is "too large" for the particular project may also prove unwise. His overhead, his fixed costs attributable to each job, his standard profit margins, and indeed maybe even his cost-intensive ways of doing things, will typically make the "large" contractor who does not specialize in "smaller work" a poor choice for anything but the "large" job. Even his basic unskilled labor costs will be dramatically higher; smaller jobs do not always require the bloated costs of Union-scale salaries and labor practices.

While the investor should cover himself and carry liability and workmen's comp. Insurance whenever work is in progress, his contracts should also require both GC and Subs. to obtain primary coverage and furnish certificates of insurance naming the investor as co-insured (the "reputable" GC or Sub. who cannot provide coverage may not be so "reputable" after all). Where a "good" small Sub. who is not equipped to provide insurance is engaged, the investor should obtain the necessary coverage and factor in the costs as perhaps a credit from the contract price. Additionally, it is always important to maintain your own owner's policy on the property to cover the value of work product in progress or completed, and the cost of materials on site.

Work Proposals submitted by Contractors – the generic Offer and Acceptance Form, or a more detailed Agreement, should be reviewed carefully and compared with standard local (usually Statewide) "owner's form" Contracts, or one of the many Architect i.e., AIA, American Institute of Architect, forms, which are mostly owner-friendly contractual frameworks.

Basic simple Agreements are sufficient for smaller projects. Contracts which give the GC or Subs. too much latitude or discretion or are replete with self-serving disclaimers purporting to insulate them and limit their liabilities, responsibilities and exposures with respect to their work product and activities, should be rejected out of hand. Where architectural plans or drawings or other detailed descriptions of the work and materials are available, the Contract should reference such Specifications and they should be annexed as Exhibits.

GC's and Subs. may be Bonded by an Insurance Carrier to ensure both their sufficient performance of the work and payment of obligations associated with the job (Performance Bond); or they may be Bonded to just ensure their payment of job-related financial obligations (Payment Bond). While the standards vary from one region to another, these bonds bear high premiums and may prove difficult for even stable experienced contractors to obtain. The scope and price of a project which might be appropriate for bonding will also vary by region, but it goes without saying that the rehab of a one family house or a modest improvement job will probably not be bonded – or even worth the trouble or cost of trying to bond.

In a Performance Bond the Beneficiary, i.e., investor / owner and/or construction lender, is to be compensated (made whole) by the insurance carrier should the contractor either: Complete the work, but in a manner deemed defective or below prevailing industry standards per contract, per local Codes, or per other inspection criteria; or Partially complete the work; and/or Fail to completely pay all job-related bills.

In the event of such "breach" the investor / owner or lender can file a claim seeking money from the insurance carrier to cover unpaid obligations and/or to retain another contractor or purchase materials to complete unfinished work or remedy defective work so it complies with applicable standards, or the claimant(s) may seek a remedy to compel the defaulting contractor to complete or rectify the work product. This is known as "Calling" the Bond.

A Payment Bond, on the other hand, "merely" provides the investor / owner and/or lender with monies to cover a contractor's unpaid obligations on the job.

In lieu of a Bond a <u>Personal Guarantee</u> from a Contractor or from principals who own a Contractor-LLC or Corporate Contractor (most GC's and Subs. enter agreements as business entities), which "assures" the Contractor's payment of bills and sufficient performance, is a fair second choice. Of course any such guarantee is only as good as the signature behind it. And whatever the value of these personal signatures, many principals will be reluctant to negotiate their individual signatures into a contract anyway. Furthermore, unlike the greater certainty of dealing with an insurance carrier, an actionable breach where the remedy is to go after a personal guarantee may lead to more costly litigation with no certainty of ever collecting anything.

Sometimes it is the construction lender, not even the investor / owner, who demands a Bond or Personal Guarantee. The bottom line is you must Check Out Your GC's or Subs. before engaging them, and you should try to deal with those who are experienced and can produce a solid portfolio.

It is noteworthy that most States <u>License both GC's and Subs.</u> – particularly those engaged in the mechanical trades (plumbing, electrical, air conditioning, heating); "specialty" contractors; and those in more sensitive / environmental areas, such as security firms, remediation companies and the like. Particularly in the mechanical trades and environmental areas, for any work of substance you should always hire a Licensed Sub., who in order to meet licensing requirements will usually have had to pass a test, have an educational background in the field, and served as an apprentice.

This of course does not mean that a handyman or a carpenter cannot change a washer in a faucet, or a laborer cannot install the shell and globe of a ceiling light fixture. No question, many GC's, investors acting as their own GC's, and investors doing some of the work themselves, frequently employ unlicensed Subs. in critical areas. But this is a mistake. Short-cuts are more common with unlicensed workmen doing jobs which should be done by licensed personnel. It might seem "cheaper", quicker and more convenient. But there are underlying legal, safety, quality, liability and insurance issues which require compliance in this regard. Save money (provided you are not misleading anybody), by putting in cheaper shrubs, by using $20.00 instead of $50.00 per gallon paint, by installing a more economical siding or by using reasonably priced kitchen cabinets. But do not try a short-cut where a Licensed Tradesman is needed.

On a related issue, it is important to understand that in every jurisdiction State and local <u>Building Codes</u> will not necessarily have identical requirements as to all matters; State Codes impose certain minimum standards and they permit the locals to impose their own higher or stricter criteria, which will supersede any "lesser" State standards.

For easy reference and perspective, the following brief <u>Checklist</u>, which is most applicable to residential and other smaller rehab jobs, should provide a superficial overview of the relevant subject areas for Contractors and Suppliers:

AIR CONDITIONING.

AMENITIES, EXTERIOR – Decks, Patios, Pools, Ponds, Spas And Tennis Courts.

AMENITIES, INTERIOR – Bars, Basement Systems, Closet Systems, Furnishings, Staging, Garage Storage Solutions, Home Theatres, Solar Products, Sunrooms, Vacuum Systems.

APPLIANCES – Laundry, Kitchen (Purchase And Repair).

BATHROOMS – Fixtures, Tops, Installation.

CARPENTRY – Structural, Framing, Finish, Trim, Custom Woodworking.

CHIMNEY – Fireplaces (Construction And Accessories), Structural.

CLEANING – Debris Removal, Services, Specialties.

DOORS – Exterior, Garage, Interior, Decorative, Sliding, Fire, Hardware.

ELECTRICAL – Fixtures, Installation.

EXCAVATORS – Site Work, Foundation, Grading.

FENCING – Types, Installation.

FLOORING – Subflooring, Carpeting, Granite, Tile, Marble, Wood, Hardwood, Linoleum, Installation.

GLASS – Safety, Standard, Decorative.

HEATING – Forms, HVAC, Baseboard, Steam Radiator, Radiant, Equipment, Installation, Fuels.

KITCHEN – Appliances, Fixtures, Cabinets, Tops, Innovative, Installation.

LANDSCAPING – General, Materials, Specialty Plantings And Visuals, Rock Gardens, Water Gardens, Maintenance, Construction, Sprinkler Systems.

LIGHTING – Interior, Exterior, Fixtures, Specialties, Decorative, Installation.

MASONRY – Structural, Foundation, Veneers, Walkways, Retaining Walls.

PAINTING – Materials, Contractors, Interior Designers.

PAVING.

PLUMBING – Fixtures, Installation.

RAILINGS.

ROOFING – Gutters, Leaders, Awnings, Canopies, Flat, Peaked, Asphalt, Tar, Paper, Rubberized, Slate, Shingle.

SECURITY SYSTEMS.

WALLS, EXTERIOR – Structural, Siding (Aluminum, Vinyl, Wood Clapboard, Wood Shakes), Masonry (Brick, Stucco, Stone, Decorative), Prefab. (Masonry, Other Materials).

WALLS, INTERIOR – Sheetrock, Plaster, Paneling, Stone, Insulation.

WATERPROOFING.

WINDOWS – Components, Replacements, Installation, Storm, Shutters, Interior Treatments.

The Roles of the investor's Inspectors and Experts have been discussed in several respects, particularly their function in Structuring The Deal (Chapter VIII). Again, they are involved in Pre-Closing activities (Locating a Property, Contract Negotiations, Contract Review stages); and their input can be vital in connection with Post-Closing assessments and recommendations. A key Role is when Experts and Inspectors assist in an investor's decision-making relative to Converting A Property To A Higher And Better Use (Legally & / Or Physically).

Such Conversions or Improvements will involve any range of Financial Planning; Cost and Feasibility Studies; Estimates; possible Legal Applications to Change the Use or Character of a Property; and Applications for routine Permits (building, environmental, etc.). Basic Inspectors (termite, structural, environmental, engineering) will often join with a host of other Experts in the

Legal Process to either Change Zoning or present routine maps and plans to appropriate Boards and Bodies. Expert Witnesses, with their many specialties, include architects, civil engineers, traffic consultants, urban planners, and landscape advisers.

The Investor and his People will also interact with <u>Official Inspectors and Experts</u>, both in the (Legal) Planning and Application Process and in the actual Rehab or Development Stages, for everything from a simple house to a sprawling commercial or industrial parcel. On the legal and paperwork end <u>Official Boards and Bodies</u> – i.e., Land Use, Zoning, Planning, Housing, Environmental – have their own staffs, experts, outside consultants, attorneys and field personnel. On the more nuts and bolts level, <u>Local Building and Code Enforcement Departments</u> have similar layers of personnel and overlaps, including field inspectors for general construction, electrical, plumbing and so on.

They all play crucial roles in initially granting (or denying) building permits, in conducting Code-mandated progress inspections (i.e., completion and pouring of the concrete in the foundation, backfilling, electrical, framing, landscaping, etc.), and, ultimately, in completing the final inspection process prior to issuance of a Final Certificate of Occupancy. Their roles, criteria, requirements as to stages of completion, schedules, paperwork regimens, punchlists, and Egos, will all be important to the "Smart" investor and contractor. They must be recognized and dealt with. Some will be reasonable, some will be sticklers, some arrogant and others accommodating.

Official Inspectors play a huge role in the progress of any project, not just the larger ones. Their approvals are often a pre-requisite to confirm compliance with any unusual requirements (which may be above and beyond those of the Code). Code-mandated progress and final (completion) inspections are important in their own right, and with regard to the investor's or lender's disbursements of draws. Again, approval of a contractor's draw requisition may hinge just as much on the Code Official's signing off on an inspection as it does on the architect's certifying some specified degree of completion.

A great deal of financial timing in a contract is often dependent on the pace and results of these Inspections. Their findings can also prove an effective arbiter of contract disputes where there may be questions as to completion, work stages or quality issues concerning materials and workmanship.

When dealing with Conversions and Changes in Use, always Be Cognizant Of Your Area, the local and regional environs of your Property. This impacts everything, including the Potential and Mechanics involved in any attempt to Convert to a Higher and Better Use (Legally & / Or Physically).

"What's doing, coming, going and happening in the Area?" Be aware of what matters: Direct Competition; the Status of Other properties and projects; local real estate Development; general Commerce; the Status of industry, strip malls, and public projects; local Technology; Schools, the Presence of higher or specialized Educational facilities; Mass Transit; Access to highways and airports. These are part of the Components of the Bigger Picture and the Potential of your own Large or Small Venture.

Socio-economic trends (Chapter IV) and the Diversity and Composition of the community are also pertinent. As are Regional Official and Popular Sentiments on subjects like local growth, use and coverage density; towards construction of additional multi-family units or industrial facilities; and concerning matters like suburban sprawl and urban renewal.

Always a pertinent question: "What, if any, Laws and Regulations are on the books concerning issues like Urban Renewal, McMansions (zoning), long-range Master Plans, and Senior Citizen Housing; and how are such broader considerations relevant to my own (small) stake and plans for a piece of the pie?"

The Composition of Local Governmental Bodies, their politics, educational levels, professionalism and biases, is also important. Precedents; recent actions, rulings, and opinions; leanings; and pending Court and Regulatory decisions, can all be telling for you and your Project – in terms of policy, legal issues which may arise and in day-to-day activities and procedural matters relating to the logistics of the Rehab or Development Work. All levels come into play – Legislative (Town Council, Commissioners); Executive (Mayor); Judicial; and Regulatory and Compliance (Boards, Commissions, Inspectors).

A relevant point, in rural and developed areas alike, is Local Sentiment vis-à-vis Environmental Issues. Here again we are dealing with regulations imposed Judicially, Legislatively, and Administratively by Boards and Bodies at all levels of Government.

The myriad of Environmentally-related matters which can impact your costs and progress on affected projects, and whose resolution might be partly shaped by Local Sentiment and precedents can include: Expansion or new

211

construction into or in close proximity to designated wetlands; Land Use in proximity to public waterways; Density; Tolerance of smokestack industries; Water runoff (detention basins) from expansion, renovation or new construction; Removal of asbestos siding or insulation or other hazardous substances from existing structures; Removal of underground oil tanks and soil / water remediation; Removal of lead paint; Clean-ups of industrial facilities and oil polluted parking areas and driveways; Contaminated drinking water (including wells) and waterways, as in the case of a waterfront bungalow or well close to a leaking septic system.

You must Learn about Your Property and its Issues. You must Explore Environmental Matters relative to Surrounding Properties. And get <u>a Feel For Local Thinking, and Enforcement Policies relative to Environmental matters</u>. A given Problem or Board Application might be a minor matter in one town and a major headache someplace else.

A point of great importance and a frequently overlooked matter is the need to investigate whether there are current or anticipated <u>local Moratoriums or other Regulatory or Legislative Restrictions</u> of a continuing or temporal nature which may adversely impact your present or future Plans for Rehab or Development.

Moratoriums and the like may present problems (losses, price reductions, delays) in the resale of property (particularly raw land), and in its use and rentability where you are Holding for the longer term. Chief among possible impediments would be partial or complete restrictions on new hook-ups to public water and other utilities and sewerage systems.

<u>Eminent Domain</u>, the "Public Taking of Private Property for Public Use", should be another point of inquiry when making many types of realty purchases, and certainly wherever you might have Plans for some type of Conversion. The Eminent Domain process, with its State by State variations stipulates, at least in theory, that the use of certain parcels of private property (the designations and "rationales" will differ from time to time and place to place), for a necessary public purpose constitutes such a superior and compelling public need that it entitles an appropriate Governmental body to force the sale of that piece of property to a public body or its designee at an agreed ("fair") price pursuant to appraisals and negotiations. If agreement on price and other terms of the "taking" cannot be reached, the Governmental entity can try to compel the sale through the Judicial process commonly known as <u>Condemnation</u>.

The price to be paid for the realty and any associated businesses which will be forced to close or be diminished as a consequence of the "taking" is supposed to reflect current fair market value and the Public Taking is supposed to be for a true public need – schools, hospitals, highways, parks, official buildings, urban renewal and the military, for example.

In many Eminent Domain cases politics and favoritism are never far behind, often to the detriment of those who are not-so-well-connected. I have seen more than one Taking of private properties for what was in reality nothing more than an Official scheme to give a preferred developer the inside track on a lucrative high-density project in a "newly-designated urban renewal" or "urban blight" zone. Recently I saw a municipality Condemn an old shuttered theatre in its downtown retail district when there were rumors that an "undesirable" ethnic minority had plans to turn it into a church and social center. In this case the town disguised and justified its action by building an unneeded out-of-place and previously unplanned "park" on the site.

The original piecing together of the World Trade Center in New York City was rich in debate and litigation over the purported "propriety" of "taking" for the then-stated public use, which "public use" was in fact more of a private use – under the auspices of the "public" Port Authority of New York and New Jersey. In both Court challenges to the Condemnation and public debate, the issue (as it is in many similar cases today), was "What does or should constitute a public use?" Today public use often seems to mean whatever the Governmental body wants to say it is.

The point is that Eminent Domain proceedings which might involve your piece of property (probably along with others), or which might involve properties in a reasonable proximity to your's, <u>can significantly impact your Plans and Potential Profit or Gain associated with Conversion or Development</u> – as indeed they can impact Profit absent any Plans for Conversion or Development. <u>The effect might be positive or negative.</u>

What if you were going to renovate or demolish and rebuild your site into a retail shopping strip, "a one of a kind new use in town", "a sure thing", a seemingly absolute Profitable Conversion of some tattered factory that you were buying, and a new Eminent Domain deal down the road could establish a far superior mixed-use retail development with real estate tax abatements and a reduced sales tax and other Governmental perks, that could steal your thunder and squash your Potential Gain?

What if you had Plans to Convert a restaurant or hotel complex on a well-traveled road while the State was Condemning nearby properties for a realignment or jughandle, or even a new major highway, which would have the bulk of the existing traffic flow bypass your site in a few years? (As happened up and down the East Coast when Interstate 95 was built.)

In either case your Plans and Potential Profit, perhaps the Only Real Potential Profit in your Purchase, would be destroyed; and the Government would owe you nothing, no compensation – because it did not "touch" your Property and thus, in the eyes of the Law, it did not "take" anything from you.

Eminent Domain can be a destructive force in still another way: for example, if you paid $200,000.00 for a parcel with an "as is" fair market value of $225,000.00 or even $190,000.00, but you "knew" there would be an additional fantastic Profit once you turned the place into six apartment units or a super-sized gas station and convenience store (perhaps it was already zoned for your Plans), and the Government Condemned your parcel, where would you be? Give or take a bit, you would receive the present "as is" fair market value – the Potential of your "Great Buy", the Buy Low, Buy Right Success Story, would evaporate.

It is very important to have an awareness of pending or rumored Eminent Domain proceedings in your area. They can take your property or they might be taking your distant neighbor's – either way you can be hurt (or helped). But all of this is a real and often overlooked matter. Eminent Domain Takings are not all that uncommon: in urban and developed areas, in newer and older areas, in areas with expansive farmlands and forests.

As noted earlier and set forth in more detail later in this Chapter, an Awareness of the Workings of Local Building and Code Officials and Enforcement Departments will also prove very useful. Getting an Idea of Who's Who, the Inspectors and their Superiors and Hierarchy, who you will be dealing with, is never a waste of time. Do not compare today's world to the "old days" when it was quite acceptable and even expected for the investor or contractor to give Inspectors a case of Scotch at Christmas and cash gifts as a routine gesture in the course of a job. Today this is legally and politically incorrect.

But proper Familiarity, Discretion, Professional Respect, Courtesy and Deference to the official position and authority of the Inspectors goes a long way to creating Harmonious Relationships and preventing unnecessary official "harassment" like delays and nit-picking.

Never under-estimate possible positive and negative impacts of "Privately-Legislated" Rules such as Restrictive and other types of Maintenance and Appearance Covenants, previously discussed, on your Use and Potential Rehab of a Property. Again, they may or may not be in the deed or run with the land. But whenever a property is in close proximity to or a part of any entity or community which is a "Condo Association", "Homeowner's Association", "Lakefront Village" or the like, inquire as to whether any such Covenants are on the books.

They may restrict your discretion and flexibility in Rehabbing. They may impose constraints and conditions on your use, choice of materials, or even the color or design of your work product. They may dictate any number of issues which are relevant to Rehab and Use of an affected property – quite apart from the parameters or restrictions inherent in Official zoning and other Land Use regulations.

These Private Covenants cannot diminish the rule of zoning or other Official standards; for example, by giving an owner greater Rights than the Government gives him. If the zoning says the dwelling can be used only as a two-family, no Community Rules can give license to use it as a four family. However, as long as they do not violate Constitutional guarantees (discrimination, etc.), or "Public Policy", they may limit the number of vehicles that can be parked in a driveway overnight and generally be stricter than applicable zoning and maintenance Codes.

And yes, they can require that your fence be painted green with a band of white across the top!

The Threshold Question Is: "How, If At All, Should The Investor Either Rehab, Renovate, Or (Re)Develop His Property?" The Broad Issues For Consideration Include Making Primary And Overall Determinations As To Best Uses, General Utilization, And Strategy For The Property. "Should it be left basically 'as is,' with perhaps some clean-up? Is a modest Rehab, or a more superficial fix-up, in order? Or can or should the property be Converted And/Or Otherwise Improved To A Higher And Better Use, Legally &/Or Physically, In A More Substantial Way?" That Is The Key Question.

The Notion Of A Legal Conversion Or Change Can Be A Wide-Ranging Concept. First and often foremost is the matter of Variances. A Variance is a change from existing zoning laws which is granted to a property owner, occupant or other party having a Proprietary Interest in a parcel of property, pursuant to statutory application, hearing, and review process (usually before a

Municipal Board of Adjustment or Planning Board). Changes which may be granted concern (1) the permitted Use of a property (i.e., residential, retail, office, industrial, multi-family, rooming house, parking lot); (2) the permitted Level Of Occupancy (sometimes a different matter from Use); (3) the permitted Deviation or Scope of Activities or Use within permitted overall Use Categories; and (4) the permitted Deviation in "Construction" and Material Standards and characteristics of new or renovated structures.

A retail use will not ordinarily be permitted in a residential zone – depending on its type, i.e., one or two-family, etc. But the granting of a Variance can change this legal status and permit the Use. Or a particular zoning might limit the number of seats in a 5,000 square foot restaurant to, say, 300, and further require perhaps 80 off-street parking spots for the establishment. The granting of a Variance might permit either a new construction or maybe 400 seats in the existing building with only 50 off-street spots, even with the site remaining untouched and unimproved at its original 5,000 square feet. Or a Variance might permit, let's say, a two-family house to be renovated and expanded into a legal four family dwelling in a neighborhood which is otherwise zoned for only one or two-family units.

Permitted Density coverage of land area is a common topic of Variances and "changes" can be very lucrative. By way of example, given a sufficient Variance a 40,000 square foot parcel zoned for 31,000 square feet of warehouse might see an increase to perhaps 37,000 square feet of permitted land coverage. And the difference can represent a windfall. In a given District with more 50 by 100 than 60 by 100 foot lots zoning might require 60 by 100 foot lots for construction of new two-family homes; a Variance could pave the way for issuance of a building permit for the same dwelling to be built on a 50 by 100 foot lot, thus making that 50 by 100 lot much more valuable. Where zoning mandates specify front, rear, and side yard setbacks (points at which construction may begin), a Variance might allow new construction or an addition to an existing building, or that new pool or deck or delivery area for a retail complex, to instead be located closer to the front, rear, or side property lines.

Zoning laws which regulate Construction and Aesthetics, restricting specifications like the height of a structure; specifying the location (visible to the street or not) of a loading dock in a commercial building; requiring a masonry veneer on new or renovated residential properties in a certain area; dictating where a fence can be erected or how high it can be; or requiring certain landscaping and exterior lighting in a parking lot, can all be changed in a Variety of Ways through Variances. The Granting of a Variance can allow the investor to Better, More Fully, More Profitably, More Economically Convert Utilize Rehab Build or Develop a given Property.

Subdivisions, a common topic in land use texts, are the basic means whereby larger parcels of vacant or developed land, or existing structures, can be Legally divided into two or more smaller parcels or structures to facilitate a sale or other disposition or use (new construction, renovations, occupancies), of a Property. Subdivisions are granted by local Boards and are pursuant to an application, hearing and review process. And they are a major component in the investor's arsenal of tools used to facilitate Legal Conversions.

Civil Engineers and Use Experts (traffic, landscape), who may be employed in connection with a Variance application are similarly engaged here. The granting of a Subdivision creates new Lot and Block numbers and in the case of larger parcels, new streets, parks and other infrastructure. The Subdivision process is the fundamental method used to separate and "assemble" tracts of land, from the smallest two lot situation to the parceling of sprawling farmlands and forests.

In a more modest context, albeit a bread-and-butter scenario for the investor depending on a property's physical characteristics and zoning requirements, the length and continuity of use or occupancy of the premises, and the manner in which the tax assessor has carried the property (perhaps as a single or multi-tenanted building, or as two separate lot and block numbers), "single" structures with pre-existing interior dividing walls may be Subdivided into two or more separate legal pieces of property having a common or "party" wall. Likewise one or more "additional" building lots may be created by Subdividing "extra" land from a property which had been deeded as one parcel and may also happen to include, say, a one family home or retail complex.

When seeking a Subdivision to create new parcels which might violate existing zoning requirements, the Subdivision application should be coupled with a request for any necessary Variances.

The Legal Conversion Of An Existing Structure To Condo Status (as opposed to new construction of a pre-designed Condo Regime), can be a Lucrative and Ingenious Way to Create Enhanced Equities and Profits by virtue of the Condo Conversion itself, and this Conversion Route May Also Enable

The Investor To Circumvent What Might Otherwise Be Costly, Insurmountable Or Deal-Killing Zoning And Other Land Use Requirements.

As we know residential, commercial (office, retail), and industrial property and sites like parking lots, can be Converted from their "as-is" aggregate form into either an identical, a larger, or a smaller number of Condo Units. The 80-unit apartment house or the townhouse-style complex can be turned into 80 or more or fewer Condo Units; the multi-story office building can be turned into individual Condo office suites; the contiguous row of retail storefronts can be separated into Condo stores; the sprawling industrial complex can be split into individual Condo sections; and indoor or outdoor parking lots can be reinvented as Condo parking spots. All such Condo Conversions come with their respective pro-rata Shares and use privileges of the appurtenant Common Elements – i.e., driveways, roofs, exterior walls, sidewalks, mechanical systems, gym facilities, laundry rooms, hallways and the like – as discussed earlier.

The Utility, the Economic and Pragmatic Beauty of this Technique, lies in the fact that the Condo Conversion Process amounts less to a matter of trying to wrestle and conform with possibly impeding, stifling Municipal and other Governmental zoning and other laws and regulations, and is usually more a matter of rote legal paperwork, surveying and engineering studies, marketing, and physical rehab or alterations which are often cosmetics or refurbishing.

As noted earlier, this Legal Process creates a new deed, called the Master Deed, which contains a "new" and detailed description of the property, with specificity in describing the Units and Common Elements, pursuant to a new survey and engineering drawings. The Condo Association, with its Rules and By-Laws, is also created. Again, the Common Elements are deeded out to the Association; the sale of the Units to Unit Owners is facilitated through conveyance of Unit Deeds whose Unit descriptions correspond to language in the Master Deed; by each Unit Deed the owner / grantor of the entire complex will progressively divest of the totality, piece by piece, of the Master Deed.

A Conversion to Condo Units will typically mean a large increase in the aggregate value of the entire parcel, an Enhanced Value resulting from creation of "more valuable" Individual Units. It is all an "artificial" yet very real means of "Creating Wealth". Through a Condo Conversion a larger, an already physically divided or a not-yet-physically divided (by walls or individual sections) multi-unit (or soon-to-be multi-unit) property or a single unit property, is

Legally Divided into Units, individual properties, in <u>a procedure which Circumvents the need for things like Subdivisions or Variances. A very Clever Legal Paperwork Maneuver!</u>

Thus can we turn an otherwise costly and potentially deal-killing failure or inability to gain approvals to divide properties via the traditional route into a non-issue.

Example: The 50,000 square foot warehouse may be Condominiumized relatively easily and sold off as individual Units (after some sprucing up and wall changes), at a huge Profit over its original purchase price or "as-is" aggregate pre-Condo status value; whereas in an attempt to split the building through Subdivisions into separate non-Condo properties sharing certain common walls (as in the Condo Conversion) the many Variance, Subdivision and related issues and costs may prove an impossible hurdle (assuming approvals would even be granted).

<u>"Legal Conversions" by Obtaining Waivers From Environmental Restrictions</u> – such as prohibitions against building in designated Wetlands, prohibitions against expanding structures or paving parking lots which may create excessive runoffs near public waterways, prohibitions against particular activities in close proximity to natural preserves, or prohibitions on the emission of manufacturing related pollutants – can be a boon for any developed or undeveloped site. Such Waivers usually translate into a green light and Big Profits. Waivers are issued by applicable Federal, State and Regional Regulatory bodies in accordance with a legal / administrative process premised on "best use, public need, public good, least detriment and supporting scientific data" per studies commissioned by the applicant.

In the appropriate circumstances having an individual structure or grouping of properties designated for Legal purposes as <u>A Blighted Or Urban Renewal Zone</u>, can prove a profitable twist for an ordinary, drab, older worn or decaying property or neighborhood. A variety of Governmental bodies are empowered to bestow such designations and channel funding and other privileges that go with them. Designated areas can obtain favored zoning status (use, density); real estate tax abatements; Enterprise Zone designations which entail reduced sales tax and other incentives to assist merchants and manufacturers within the zones; and low-interest loans and grants for rehabs, new construction and businesses housed in the realty.

It will behoove any investor who plans to do <u>Legal Or Physical Conversions</u> to scout properties in designated <u>Urban Blight and Renewal Zones,</u> or areas which in the future might lend themselves to such designations. With label in hand, the owner of such "depleted" properties can more easily and profitably refurbish, rent or resell. Be a buyer or partner in overall rebuilding, rehabbing, or assembling of properties in the Zones.

There are also <u>Judicially-Mandated Arenas, Defined Geographically and/or by Subject, where a Legal Move by an investor can, either in and of itself or in concert with a subsequent Physical Improvement to his property, lead to strong financial Gains which will enable him to further Capitalize on his original investment</u>. (In this sense, by Judicially-Mandated we do not mean Court Rulings or Appeals which might overrule adverse decisions against an owner-applicant by a lower court or board or agency "down below".)

By way of illustration, one still vibrant wide-ranging area of Judicial Activism, or Scrutiny, which gained steam in the 1970's-'80's is the practice of <u>Compelling Construction Of Affordable Or Low Income Housing Units, For Sale Or For Rent, Regionally (including affluent suburbs)</u>. The diverse rulings throughout the country on this topic carry over today, and have had a great impact on real estate values in affected municipalities. The essence, or original Rationale, of most of these decisions was that those municipalities which fell short in their quotas or ratios of Affordable Housing Units, had an obligation to set aside portions of their undeveloped land for future construction of "affordable" units.

At first glance one might expect such a requirement to adversely impact values of both raw land and existing residential units in affected areas. But some rather "complex" notions of "owner rights" and "methods" used in calculating a municipality's Affordable Housing "obligations" have instead proven to be a boon for land owners who are "pulled into this web", or who sometimes "seek out this web!"

Thanks to a layer of super-imposed Judicially-Permitted "privileges" which enable affected land owners or municipalities to "convey" their Affordable Housing obligations to neighboring towns (which "privilege" obviously defeats the purported intent and purpose of imposing the Obligation in the first place), the tables get turned rather easily. The so-called Obligation to build Affordable Housing may even be conveyed out to a municipality which itself already has an over-abundance of urban problems and low-income housing.

Thus, instead of the suburban land being used for this "purpose", paradoxically the "privileges" often give land developers in many "desirable" towns which supposedly "need" the low-income housing a powerful money-making lever over their own Town Fathers, to wit:

> "Give us zoning and other concessions (to allow us to overbuild our land with 'our' type of dwellings and make more money than we could if we built within the confines of the Affordable Regulations), and we will convey our Affordable Housing Construction Obligations to some other town (and thus heap on those who probably already have loads of such housing, outside of suburbia) or we will build those low-income units here, flood the town with a type of housing stock that you would rather do without, and over-populate your schools and town with people who you would prefer not live here."

So we have a major area of <u>Judicially-Mandated requirements, Affordable Housing</u>, being transferred by another Judicially-Permitted privilege – the ability to unload that obligation, making dollars for Lucky or Savvy investors who have or who seek out land in affected areas, precisely for the purpose of playing the Court decisions to manipulate the System and create a Windfall in a Conversion of their Property – either by building themselves with the benefit of their new-found sweetheart incentives, or by selling their land with its newly-empowered Legal parameters for superior development. <u>A Classic Profitable Legal &/Or Physical Conversion Empowered By Court Decisions, And The Savvy Investor Who Understands What's Going On In His Area Can Capitalize On It Quite Handsomely.</u>

Additionally there are a multitude of <u>Constitutional Challenges</u>, grounded in Due Process, Equal Protection and other guarantees (real or supposed), which can be asserted in State or Federal Court to try to alter existing local regulations or "persuade" a municipality to promulgate more "favored rules", which "rules" can then be "used" to facilitate a given type of development or redevelopment of raw land or existing structures.

We are not talking about a Court Appeal of a zoning or other board or regulatory decision or denial. We are talking about a real or threatened wholesale challenge to existing local laws or regulations, a Challenge to a certain state of affairs. For example: "I have the Right to Convert my one family into a legal rooming house, even though this use is not permitted where it is located, because such a converted use will make it a rooming house for people of a particular orientation, or for single mothers, etc., and to deny me when this is a locally 'needed use' and there seems to be no other suitable place for such a facility, is Discriminatory and Unconstitutional."

On a more functional level it must be noted that any Physical Or Legal "Tinkering" with a parcel must nevertheless be done in Strict Compliance with those more mundane Legal Requirements which affect all owners and projects; Obey local Codes, Permit Procedures, Inspections, Rules and Regulatory Decrees.

It ultimately comes down to Fundamentals: "What will be the scope of a Legal Maneuvering &/Or Physical Work? What degree of effort and costs are called for? Should any of the contemplated Work be cheap and barebones, should it be new construction, expansion, major renovation or less?" One Must Think Outside Of The Box, And At The Same Time Inside The Box, with Knowledge, Prudence and Ingenuity.

Crucial – Remember – In Any Project: "How Far Do I Go, And What's Best At The Particular Location And In The General Area?" Basic Factors to be Considered – Purchase Price; Present Property Value; Local Comps; Market Trends; What Your Locale Does And What It Can Support; Rehab Costs; Other Costs; Your Budget; Your Resources; Your Abilities; Your Goals; Other Possible Deals And Opportunities; Your Margins And Rules Of Thumb; The Scope Of Any Undertaking; Socio-Economics; Local Sentiments; Local Official Policies; Potential Competition And Cost Overruns; And Potential Value Or Gain Upon Completion.

Again And Again, To Reiterate: Create Wealth – Buy Low, Buy Right; Try To Avail Yourself Of Market Cycles; Try To Capitalize On The Upswings; Avail Yourself Of The Basic Core Gains And Yields Of Any Sensible Speculative Or Longer Term Investment; And Know How To Take Whatever It Is That You Have, However Much Or Little, Do Those Physical And/Or Technical Legal Things To That Property; And Make It All That It Can Be, And, With Foresight (Chapter X), Manage And Maintain, In A Businesslike And Intelligent Fashion, Whatever It Is That You Bought And Perhaps Embellished, If You Are Holding For The Longer Term As Opposed To Flipping.

My own experiences both personally and as an observer, are not woven from that same silly cloth which is the basis for many TV infomercials and certain Rehab Shows which would have us believe they reflect what real-life Deal-Making and

Rehabbing is all about. To be sure, the flukes are out there. Just as the wildcatters hit oil gushers and the prospectors find those Alaskan streams sparkling with gold nuggets. There is pure chance. Anybody can stumble into a real estate windfall in a strong Up Market or even despite themselves.

But that is not what <u>Learning</u> and <u>Trying, Doing</u> and <u>Striving</u> are about. Luck is Luck. In the real world we can hope for Luck, for Good Timing or Success by Happenchance. Though the reality is a world where <u>Positive Results</u> flow from <u>Toiling</u> in <u>a Fertile Arena (Real Estate)</u>, with <u>Knowledge</u> and <u>Insight</u>. No real estate magic with the snap of a finger, and I am no "teacher" with "investors" basking on the yacht as they recount fairy-tale "success" stories.

<u>A sampling of same Actual Conversions to a Higher and Better Use Legally &/Or Physically, in small and large Projects – Classic Cases; Combining Physical Work And The Legal; The Changing And The Marketing (Alone Or In Combination); To Convert To Make Something "Different" And More Out Of A Purchase</u>.

Not too long ago I Flipped a modestly priced property, which I Knew was a Good Buy, a Good Deal, yet which on the surface might have seemed anything but to the novice. Just as Values were starting to soften in the area, I bought a vacant one family house with some extra land in an older working class neighborhood of a tired industrial city in Central New Jersey. My purchase price was just about 10% less than the retail net which my seller's broker had "guaranteed" him. But I saw a <u>Gem</u>, and more than enough <u>Possibility</u>, that I still happily paid close to "fair" market value in a Market which I knew had already peaked. And it was clear that quick action was a must if I was to have any chance of Success.

The house was situated on a lot whose original deed dimensions (on two separate deeds) were a total of 75 by 100 feet, and my seller would also be conveying some adjacent vacant land to the left of the house, which he had acquired through still a third deed 40 years earlier, a sliver of land measuring 5 by 100 feet. Current Zoning required a 40 by 100 foot lot to build a new one family dwelling. Based on the character of the Neighborhood and its existing housing stock, the extra 5 feet of land would add very little, if anything, to the value of the property if it were retained in its existing form of just one parcel, one dwelling. But an extra 40 by 100 foot lot could constitute a separate legal building lot, and as such would be worth at least $110,000.00 "as is" with a building permit in hand, in a quick sale.

Further complicating the picture the existing house, a modest, mostly brick pre-World War II structure in need of some renovation and clean-up, had an "addition", vintage 1950, which added a bedroom to its second floor and was built in a canter-leavered (overhang) fashion. And it encroached some 15 feet over and above our "would-be" new 40 by 100 foot adjoining building lot.

Based on a quick estimate of probable costs, I decided that the best route would be to demolish part of the existing structure, namely the overhang; rehab what remained appropriately to the prevailing Character of the older neighborhood (without trying to over-improve or burn up money and time to no avail); finish and market the house as soon as possible in order to catch the Market and avoid incurring additional carrying costs; bail out as much of my investment as possible from the house itself; and net my "Profit" out of the building lot.

The purchase was consummated before the seller listed with his broker. He saved on the commission and, based on the comps which his broker produced, he netted a fair price from me. My Research (Due Diligence) had convinced me that I was dealing with a mature, strong, reliable seller who had a tiny mortgage balance on his property.

Under our Contract I advanced a 20% Deposit which was tendered directly to the seller and not held in escrow (as it ordinarily is and ordinarily should be pending closing). The Contract gave me carte blanche to demolish the old "addition" and start rehab work immediately, operating as PUC, and the Contract also contained the seller's Authorization permitting me to apply for necessary Permits and make other legal applications prior to closing. It further gave me a four-month closing date; a longer than average window, which I had bargained for. And it also contained a Hold Harmless and other Insurance provisions for the seller's protection in connection with my anticipated Work.

I would thus bear the Risk of tendering a deposit, which itself was larger than the average 10%, out of escrow, and investing in a Rehab prior to closing. But in proceeding as Purchaser Under Contract, with Valuable Rights, it all made sense. Sure, there was a gamble. But I had reason to be convinced that my deposit was safe. My seller was a stable long-term owner, and I had reliable references. And immediate access to the deposit was an important factor in his making our Deal.

I wanted to minimize my Transaction and carrying costs, move money from another Deal which had yet to close to this one, act quickly in a softening market (again, as noted earlier, avoid the Cliffs in a Boom Market and when Negotiating leave something on the table for the other side), and I just wanted to Leverage In and Out, A.S.A.P.

I acted as my own GC. I needed only one Licensed Sub., an electrician, to do minor capping of wires which led to the bedroom that was being demolished. With day labor, some basic hand tools, two 40-yard roll off dumpsters for masonry debris (which would be recycled; by dumping masonry in a separate dumpster you save money), and three 40 yarders for the balance of the demolition debris and Rehab aspect of the job, we completed the demolition within one week of going into Contract, at a total cost of under $4,500.00 ($11,000.00 less than the best demo contractor estimate that I had for the job). And now "potentially" (but "really", I Knew) I had an extra Valuable building lot.

Before we began Work I obtained the necessary Demo and Rehab Permits from the Municipal Building Department. Since there were no stumbling blocks, no mechanicals involved, no bearing walls to deal with, and thus no formal architectural drawings needed, with only a simple diagram of the area to be demolished and a brief written summary and general total cost estimate of the anticipated Work to be performed, the Permit was stamped within one day (in a business-friendly city), and all that would later be required of the City was a Final Building and Code Inspection. Before starting Work I had also obtained the appropriate liability and workmen's comp. Insurance, and as the Rehab got underway I quickly listed the house for sale with a Broker (Work in progress, still as PUC), and put a "for sale by owner" (FSBO) sign on the adjacent lot (it would be easy selling such a lot to any number of local builders, no need for a Broker here).

I saved on the expense of an extra dumpster or two in the clean-out process by giving a lot of still usable furniture and appliances to some of my workers and a couple of neighbors, who greatly appreciated their "gifts". After some economical siding was installed, along with two new windows, thus sealing the void in the upstairs wall where the demolished bedroom had been attached, the same siding was wrapped around the rest of the second floor, replacing some old frayed and discolored shingles. The old brickwork on about two-thirds of the house was solid, but tired in appearance.

The brick was acid-washed (my total cost including labor, about $250.00), and together with the bright new siding we now had a solid, classic rich-looking veneer. The exterior trim and windows were puttied and painted, some fresh plaster applied to the small area between the brick veneer and the ground level, some exterior spotlights were placed on the house, and the old-fashioned enclosed rear sun porch was reinvigorated by removing its fragile aluminum partitions (from another era), installing a wooden banister and some cheap new indoor / outdoor carpeting. The dingy old porch became a bright, fresh, open usable amenity which was a natural aesthetic draw.

The old broken concrete driveway which ran the length of the right side of the house around and into the back yard was partially removed (with a couple of sledge hammers and wheel barrels), and covered with new blacktop, as was most of the yard, where an old peaked-roof three-and-a-half car garage spanned almost the entire width of the property along its rear line. Based on the Character of the Neighborhood (many homeowners with small home-based manual businesses requiring garages, many owners with extended families and trucks in an area of small lots and scarce on-the-street parking), I realized it would be more cost-efficient and at the same time a better selling point, to repave most of the rear yard, which in fact provided access to the garages, and paint the garages and fix their overhead doors instead of turning it all into grass.

Our landscaping (a small front yard and essentially one narrow side yard), consisted of a dozen or so miniature bushes and plantings, a small crate of stones, eight bags of mulch, and a pick-up truck load of sod – and with about five man hours of labor, it looked better than anything on the block – for a modest material and labor cost at that.

The interior of the house revealed magnificent pristine 65-year-old hardwood floors beneath some ragged carpeting. I had them refinished by a hardwood floor Sub. (using a Sub. who knows the business is the way to go if you want to avoid a botched job when refinishing hardwood floors, which should be a center-piece), and they bore a rich, shining polyurethane sheen when dried. (Refinishing hardwood floors is a labor-intensive skilled process which requires experienced hands and proper equipment, and is certainly not one of those areas where you want to "save" by using a seemingly less-expensive amateur or by renting a machine yourself.)

Some spackling on the walls, a lot of paint, preservation of the classic stained doors and their crystal hardware with some TLC and polyurethane, some nice new cheap light fixtures (globes) in the ceilings and a few spots in some of the corners, new plates for the wall light switches and outlets throughout in shades blending with the new paint, inexpensive new tile floors and some reasonably-priced fixtures for the two small bathrooms, a new vinyl stick-down kitchen floor, resurfacing of the kitchen cabinets and a new ceramic countertop and backsplash, and paint, sheetrock, a lot of cleaning and some minor waterproofing in the mostly finished, already partitioned older-style basement.

A second (and illegal, it was a one family house), kitchen on the second floor went into the dumpster along with the bedroom demo, and that kitchen area became a fourth bedroom (a very important selling point in such a Neighborhood). The Conversion to a bedroom required only some more sheetrock, a new door and paint. And this would become the only newly carpeted room in the house (carpeted because its ancient vinyl flooring had so severely damaged the underlying hardwood floor that it was cheaper to carpet over; and the carpeting also added a bright touch and broke up the monotony of the room flow on the second floor at the same time).

Smoke and carbon monoxide detectors and a portable fire extinguisher in the kitchen paved the way for the mandatory pre-closing Fire Department Inspection. The Certificate of Occupancy (CO) Inspection, which I had not ordered in a timely manner and was thus left for the last minute as we were scheduled to close, resulted in a few minor items which would need further attention, so I secured a Conditional CO (sufficient to close), and arranged with my buyer to allow me to have the Inspector's Checklist attended to within the required 60 days after closing. And on his Final (and only) Inspection, the Building Inspector had no problems with the workmanship pursuant to our Permits, and accordingly closed them out.

After the exact time and date for closing was scheduled between the attorneys, and long after my buyer had Waived his Contractual Mortgage Contingency (he never notified me of any failure to obtain the stipulated financing even after the date set for notification in the Contingency Clause had passed), at literally the last minute his mortgage broker (a mortgage banker funds loans, a mortgage broker places deals with bankers for a commission; it is best to deal directly with a banker for more certainty and better rates), advised that there was no firm closeable commitment.

The buyer was bound to perform and his 10% deposit, still in attorney escrow, was at risk. All the other Contract Contingencies had been satisfied, and I, as the seller, was Ready, Willing, and Able to perform. In discussions between respective counsel and the broker, buyer and myself, it became clear that the buyer had been less than diligent in his mortgage application process. And his mortgage broker had been much less than competent and truthful.

In a deteriorating Market, going into the traditionally (at least in the Northeast) slower winter / holiday season, and seeing an ever-increasing supply of unsold inventory on the market I was anxious to close on this resale and avoid incurring additional carrying costs, going forward with Capital tied up in the Deal and risking a sinking Market. The ultimate sales price which I had agreed to, and which included a real estate commission negotiated down at the time of Contract, was somewhat lower than I originally anticipated, but still satisfactory.

The buyer, the party in breach of Contract, nevertheless tried his luck in demanding seller concessions to obtain his financing. A Time of Essence Notice was served in an effort to compel him to close in accordance with the Contract terms (typically, unless a Contract specifically Makes Time of the Essence by its very language, Contract closing dates are legally only target dates, and a delay in closing by either party does not constitute an automatic breach but it may entitle the other party to Make Time of the Essence, meaning the party who is served must perform in accordance with the Time of Essence date or the Contract is void, the deposit – in those cases where there is a breaching buyer – is forfeited, and there may be additional damages against the breaching party).

My buyer did not close in accordance with the Notice, though he said he did still want to close. We negotiated a moderately higher sales price to compensate at least in part for my additional carrying costs and legal fees caused by the breach; the deposit monies, at my request, were transferred from the buyer's attorney's trust account to my attorney's account (as an added measure of comfort should the breach continue and lead to litigation over the deposit); and pursuant to a second Time of Essence date being served, we finally went through a rocky closing.

As for the lot next door, within less than a week after beginning my "marketing" efforts, again without a broker (lawn sign, Internet listing, calls to several local builders), I had a Contract and it closed long before the house. The assemblage of this small 40 by 100 foot lot could have been a complicated if not impossible task for the novice. Three separate deeds. A 40 by 100 with a structure on it; a 35 by 100 with part of that same structure encroaching on it;

and a 5 by 100 foot strip. The existing house itself needed 40 by 100 in order to be Conforming, as did the vacant lot.

Fortunately, the City had been carrying the three parcels as separate lot and block numbers for tax purposes and issuing separate tax bills for each parcel for decades, all of which I was well aware of. The bills really should have been issued only for lots which had minimum dimensions of 40 by 100. (Original plot plans when that area was first sectioned off in the early 1900's had 20 by 100 foot building lots.)

The fact that this taxing process had continued over many years, due probably to the same clerical error being repeated annually or the result of a carryover of the original dissection and conveyances of the parcels, should obviate any need, I successfully "argued" in my informal discussions with the Building Department, for any type of Subdivision at this late date. The tax assessor had never combined, or at least on paper he had not combined, or merged, the original 40 and 35 foot lots. Thus, I contended, there could be no need to divide anything today.

I had done some research and knew all of this before my purchase contract was finalized. And I also knew that the legal implications which would flow from this fact should confirm the existence of the second, buildable 40 by 100 foot lot. Even though a Subdivision, had one been deemed necessary, should have been a perfunctory proceeding (with some expenses and costly delay), one can never be sure of the extent or impact of local opposition or other resistance which might lead to large problems and costs and possibly scuttle plans in the end.

Indeed, at the time this was an older City in a state of change. With urban problems creeping in, overcrowded schools, and a declining core tax base which historically had relied on long-since fading heavy industry, the Climate was not conducive for getting Board approval to squeeze in more houses which would probably produce more school-age children, and it was certainly not conducive to this where the applicant (me), was not one of a select few with an inside track at City Hall. Some districts in the City had recently been rezoned to require 50 by 100 foot building lots for new one family construction. (Prior to signing my purchase contract I confirmed that no rezoning was under consideration for "my" part of the City.)

My Research of the updated Municipal Building Code / Land Use booklet (usually available for purchase from local building departments), also confirmed my belief that no legal proceedings would be needed to combine the 35 and 5 foot lots into one parcel for building purposes. (Certain jurisdictions do require a form of Reverse Subdivision, if you will, to assemble separate lots into one buildable parcel on one deed.)

So there we had the two parcels – one containing a house, one just raw land. A preliminary survey which I had done as I was going into my Purchase Contract revealed that the house on the 40 by 100 foot lot, even after demolition of its old addition, would still "encroach" several inches, not onto the adjacent lot, but over and into its own left side "side yard", the side which was contiguous to the vacant lot.

Requirements for the front, rear, and both side yard setbacks (land which cannot be used for actual building coverage), were more stringent than when the house was built. The footprint of the original construction conformed to Code when it was built. And absent any subsequent new construction or Variance or Subdivision requests which would impact the parcel containing the house, this "aberration of the side yard encroachment", an aberration only in the sense of new activities in an era of different Code requirements, would have meant nothing insofar as the house or its use was concerned.

It was there; it was okay; it was pre-existing to the then-current Code requirements; and it was thus "grandfathered" in – as long as no changes were sought which would require the side yard to Conform to a different "newer" standard.

Had I needed to apply for a Subdivision or Variance to facilitate my assemblage, there could have been issues: I would be legally changing properties common to one owner in a manner which would leave a "new" or "changed" 40 by 100 foot lot with the pre-existing structure, and which would have to conform to current requirements. And it would have been in violation on its own side yard. That would have called for a Variance Use application to hopefully Cure any legal issues stemming from this "encroachment" onto its own side yard.

The Code Inspector viewed the properties (AFTER demolition), and agreed that I had a new building lot and an old conforming parcel with a house on it. The several inch encroachment onto its own side yard would be of no concern, and he would issue a Certificate of Occupancy for the existing house and, upon submission of architect's plans, a Building Permit for the vacant lot.

Of course it was all made possible by the immediate demolition of the "addition". Had I sought verbal approval of preliminary plans prior to demolition, perhaps to see if issuance of a building permit would later be a problem, and had I told the officials there was to be a demolition to clear the 35 foot lot, the City may have required an entirely different application process involving Variance requests, money and time, which could have ultimately resulted in a denial.

The builder who bought the lot had his shell up by the time I closed on the resale of my house. In my view he overbuilt for the neighborhood, but he put up a nice residence and a solid comparable for mine.

My Net Profit? About $72,000.00. The lot was "my Profit". Had this Deal matured ten months earlier, the Profit would have probably been more like $140,000.00 - $30,000.00 more on the lot, and $40,000.00 more on the house. Ten months later – who knows – it would have still been a decent Flip, but I would have been bucking a strongly declining Market after having bought on the Cliff of a Boom Market.

With market trends becoming clear even as I went into my purchase I was still looking at a bread and butter Deal which was an easy fit for me in an area that I knew well. I understood the entire Process had to be rushed – and that is exactly what I did, from operating initially as PUC to closing. Legal. Quick. Clean. Maneuver. Watch Costs. Do Not Over-Improve For The Neighborhood. Do Not Hold Out For The Last Dollar In The Deal – (If you want to push it, save your efforts for a better Market).

Why did I not build myself instead of selling the lot, and try to make an additional Profit on the new construction? Where time is short, when you know you have to move a Deal fast and you do not have the necessary apparatus in place to accomplish something that you would have to do effectively and quickly, "quit while you're ahead". Know Market Trends And Your Own Limitations. Focus On What You Know And What You Can Do Best, Unless The Market Is On Your Side And You Want To Expand And Explore. Half A Loaf Is Often Best, Especially If It Is Relatively Easy And You Can Minimize Your Risks And Look For Another "Easy" Half A Loaf In Some Other Deal.

When I approached this venture I first explored my original Idea to demolish the entire existing house and assemble one 80 by 100 foot lot for construction of one-bedroom age-restricted Condos. Such a Project would have required multiple Variances and introduced a new Density to the immediate Neighborhood, but with a commercial district only a couple of blocks away and multi-families and retail just down the street, at least on the face of it I should have had a fair shot at getting approved.

But I saw the Market declining. I knew the next door neighbor and a family across the street would oppose my applications. True, the City would have been assured of no additional school-age children, no significant on-street resident parking, and good tax rateables. But any approval could be a long and costly process. Plus, it did not make sense to carry this type of property into a deteriorating market while chasing an approval to build something, a concept which was already peaking in popularity locally, perhaps reaching its saturation point for the moment, and one which would seek to draw buyers from a pool of older local residents who themselves would need to sell their own homes and might hold off in a poor market.

The required construction, with underground parking on a tight lot, would have also been time-consuming and expensive when pro-rated by the number of Units. <u>The Risks, the Downside, just did not seem to justify my Idea and its Possible Rewards</u> (though once I finished the Project, I saw a couple of new age-restricted developments nearby which had me second-guessing my decision. But just because somebody else built something does not speak to the shrewdness or success of their venture).

Another Deal which I did a few years ago also Yielded just a part of the Loaf, but in this one, save for my pre-occupation with other projects at the same time and my seeming clueless assessments, the Deal should have been a much bigger Windfall than it was. I should have been more substantively involved in trying, within my own Abilities, to Maximize its Potential.

I bought a small beat-up one family in a prime town from an absentee owner residing in the Virgin Islands. Not a Foreclosure, she had only a small mortgage, and her cousin was renting the house at a nominal figure. She just wanted to sell. The house had been sitting on the multiple listing system for months with a few price reductions. Nobody was showing it. The interior was dingy, the house was falling apart with voodoo dolls all over the place and a pictorial display of deceased family members in open coffins plastering the upstairs walls.

My purchase price for the house, which was situated on an oversized lot, was $55,000.00 and I Structured the Deal to Assume my seller's own small FHA mortgage, with a mere $500.00 down payment and the seller Holding the balance in a Second Mortgage at a slightly above market interest rate, interest only, for a two year term. The seller had the house vacated, and she was happy with her monthly interest income from me and in getting the Town Code Officials off her back in an "as is" sale of her wreck.

With basically no Money Into The Deal and sensing the Market was on a modest Upswing, after having a few repairs done I rented the house out for eight months at a cheap price to a tenant who was in construction and could work with me on repairs as we went along. When my tenant left I started to Rehab with an eye towards Resale. Only basic Permits were needed (roof and the like), and Town Code Officials were happy to see the eyesore getting cleaned up. I did nothing that was not necessary as I economically completed a ton of cosmetics both inside and out.

Too extensive, too substantial a renovation of a tiny older house like this one would have been a never-never land; everything could have been replaced, and everything that would have been touched would have led to an ever-spiraling number of new problems and costs. Sometimes it is better to do a modest Rehab and sell a more modest product, recognizing a particular product, a particular property, for what it is and not pouring in a disproportionate amount of money to try to make it something that it is not and never will be. The entire transaction was uneventful. The Market was good. I listed with a Broker and quickly received a satisfactory "as is" offer on a somewhat anemic Rehab.

Only as I was going to closing however did I realize how negligent I had been. I had gotten a terrific Buy, with ideal Leveraging. I was looking at a nice Profit of $50,000.00 at closing. So what did I do wrong? I realized that my buyer was a teacher-turned-builder who lived a block away from the property. He was about to demolish my Rehabbed house and apply for a Variance to split the land into 2 two-family building lots (very choice and Valuable) and he would proceed to make a fantastic Profit. The Town would welcome two new clean dwellings as a replacement for the old house.

Had I really done my homework (Due Diligence), I would have better studied the complexion of the Neighborhood, Zoning Codes and Local Development, and I would have realized that instead of a Rehab, even if I did not want to build myself, I, too, could have obtained the Subdivision and in this two-family zone taken a shot at a Variance for the slightly undersized two-family building lots. Had I done what my buyer did, I could have sold the two lots and realized a Profit not of $50,000.00, but instead about $175,000.00. And a lot more had I built, or Partnered with a builder (in an LLC), even using the Equity in "my" two lots as my Cash Contribution to a building Project. Quite a difference!

If I had built in the solid Market that it was with new two families selling off pre-construction plans, my Profits would have been huge. (After our Deal, my buyer called me for years to see if I had anything else for him.)

In the alternative if I was on the ball and proceeded as the applicant, an application could have been made with the old house still standing "as is", without having first been Rehabbed. I would have ended up with 2 one or 2 two-family lots (which are more valuable), and whatever the outcome, however unsatisfactory it might have been, I could have always then done the Rehab and sold the eyesore later, or tore it down and come out with 1 two-family lot, which would have still Yielded a larger Profit than the Rehab did, anyway.

Most of my Rehabs have been one family homes and smaller commercial parcels, often purchased in Down Cycles or slower Markets, sometimes the proverbial shop-worn sleepers on the multiple listing system, sometimes properties in Foreclosure, or Deals otherwise in Physical and/or Fiscal Distress. Many times I have maintained (nursed) them along with short-term tenants, waiting for the Right Time to Fix and then Hold, to Fix and Flip, or to Flip "as is".

One of my most eye-opening experiences involved a larger industrial facility which I was involved with and preparing to market for sale. This was not a fixer-upper or a steal. It was a solid long-maintained property; two separate 11,000 square foot buildings, masonry construction, brick fronts, loading docks, ample parking, clean clear-span (no interior columns), featuring modern office suites.

Built in 1965 the buildings were erected on a one acre plot in conformity with then-prevailing Building Codes, and through the years were operated with Certificates of Occupancy for up to four tenants – two in each building, each building being split down the middle by a cinder block wall. The buildings were maintained in compliance with local Fire and Building Codes.

Interestingly, with no Subdivision for the land having been required when they were built, the Town permitted the two separate structures to be constructed on a single lot and block number. With the builder remaining in title going forward, apparently for the sake of expediency the local tax assessor taxed the buildings on individual bills as two separate and distinct parcels, by arbitrarily assigning a second lot number to one of the buildings – Lot 20.1 (the other being Lot 20) – both on Block 5.

So with no Subdivision and therefore no clear delineation as to how much land, or how much land value, actually went with each building, decades earlier the assessor and collector took still another short-cut: they began assessing and taxing one of the buildings based on its Improvements (the value of the structure), and proceeded to assess and tax the other building based on its Improvements, also, but added onto this second assessment the valuation, and thus the tax that went with it, for all of the land which was under and around both of the buildings. So for decades the tax bills would reflect one building as having all of the land, and the other as having no land and no land value. And quarter after quarter the bills were thus paid.

With such a long history of the Town's sloppy "approach" and seeming tacit approval of the status quo, indeed the Town was a *de facto* "actor" in the "creation" of the two "separate parcels", and with the legal indicia for individual properties well-established, one would have thought it should later be a routine matter to secure a formal Subdivision, if one were even required (as it would be to sell either part of the property in 2006).

The Town was more than negligent in its record-keeping. It issued two tax bills and separate Certificates of Occupancy for decades, and repeatedly conducted individual Code and Fire Inspections on two separate addresses (the buildings being some 20 feet apart).

But this was a Town with a strong industrial base which in recent years wanted to make believe that its lucrative industrial parks were not really there. Residents in a neighboring section of Town, built up after the industry was already around the corner, would constantly complain about truck traffic. The Town would issue a maintenance summons for the slightest infraction by an owner or tenant in its industrial parks. The Town Council always appreciated the tax revenues from these buildings, which constituted a strong base and kept residential rates low, but would routinely side with their constituent voters on issues which involved absentee industrial landlords.

Amazingly, after all those years, in order to effectuate a separation of the property the Town was going to still require not only a Subdivision, but also a slew of Variances with conditions to "upgrade" the buildings and parking areas. (Stipulations which mandate physical alterations and improvements to existing structures or land are often tacked onto Use, general Variance and Subdivision approvals.)

Off the record and prior to my submission of formal applications the Town confirmed that costly and involved work would have to be done if we even hoped to get a shot at the necessary approvals. New landscaping and exterior lighting, curb cuts and signage, and extensive upgrades to the buildings' exterior facades were the least of it.

The Town would also require fresh paving, underground piping of runoff water, and surface water drainage systems including a retention basin. The cost of such work would have severely impacted the dollars per square foot that we hoped to realize on any sale. The work would take many months to complete after approvals were granted. And approvals were far from guaranteed.

There would also be local opposition – any number of additional costly conditions could be imposed. Legal fees and costs, fees for expert witnesses and engineers, would all be sizeable. And in anticipation of marketing (properties like these usually draw self-users as optimal buyers), we had been maintaining the buildings with shorter-term, lower-paying warehouse tenants, who themselves were in the process of vacating. So a long delay with no rental income and huge costs was not what we wanted.

Selling both buildings as one larger parcel would limit the pool of prospective buyers and bring a much lower per square foot sales price. Buyers could also argue, and quite rightfully so in such a case, that the buildings were not Subdivided and should thus sell for less than what their value might otherwise be, since the absence of a Subdivision would work a hardship for them in any future attempt to resell. Any buyer could easily negotiate this point against us.

We came up with a rather novel approach, one which at once would avoid many of the above potential costs and problems, eliminate any need for a Subdivision or Variances, and enable us to immediately start marketing the parcel as four smaller, separate 5,500 square foot buildings, which could bring an even higher price per square foot than we originally hoped for.

The Idea was to Convert the entire property into four Condo Units together with Common Elements. By so doing there would be no need for Municipal okays, no need to placate politicians or neighbors, no need to bleed money. On a pro-rated per square foot basis in a Condo Conversion our transaction costs would be quite minimal.

We had to get some civil engineering work done; obtain a metes and bounds survey description of the dimensions of each of the proposed four new Units; clearly define the Common Elements (driveways, parking, and roof;

but not plumbing, heating, or electrical, as each Unit had its own systems); and assign parking spots within the Common Elements for each of the Units.

A Master Deed would be drafted and recorded in accordance with the four new Unit descriptions; the property would be deeded from the current owners to themselves in this new form, and a Condo Association – with its Rules, By-Laws and other components – would be Incorporated. And thus would we have our four Condo Units, to be marketed "as is" at a higher-than-ever-hoped-for per square foot price after a bit of essentially cosmetic work was completed.

I understood that a Condo Association consisting of only four Unit Owners would be more difficult to manage and less attractive to some prospective buyers than the more common Association of, say, 40, 60, or several hundred Unit Members. In larger Associations there is more room for reason to prevail and true majority-type voting, and less room for the few to bully a "minority". There is also a greater distribution of duties and a greater ability for Unit Owners, should they so wish, to sit on the sidelines and limit their own time commitments to Association affairs.

But the four Units sold quickly and at good prices. This <u>Conversion Trick</u> saved and made a lot of money for the sellers. <u>It Legally Changed the property to a Better and Higher, to a more Valuable Status, while short-circuiting the ordinary Legal Procedures</u> which in this case could have been a disaster.

A Conversion in which I had a small role saw an associate of mine purchase an abandoned multi-unit "new construction" Condo Project in a scenic North Jersey lakefront community. The original builder had poured over $2,000,000.00 into the project and virtually completed 18 of its 30 planned units. He complied with local Codes and thought he was in a position to obtain his Unit and Project CO's. But he did not adhere to the New Jersey State Department of Environmental Protection Regulations for construction of the septic system. And he had based his costs and anticipated Profit, the validity of the entire Project, on the construction and sale of 30 Units, not 18.

After completion of the first 18 the State DEP shut him down for being in violation of their Regulations. Curing the violations would have entailed remedial costs that he could not afford without first selling a number of the Units, which he was now barred from doing. Construction on the entire Project was halted, he defaulted on his construction loan and the bank ultimately took the property back at Sheriff's Sale, only itself to soon fail and be taken over by the FDIC.

The FDIC Dissolution Department took almost five years to liquidate the lender's assets, and during this time the property fell into severe disrepair. The Town had a terrible eyesore, a deserted hazard which was producing no appreciable tax revenues. (To be sure, the Town had a cash flow from the Project as the Tax Liens had been bought by a third party and taxes were being maintained; but since no CO's had been issued the Units, the entire Project, was still being taxed based on its (incomplete) land status, and hence the taxes were a far cry from what they would have been had the Project been completed and issued its CO's.)

Due to the Market the initial FDIC auctions which listed the parcel drew only a handful of bids; and my friend's $500,000.00 All Cash No Contingency "As Is", 30 Day Closing Offer eventually took the development. The property looked like a mess, but it was a Genuine Steal.

In order to turn this seeming monstrosity into the marketable gold mine that it really was, he had to apply some Smarts. The central problem for the original developer had been the septic system and DEP compliance. But now, down the road: <u>Step One – Buy Low, Buy Right – was accomplished. A Shrewd Offer had been Structured and accepted, Next, "What to do with the Deal?" My friend had to comply with the DEP, obtain the necessary local approvals, clean-up the site, refurbish the Units, and Market them in a sensible manner. Comply and Complete, in a Cost-Effective Way.</u>

<u>The Plan was to work with the Powers That Be, Get In and Get Out, Minimize future exposures, Keep it all uncomplicated, and Try to make a Good Profit on the Flips.</u>

He decided to stop at the 18 Units which were already "completed" (his Offer had pre-supposed this), devote the excess remaining land to some extra-nice Common Elements for future Unit Owners (and to help attract them), and re-construct a septic system which would be adequate, aesthetically pleasing, and in compliance with DEP Regulations. And that he did.

<u>He got a Good Deal. He Analyzed his Potential, Kept his Costs Low, Played Ball with The Powers That Be, Moved Quickly, Turned out an Attractive Product, Marketed it Competitively, Sold most of the Units at Under Market Prices, and came out with a Tremendous Profit.</u> His basic cost per Unit was about $30,000.00 and he sold them at an average of $120,000.00

each. $90,000.00 times 18 equals $1,620,000.00 Gross Profit; less Rehab and other Costs totaling about $450,000.00; leaving a <u>Net Profit of almost $1,200,000.00. And this development had sat, it had brought no offers for the longest time; the proverbial drug on the market</u>.

A few years back I saw an absolutely incredible real estate <u>Conversion Success Story</u> unfold in one of New Jersey's most prestigious towns, again beginning with the purchase of a shop-worn "white elephant". The buyer / developer was one of the State's larger builders. <u>And virtually all of the elements which could ever apply to the largest or smallest of projects came into play here</u>.

Like the Lakefront venture, this site was also sitting on the market for over a year when the buyer placed his winning bid. It was <u>Foresight, Ingenuity, a bit of Lucky Timing, an Understanding of all Facets of the Business and a lot of Cash</u> that made the Deal possible. <u>But whatever its scale, this Project epitomized so much of what we need to Know regardless of the depth of our own Resources</u>.

The property was once the corporate headquarters of one of New Jersey's oldest banks. During a Cycle of bank failures the FDIC had taken the thrift over and proceeded to liquidate its assets – which of course included its foreclosed collateral inventory, its mortgage paper and other receivables, and the realty and personalty formerly used in the bank's own business operations.

Its corporate campus consisted of a magnificent, sprawling three story office building with state-of-the-art features and amenities too numerous to mention, with rolling acre upon acre of park like land and a picturesque plot of woods which included an Environmentally-sensitive Designated Wetlands area (off limits, "usually", for new construction).

So the Deal started with the developer bidding approximately $4,000,000.00 for the entire complex, his Offer coming after (repeated) listings of the parcel by the FDIC had met with little interest and no solid bids. This was a true sleeper.

The vacant office building, with its cafes, cafeterias, marble hallways, and conference rooms which boasted panoramic views, was strategically located in an affluent town; close to a major mall and mass transit connections, regional and Interstate highway exchanges, a host of other commercial and professional buildings, and one of the State's premier hospitals.

At the moment the real estate Market was Down, but to the seasoned eye it was clear that the Possibilities for this parcel were virtually unlimited. Upscale socio-economic trends in the area, all sorts of local needs and activities, and such a building situated where there was a scarcity of buildable land so choice. Yet a Project so vast, although we see all sorts of mini-versions every day, that it would require deep pockets and expertise in basically every facet of Legal and Physical Rehab and Development.

It would not be long before the developer was petitioning the local Building Department and Planning Board with a host of Use, Density, and other Construction-Related Variance requests and Subdivision proposals, accompanied by all sorts of studies and expert witness reports as to traffic, engineering and landscaping issues. Next came the Permit applications and drawings for a major Rehab and add-ons to the building and construction of a new parking deck – all to the overwhelming accolades of the town. For the developer had already Negotiated an agreement with the local hospital to turn his white elephant into what would be a bustling out-patient center, together with suites of specialty medical offices.

The anticipated immediate and longer-term Profit Streams from the joint venture with the hospital on the building and some adjacent land would cover the developer's total investment in the entire parcel countless times over. Furthermore this meant that the balance of the undeveloped land was basically free to the developer. But it did not mean that he had any intention of leaving it fallow as perhaps a nice appurtenance to the new ambulatory care center, or donating it to the Town for some sort of recreational center or natural preserve.

Even before making his Offer to the FDIC and going to the Town with his benign, acceptable plans for the office building, he had some additional Ideas in mind – which he would hit the Town with AFTER he got what he wanted on the "Easy End". And this was his second ace in the hole, his even bigger money-maker than the Rehabbed out-patient complex.

Due to its Wetlands designation much of the land was supposed to be non-buildable. Moreover, local Zoning required one acre plots for its only permitted use, which was one family housing, and in any such contemplated development the land would also have to be further cut-up by roads, by-passes for the Wetlands section, and other requirements. The developer understood the huge potential for an Optimal Use of such a tract. It was the largest remaining undeveloped piece in Town and mostly clean and flat.

And the developer also Knew that the Town was already over-built in terms of school census, its property taxes were sky-high (in part because of substantial County urban burdens impacting the local tax rate) and were a sore point among residents; and the Town was in no mood to entertain a new flood of school-age children or still higher property taxes to fund new school construction.

And he Knew that a student influx comprised of "low-income" people would be especially unpopular, and he Understood that the threat of a Mount Laurel (Affordable Housing) litigation, with its costs and "fear factor", would turn the Town upside down (and that it did). He gave the Town an ultimatum: "Give me my approvals for a few hundred or so low-rise luxury Condos (almost million dollar Units) with the fancy clubhouse, which will bring few school-age children and cater to the local older populace, or give me my permits to build a glut of lower-income Affordable Units to sell and rent because you, this affluent suburban paradise, have not fulfilled your State Affordable quotas and this almost last remaining tract of vacant land will just have to cure a lot of that deficiency."

As we know and as the developer pointed out, the Affordable Obligations could be "conveyed" to another town (an absurd legal / societal farce which inherently contradicts the underlying reasons for New Jersey's Mount Laurel Obligation to begin with, but the Law nonetheless). By resorting to a Legal Technique which has been used in both large and small development situations throughout New Jersey, and which in reality is a Legal aberration, Judicially-Evolved from what was originally a socially-conscious Ruling, the developer was quite willing to Maximize his Gains by "squeezing" the Town and local sentiment. So the "threat", the Legal Angle, was used to further his development.

Armed with such a powerful Legal perversion, which is on The Books for no rational reason other than serving as a loophole for owners, speculators, developers and "threatened" municipalities (why impose an 'obligation" to alter the character of a municipality if it can be "sold" to some other town?), the developer in our case engaged his Town in costly litigation which led to Negotiations. Eventually there was a Settlement: Million dollar Condos and no low income sprawl.

He got his wish list of Subdivisions, Variances of every sort, and the Town's Cooperation in helping secure DEP Environmental Waivers to minimize his Wetlands prohibitions; he set up his Condo Master Deed and Association and proceeded to Build and Build, and over the years to Rent and Sell, an expensive mini-community which has thrown off many tens of millions of dollars in Profit.

Indeed, Books and Checklists can Teach the Basics – (and most of them do not even do that). It also takes a Gut Feeling, a Pulse of The Market and The Times, a Knowledge of Your Area, an Understanding of the Business, an Inquisitive Mind, and that Full Blend of Perception and Grounding, to Successfully Navigate and Reach For The Next Level, if you are to Maximize your Deals and Create Dollars.

CHAPTER X

HOLDING FOR THE LONGER TERM –
SOME LANDLORD & MANAGEMENT ISSUES

In all of my roles as a <u>Landlord</u> I have always been conscious of my <u>Attitudes</u> and <u>Demeanor</u> when dealing with <u>Tenants</u>, I tend to be too informal, pliable and solicitous of the feelings and needs of others in a business transaction to a fault. But I think my advice would be well taken when I say that a landlord should avoid airs of superiority (he is not superior, *ipso facto*, anyway), and should avoid the appearance of being stuffy, rigid or excessively formal in the way he handles both larger issues and everyday details inherent in landlord-tenant relationships.

A proper <u>Temperament</u>, best if it is natural and not affected, a certain <u>Patience</u>, a <u>Firmness</u> when necessary yet also an <u>Understanding</u> and a <u>Flexibility</u> where appropriate, are all in order. <u>A Friendly yet Business-Like Manner, a Hands-On Common Sense Approach</u> to problem-solving and more casual matters which arise and <u>a Pro-Active Nature</u>, are all helpful. Adjust your rents and demands, again where appropriate, to conditions in the market, and Adjust Yourself to those with whom you deal.

We all have our own ideas and ways, but I feel a landlord furthers his own cause and promotes necessary harmony and good feelings if he leaves his expensive shoes at home when meeting with most tenants, particularly those in more modest apartments. Is it a snobby or hypocritical façade to try to "appear" one way for the modest apartment tenant, and perhaps another way for the "sophisticated" or well-healed commercial tenant? No, no more than it is inappropriate for the owner of the local pizzeria to have his host dress in formal attire on the restaurant side which features $75.00 dinners, and his pizza maker dress a bit differently on the take-out side.

ROBERT METZ

It's called <u>Common Self-Centered Business Sense, and Respect</u>. To be sure, a more businesslike approach is often called for in the non-residential tenancy scenario; depending, naturally, on the landlord's own situation and the market; Demeanor and Approach in dealing with business-savvy wealthier tenants should be commensurate with the dollars and issues at hand.

<u>In Day-to-Day Management of tenanted properties</u> it is sometimes sensible to have a Superintendent or hierarchy of Management Personnel, and other times it is just wasteful. The size of a property, the number of units, rent roll, profitability, the type of tenancy, the amount of work involved (paperwork, on-site supervision, repairs, marketing), and obviously the abilities and desire of the landlord to work or not work the property himself, are among the determining factors.

An on-site super and staff is most appropriate for multi-unit apartment houses and commercial or office properties where, even if the tenants are responsible for their own maintenance, there is still a need for overall Management (paperwork, marketing, general maintenance, security), in the common interior and exterior portions of the complex.

Management should be a matter of Moderation. Do not overreact to problems or delinquencies. Keep problems and matters in perspective. Do not hound; handle what needs to be handled, look out for your own rights, be considerate of the tenant, and maintain a strong and clear Presence in any form of Management. Simplicity and Efficiency is the best style, whoever is managing.

<u>General Maintenance of Leasehold Property</u> is often a major worry to the novice, and neurotic, alike. Of course it is important, but again, Moderation; Keep Things In Perspective; Avoid Overkill; Bear In Mind what your Goals and Plans really are (Will it be a Flip or a Longer-Term Investment?); be Cognizant of Costs, get a Feel for what can be "Patched" and where you need to Spend Money. Think Economic Utility and Potential Profit, and the Need, if any, for a given Level of Maintenance. Unless a property is truly high-end and commands something more, you must Focus on Efficiency, Cost Control, in choosing both labor and materials. Do not skimp when it comes to Licensed Trades or Permits and Code Standards. And most Maintenance should be done in a Timely Manner.

But again, save for high-end properties where lease (contractual) obligations or standards must be observed, or where you have a property that is about to be Marketed, Remember that overkill, high-cost approaches to Maintenance,

244

are counter-productive. Where you anticipate Holding for a period of time and the application of a higher grade paint to the façade will last three years longer than a lesser brand, go with the more expensive one. If the common hallways need re-carpeting, unless the nature of the property demands a certain plushness, the inexpensive variety will do just fine. Added costs will accomplish nothing in this case; wear and tear, carelessness by those who use and work in the premises, will kill any carpeting. And the real issue is what Profit, if any, will the more expensive variety bring in either the short or the long run?

There are Three Essential Categories of Maintenance. Routine Maintenance is the day-to-day, typically wear and tear variety. Deferred Maintenance addresses those repairs and replacements which can be put off. And Preventative Maintenance is aimed at avoiding more costly repairs, problems, losses, and third party claims in the future. This will include both minor and substantial cost items, those of more import to the physical and fiscal integrity, value, and health of the real estate – i.e., work on the mechanical systems, structural components and roof. Preventative Maintenance in its own right should be "Routine", with discretion.

Repair and Maintenance Obligations may be imposed on the landlord and/or tenant by lease; by operation of law; by other agreement between the parties; or by Order of the Courts, Inspectors or Regulators. In residential situations, especially apartment rentals, Maintenance is typically on the landlord.

In the office, retail, general commercial and industrial sectors, Maintenance responsibilities will most often be allocated by Lease (below). Where tenants bear obligations the landlord should insist on timely performance and not wait until the end of the lease term to compel compliance or a credit. By that time neglected repair items can pile up and any last-minute unpaid rent might already approach or exceed the amount of security the landlord is holding, thus leaving him with little or no immediate leverage (security deposit) through which to effectuate compliance.

Capital Improvements, which are a step above the typically smaller or less costly Maintenance Items, can be compared to Mini-Rehabs. In leasehold situations Capital Improvements may or may not be productive or beneficial to the Cash Flow, Use or Future of the property. Where the subject of Capital Improvements, desired by either landlord or tenant, arises in the context of lease negotiations, considerations of who should bear up-front out-of-pocket costs and who should oversee the work (landlord or tenant), are the threshold issues.

In virtually all residential (single family or apartment) rentals, Capital Improvements, like most Maintenance Matters, are for the landlord to deal with. But in commercial and industrial relationships "obligations" during the lease term or as conditions precedent to execution or commencement of the lease, may be allocated either way in the lease.

And in such situations it is usually best to have the tenant bear all or most out-of-pocket costs and get the work done, perhaps with a contractor selected or approved by the landlord. Clearly this position will be tempered by considerations of the landlord's bargaining power in the context of market conditions, issues of supply and demand, the desirability of the subject property, the size of the transaction, the strength of the tenant, and the general terms of the Deal. As a rule, though, it is preferable to have the tenant lay out the money, propose what he wants to do and do it, subject to landlord consent / supervision.

Where necessary the landlord should make an appropriate trade-off in rent or other lease terms in exchange for a tenant's bearing large up-front costs. As a rule it is better to contribute in future cheaper dollars predicated on a tenant's continued occupancy and payment of rent.

Why go out-of-pocket today and maximize your exposure? What if your tenant goes bad? It is best to not go in heavy up-front for (most) tenants. Moreover, many so called Capital Improvements are subject to dilution of their future economic value and utility by virtue of wear and tear and obsolescence. Sometimes the big "improvement" or change which is desired by one tenant will later prove less desirable or even an impediment, to the use and rentability of the property in the eyes of other prospective tenants.

Today's improvement may be tomorrow's demolition project for the landlord, for a subsequent tenant or for a buyer. Even where the tenant fronts the costs, the landlord must still be sure that any trade-off concessions are prudent in relation to the tenant's own "contribution", depending, again, on other lease terms and the Market.

A few years back I was involved in an industrial rental where the tenant, at his own cost and with no trade-off even requested from the landlord, partitioned a 10,000 square foot warehouse into a hodge-podge of storage areas and offices. He spent a small fortune on electrical, dividing walls, floor coverings, and new ducting for heat and air conditioning. He subsequently went bankrupt (corporate Chapter 11 Converted to a Chapter 7 liquidation), and his company was dissolved. The Trustee sold the Bankruptcy Estate's assets, but the leasehold "improvements" were a part of the real estate, and thus (we) the landlord, became "beneficiaries" of all of this lumber and sheetrock.

None of his work was suited to the particular type of building, and the tenant's brainstorm became our costly demolition headache. Prospective tenant after tenant wanted the building, but only if we would first clear out the "improvements".

<u>Where as part of lease negotiations a Tenant is given permission to make significant Changes to demised premises, particularly where such "Changes" are specific to his use,</u> the landlord should get a larger security deposit to cover possible future remediation costs. The lease should clearly identify who will own the "improvements" and associated fixtures, and indicate if the tenant, at the landlord's option upon completion of the lease, will be responsible to return the premises to their original condition. It is important for the landlord to have the authority to ultimately decide whether improvements shall remain or the tenant must remove them.

Lease terms which permit a tenant to make changes to the property should be specific. The tenant should be obligated to present sufficient plans or drawings for the landlord's approval prior to commencement of the work and to comply with Building, Health and Safety Codes and secure all necessary Permits and Inspections. It must be spelled out that work is to be done in "a good workmanlike manner" and the tenant and its contractors obtain worker's comp. and liability insurance policies naming the landlord as co-insured. The tenant should also be required to Hold the landlord Harmless with respect to related claims or liabilities.

The landlord should try to ensure that changes will not work to his detriment by compromising the future status of the property – Legal, Use, Zoning or Structural Integrity. Again, sometimes a tenant's improvements turn out to be anything but. Yet excessive rigidity is not always a wise posture for the landlord, either. Proceed if the Deal warrants, but Proceed in a protective way.

<u>Environmental Issues</u>, usually most pertinent in commercial, industrial and land transactions (see below for Lease Applications), should be of paramount concern in selecting a tenant. Be they pre-existing to the purchase of your property or arising later in connection with its use or tenancies, Environmental problems should never be under-estimated. The structure (floors, walls), underlying and adjacent land and parking areas, the air, and indeed even contiguous properties and waterways, can all be adversely impacted in costly

ways. And regardless of who the tortfeasor (wrong-doer) or polluter may actually be, it comes back to the owner / landlord. Even if a tenant or former tenant is on the hook to affected third parties, and indeed to the landlord for having caused an environmental problem, the landlord is almost never in the clear unless and until all remediation work and costs and penalties have been satisfied.

Research and Select your Tenants Wisely. Be sure of their operations. Be aware of their Standard Use and Manufacturing Classification Categories, even those which apply to "mere" warehousing but which may subject your property to State Environmental Regulations, monitoring and/or inspections. Emissions, spills, runoffs, ground water pollution, odors and contamination of the structure, can all be expensive matters after a tenant is gone, and remediation costs can far eclipse any returns on that "good" rent you received from that "wrong" tenant. Environmental compliance and clean-up is costly in its own right and the problems can also cause a property to sit vacant and/or complicate efforts to resell.

It should be noted that a Variety of Laws, Codes, Regulatory Bodies and Inspectors on the Local, State and Federal Levels all shape many of the parameters of the Landlord-Tenant Relationship, and it behooves the landlord to keep abreast of prevailing Laws and Norms. (Property Owners Associations, Law School and Other Libraries, Realtor Associations, State Bar and Real Estate Commissions, and of course local Attorneys and Management Firms and the Internet, are all good sources on Laws and updates.)

The matter of Tenant Rights is paramount. Most laws and regulations on the subject pertain to residential tenancies, and the majority, particularly in densely populated regions, are often slanted in favor of the tenant. Indeed, one of the chief complaints of residential landlords concerns the increasing scope and depth of Judicially and Legislatively-imposed Tenant Rights; but on the other hand, (multi-unit) residential landlords do tend to get better returns and carry a lower risk of vacancies than their commercial counter-parts.

Where the residential landlord has a statutory or contractual (lease) obligation to provide certain utilities or other basic services (i.e., refuse removal, maintenance, security), he will usually bear a burden of Strict Compliance. Even if a tenant is delinquent in rent or an eviction for non-payment is pending, the landlord must typically still continue to furnish every utility and service that he is obligated to provide. Terminating or holding or cutting back may land him in Municipal Court or before a State Authority, a defendant on Code violations, facing sanctions that can range from fines and costs to damages and even jail, and a requirement for immediate resumption of services or utilities.

In what I initially thought was a seemingly harmless situation some years ago, figuring I was being a nice guy, I instead found myself cast as the ogre in a Municipal Court with summonses for Code violations. Following a brief ownership I was selling an old two-family in need of repair, "as is", but the dwelling was still quite Habitable. It was located in a middle class neighborhood among mostly owner-occupied one and two-family homes. I had bought the house subject to two month-to-month tenancies which my seller insisted I assume (he did not want to bother with the costs and headaches of vacating the apartments / possible evictions) so I met the tenants and figured I would let them stay. Their continued occupancy would bring in a few dollars and relieve me of the job of watching a vacant property (which would have also been subject to higher insurance rates and vandalism).

So I kept the tenants at their below market rentals on a month-to-month basis, and they understood I would be selling. In my mind our little arrangement, similar to others I had engaged in over the years, was fair and mutually advantageous. The tenants knew the condition of the property, they had been there for years and never knew it to be any different. But one was an instigator, the other one joined in, and they decided to play games with their new out-of-town absentee landlord.

As they both fell several months behind in rent (I was not even evicting them), they filed complaints with the Building Department alleging that I was withholding maintenance and the dwelling had all sorts of hazards.

So as a Thank You for giving them a break I had to go to Court, pay fines and do some quick remedial work which was not even required for my pending resale. I knew better than to try and assert a defense based on non-payment of rent in Municipal Court. But such bumps in the road are all part of the cost of doing business, and do not necessarily mean that my somewhat laid-back approach was totally flawed. Real Estate is essentially a People Business. You will run into all kinds of situations and people, at their best and worst. And the Strategy that failed me in this case has made for many other excellent transitions and is usually appreciated by most tenants in similar situations.

The range of Services / Protections which most States require a landlord to provide (at least in multi-unit apartment buildings), is a continually expanding list and includes, among other things: sanitary matters; basic safety concerns such as window guards, bannisters, gates and signage; security protection, including deadbolt locks, exterior lighting, camera surveillance, controlled access doors, and appropriate personnel; fire protection, including alarms, sprinklers where the complex is of a certain size, smoke detectors, and fire extinguishers; and certain utilities.

The landlord's obligation to provide appropriate levels of Habitability is, as a general matter, inherent in the tenancy relationship by virtue of common law, statutory law and standard lease provisions. It includes many of the obligations discussed above.

And while providing a Habitable rental unit is a functional physical matter, it is also part and parcel of the landlord's additional duty, which again is implicit in the law and most leases, to promote and ensure a tenant's Right Of Quiet Enjoyment in the demised (leased) premises. Quiet Enjoyment, a status which may be impacted by the actions or inaction of other tenants and even third parties unrelated to the landlord, is nevertheless an obligation which the landlord must deliver on.

If a neighboring tenant is excessively noisy, or somebody is cluttering the common parking lot with abandoned vehicles, for example, it may be a police or Code enforcement matter, but it is also a matter which the landlord is obliged to get involved with, on his own or in conjunction with the authorities, to set things right for the other tenants. Quiet Enjoyment amounts to the continuous, peaceable and uninterrupted occupancy, use, and enjoyment of the (Habitable) premises.

The landlord's obligation to provide stipulated utilities, general and specific services, and a certain standard of Habitability and Quiet Enjoyment, is well-established. And over the years, particularly in residential tenancies, the landlord's duties have steadily evolved and expanded in what has come to be both implied and explicit obligations; through Statutory Law (Codes, Regulations), and through Common Law (Court Precedents). The intent has been for Society and Government to hold the residential landlord to a higher standard and to impose on him obligations of care and remediation not previously addressed in lease forms or "earlier" law.

This trend has expanded the definition of concepts like Actual and Implied Warranties of Habitability and Maintenance. It has broken new legal ground and imposed additional costs on the landlord. The underlying Judicial, Legislative, Executive and Popular Rationale has been that both "innocent" tenants and the more general Public Health and Public Good must be protected and furthered, and the equitable and realistic allocation of this burden should be placed on the landlord, the one in the "superior" position to afford it. Indeed, this is not an entirely different Public Policy Statement than the now well-established doctrine of Implied Warranties of Fitness in the unrelated arena of Product Liability law.

It is akin to the requirements that manufacturers and distributors of food and consumer products work to avoid latent defects, even unforeseen and previously unknown defects, because of the overriding interests of the general Public Good – this is the essence of Products Liability (Strict Liability).

In general negligence (tort law) the norms of yesteryear stipulated that fault, which is a deviation from a certain "standard of care" by the tortfeasor (responsible party from whom damages can be sought), the prerequisite for liability for a harm occasioned on another, had to be based on some degree of carelessness or wrongdoing. It goes to theories of the "best" allocation of Societal Risks (principles underlying the concept of Insurance) – which party is the driving force in the particular arena and has the deeper pockets.

Fortunately for the landlord, however, many of these "liabilities" can be covered by Insurance and as a rule, over the years the costs have been built into the general price of doing business; the bottom line is that if you Buy Prudently and Manage Prudently, with scarce exception your costs and risks are already factored into your Insurance coverages and Yield pictures.

But for purposes of the instant discussion Implied Warranty means that even where the residential landlord has no Knowledge of a given type of "hazard" (i.e., lead paint on apartment walls), he may nevertheless still have an affirmative obligation to remediate, under threat of civil damages from his affected tenant and/or criminal and civil sanctions for "non-compliance" from the State. The Known or Unknown hazardous situations which a landlord must recognize and deal with or remediate can range from the discovery of fumes being expelled from some long-forgotten substance buried under the property by some unknown prior owner or tenant, to security matters imposing an obligation to install "appropriate" (but maybe still undefined) fencing or other apparatus around the property – all means to protect tenants (the landlord's "duty") against hazards, again Known or previously Unknown, new or old, even dangers which are the doing of third parties who never even had an interest in the property.

Such imposed obligations have become a Public Policy discussion articulated by the Courts and Legislatures, directly and indirectly, by "expanding" the Maintenance Codes and boilerplate content of Lease Agreements. The System has been imposing new and changing standards to cure, to avoid, to affect, to do, to abate a variety of substances, events and societal circumstances, on the landlord.

In most jurisdictions <u>Security Deposits</u> under residential leases must be held in interest-bearing segregated escrow accounts, with (typically) most of the interest going to the tenant, and the landlord must advise the tenant, in advance, of the name of the bank and the account number where it is deposited. Failure to so notify and maintain the Security may subject the landlord to penalties, including treble damages in some States.

In non-residential leases the amount, manner of holding, and allocation of any interest on Security Deposits are generally matters to be agreed upon (per lease) between the parties, with few statutory requirements. Security, which is often "used up" by tenants in lieu of paying their last month's rent, is supposed to remain on deposit with the landlord, in full, for a certain period after the lease has expired and the tenant has vacated in order to serve as a fund from which the landlord can be made whole, or at least partially whole, with respect to unpaid rent or other financial obligations which the tenant has not fulfilled – including repair or remediation work to the premises and any other costs associated with the occupancy which were the tenant's obligation. Any balance is to be returned to the former tenant in accordance with statutory requirements or terms of the lease.

<u>Leases – Commercial, Industrial, And Residential</u> – Especially in the more populous States, are modified by Legislative enactments and Judicial decisions which act as insulating buffers to ensure certain <u>Tenant Rights In The Event Of Non-Payment Of Rent</u>. Breach by failure to pay entitles the landlord to his remedies at law, in equity and under the lease itself – including eviction and suit for any deficiency. A tenant, particularly a residential tenant, however, who seeks Delay, who wants a Free Stay, who wants to Bargain with his landlord, can resort to a laundry list of remedies and legal ploys which are at his disposal, again – at law, in equity and under the lease.

<u>None of this should discourage would-be landlords; Just Buy Low, Buy Right; try to Choose Decent Tenants; be Fair with Them; Manage Them and Your Property Prudently; and any Problems and Losses will Typically be far</u>

outweighed by the Yields and Gains of your Real Estate Investment and Spec-ulation. Knowledge and Prudence are the best weapons in confronting those problems which from time to time are bound to be a thorn in the side of any landlord.

As for the Tenant's Remedies and Ploys upon his non-payment or other breach: First, a defaulting tenant is entitled to written notice of failure to pay or other breach, and is given specific opportunities to cure, with or without payment of a late fee or other penalty, as the law or lease may provide. In the case of non-payment, the tenant may also then seek to negotiate a resolution with the landlord (including a repayment plan), or avail himself of any alleged offsets for claimed prior breaches by the landlord – i.e., failure to provide serv-ices or otherwise perform in accordance with the lease. But Remember one of the Cardinal Rules; the landlord may not withhold services in retaliation for non-payment.

The landlord's basic legal remedy in the event of breach by the tenant is to file an eviction to terminate the tenancy and "remove" the tenant. The ob-jective may be to effectuate the tenant's immediate removal and perhaps later seek payment of arrears and damages occasioned by the tenant's breach (through the eviction or subsequent proceeding, as local law may direct); or the objective may be to use the eviction proceeding to bring the matter to a head and try to compel the tenant to pay or settle or otherwise comply with other non-rent terms, while permitting him to remain in possession. Filing for eviction moves the matter closer to finality while at the same time opening up avenues for both parties to settle, or for the tenant to "deal" with non-pay-ment issues or otherwise play the situation out.

Typically where the tenant goes to Court with rent arrears in hand or oth-erwise agrees to a Court-ordered or mediated lump sum payment and/or re-payment schedule, he stays and maintains the status quo of his lease. Or he may remain based on mutually-agreed new terms and the eviction proceeding can be dismissed.

Where the tenant asserts a defense based on property-related or other al-leged setoffs as his reason for non-payment, a Judge or Mediator may order that all or part of the back rent be paid into Court escrow pending the land-lord's compliance with "required" repairs or other obligations, or he may bro-ker a settlement calling for perhaps partial or full payment of arrears together with compliance by the landlord.

Depending on the particulars of a case, the jurisdiction and the economy, the Eviction Process can be time-consuming and cause costly delays for the landlord – Service of the Summons; Scheduling Court dates; Adjournments; Hearings; and additional Tenant-instigated Delays through frivolous defenses, motions for the sake of legal maneuvering (aside from bona fide issues), and the like. (A mini-version, if you will, of some of the ploys which a debtor may assert to stymie his lender in a Foreclosure action.)

And just as the mortgagor can do in a Foreclosure defense / delay tactic, at any time as late as the point of physical removal pursuant to a judgment in favor of the landlord, the tenant may apply the brakes in an Eviction proceeding by filing a Chapter 7, 11 or 13 and serving a copy on the Court or Sheriff. He may be in arrears, he may have paid nothing. But pending resolution of the Chapter 7, 11 or 13 or the landlord's otherwise going to Court and getting the Automatic Stay lifted, the tenant remains in possession and may at least temporarily continue to ignore his rent obligation. A resolution of the Bankruptcy on its merits, a negotiated settlement which may perhaps call for a schedule of payments and permit the tenant to remain, or the landlord's getting the Stay lifted, can all take weeks or months after the filing.

To add insult to injury, unless the Court lifts the Stay or dismisses the Bankruptcy "with prejudice", which it may do even with a first filing in eviction cases where the filing is clearly frivolous and not properly prosecuted, the tenant may refile a second time, thus causing the landlord still more delay. Or, again similar to the Foreclosure situation where a spouse named as co-defendant may file after the defendant has been barred from refiling, any other party named on the lease can file in his own individual right and thus further delay any departure.

But where a Bankruptcy Judge smells bad faith in a filing, especially after judgment for possession has been granted to the landlord in State Court, he may prohibit future re-filings and strike a tenant's pleadings more quickly than in a Foreclosure proceeding where it might also be clear that a filing is in reality nothing more than a Delay tactic. Still all of this can cost the landlord in legal fees and lost rent.

Caveat – in the non-residential context where a corporate tenant files Chapter 11, even when the filing is unrelated to an eviction proceeding, by law the landlord becomes a secured or priority creditor with respect to distributions from the Bankruptcy Estate, should the filing result in dissolution or reorganization of a tenant who in fact has net assets.

Self-Help is not permitted. You may not remove your tenant's or former tenant's possessions on your own volition, no matter how right your thinking may seem to be. In most jurisdictions removal must be pursuant to Court Order, and carried out in accordance with the Statutes, typically by a designated Court Officer – Sheriff, Constable, etc. The landlord who takes matters into his own hands and resorts to "Self-Help" will possibly subject himself to both criminal charges, including trespass, and compensatory and punitive damages at the hands of – Who Else? – "his tenant in arrears". This is a serious issue, particularly in residential tenancies.

Recently a friend of mine who is a local real estate broker decided to move things along with a tenant he was evicting by putting what he honestly thought was debris left behind by the tenant, at the curb on garbage day. The tenant had his Rights. The proper procedure for Removal – Court Order carried out by a Court Officer – was not followed, and regardless of his understanding or intentions, it was an Illegal Removal, a violation of the deadbeat tenant's Federal and State Rights. The tenant got an attorney to handle the case on a contingent fee basis and ultimately won punitive damages against his former landlord in Federal Court – after first having beat him on the rent.

Among the issues a landlord must deal with in residential situations is The Extent of Permitted Occupancy. And this can be a thorny one. There are situations, senior citizen housing among them, where in a benign non-discriminatory fashion a lease may limit the number and "type" of full time occupants in a Unit (The number of "guests" is a function of local Health and Safety Codes).

If the lease does not cap the number of occupants or identify them, unless the Zoning Official finds a violation a landlord may be hard-pressed to determine who is and who is not a member of an extended family or a casual guest, who has the right to occupy. In order to sidestep the possibly litigious tenant, if a tenant is in good-standing and his "guests" do not disturb the peace or annoy other tenants, a landlord is well advised to focus his energies on more important issues instead of worrying about how many people are in the apartment. Yet many landlords overly concern themselves with such issues, as if they have a "territorial thing" about "their" property.

Rent Control, that storied tale of New York City and some other metropolitan areas and historically the bane of many of their landlords, was born of a need to protect tenants of limited means from greedy landlords. Its function as a "necessary" protective mechanism in some sort of benevolent almost humanitarian manner has always been tempered by criticisms that Rent Control is a political expediency designed to get votes; that it is an unfair intrusion and restriction on a landlord's rights; that it is a prescription to impede growth in property values; or that it is a vehicle which inhibits a landlord's initiative and tends to destroy neighborhoods.

True, it has had its purposes and certain good points, but it has also been a misapplied tool. Where rents are kept artificially low for luxury apartments, where suburban apartments are kept well under market when there is no "compelling need", where people with decent incomes can skate by and pay a fraction of what their true rent should be, it has become politicized and is no longer serving any Public Policy. Restrictive Rent Control which hurts landlords, dampens Yields, causes operating losses or depresses values, is neither sensible, Capitalistic, nor fair. It is the Government taking out of the pockets of one group in the business community, in Society, and using their money or entitlements as direct in-kind subsidies to others.

Housing is obviously a vital need, but so is food, fuel, clothing and countless other things. And aside from fulfilling a role as guardian of the Public Good in a fair and equitable manner, there are areas where Government over-regulates sectors of our supposedly free enterprise economy. Yes, regulate health standards in restaurants. Compel the landlord to install window guards on the tenth floor. Prevent the local paint factory from dumping its waste into neighboring waterways. But force a landlord to rent an apartment for a fraction of its market value when nobody is capping his costs, and thus take his legitimate Profit and depress the value of his property, and let some tenant stay "forever" at a bargain rate?

Whatever its origins, pros and cons and abuses – for the Prudent Buyer / Landlord or Buyer / Flipper, the bottom line is to Know What You Are Doing, Inquire if there is Rent Control or other restrictive guidelines which affect your purchase and its operation. And where there is Rent Control its future impact must be Analyzed and the prospective investor, with the benefit of professional input, should look at the Entire Picture and make a Decision. The Purchase Price, the long range Potential of a property, and the applicable Political Climate must all be right to Justify a foray into Rent Controlled apartments.

Any discussion of <u>Residential Tenant Rights</u> must recognize that most States have either Regional or Statewide regulatory arms which, pursuant to statute or regulation, mandate <u>Strict Standards and Inspections for Multi-Fam-</u>

ily Dwellings, usually defined as three or more units, above and beyond those of any local Codes. Most States have regulatory departments, in New Jersey it is Community Affairs, which can issue lists of violations (giving reasonable time to cure), and promulgate their own sets of health and safety standards for buildings with three or more units.

In a different vein, it should be noted that the standards and operating procedures for Rooming Houses are usually regulated by local ordinance. Even their "eviction" process is typically different from the procedures for "other" types of tenancies. Code requirements, where properly enforced, as to health, fire, sanitation and safety issues, are usually very strict for Rooming Houses, where there are numerous occupants (not tenants per se) living in close quarters. Rooming Houses must be run with a tight rein and can be likened more to a "going business" in their daily operations as compared to the less intense, or more passive, management of well-oiled apartment units.

As a rule the novice should defer to counsel in drawing or reviewing his Initial Leases. The landlord should familiarize himself with the laws and business and procedural matters concerning basic leases. Again, one needs to develop a Conceptual Understanding of Terminology and Issues in order to gain a Solid Handle on things. One Real Estate Truism to always Remember: Knowledge (REALLY) Is Power – Knowledge, as in Certain Factual Information, AND as in How And Where To Find Out The Rest, and Knowledge as in Smarts and Understanding, and not necessarily of endless minutia and trivia.

The point is not much different from the Approach that should be used in determining neighborhood property values – the Goal is not simply to memorize Main Street's comps as of January 1 and Wall Street's as of February 1. Yes, Details are important, but having a Grasp of the Science and the Subject Matter, Knowing How And Where To Get the comps, and What To Do With Them when you get them, that is what you call Smart Working Knowledge.

Generally speaking, the Broad Categories of Form Leases include Residential; Condo; Office; Commercial / Retail; Shopping Center / Strip Mall; Industrial; Land; and the more esoteric Air, Mineral, and Riparian Varieties.

By way of Sub-Categories of Leases, we have the Gross and Net (with its Variations), and the Hybrid; be they for Residential, Industrial, or other type of tenancy. These Sub-Categories differentiate the allocation of a tenant's responsibilities with regard to payments and fulfillment of other obligations under the lease (as set forth below).

Additionally, by their language Leases may be <u>Assignable</u> as written with no need for further review or permission; they may be <u>Assignable on Condition</u> that a stipulated event occurs first (a Condition Precedent) which, for example, might be payment of a certain consideration or some other requirement and which condition must be satisfied for the tenant to Assign; they may be <u>Assignable with the Consent of the Landlord</u>, possibly stating, for example, that "such consent shall not be withheld unreasonably"; or they may be <u>Non-Assignable</u>.

Leases address a tenant's right to "<u>Sublease</u>" to a third party similarly to how they address Assignability – with or without conditions – i.e., a tenant may Sublease, period; or a Condition Precedent must be satisfied to obtain the landlord's consent to Sublease; or landlord's consent to Sublease is necessary, and such "consent shall not be withheld unreasonably" or the lease may simply prohibit any Sublease.

While an <u>Assignment</u> is essentially the wholesale transfer of rights and obligations under a lease from the tenant to a third party, a Sublease involves the tenant's (Sub) "leasing" of all or part of the demised (leased) premises to a third party, for all or part of the balance of the term of the lease, for a greater or lesser rental than set forth in the lease, with the original tenant remaining more involved in both a legal and day-to-day sense with the landlord and the operation of the premises.

The tenant will prefer that his lease contain an Assignment or Sublease clause which is either absolute or which hinges on the landlord's consent with the proviso that said consent "cannot be withheld unreasonably". This obviously gives the tenant more latitude in making future adjustments which may be necessitated by either good or bad fortune; it gives him an ability to try to profit or minimize losses in connection with his leasehold situation generally.

Where Assignment or Sublease is conditioned on "landlord's consent" and there is no qualifying language that it "cannot be withheld unreasonably", or where the lease simply prohibits Assignment or Sublease, the landlord has the upper hand and depending on the circumstances, he may thus sometimes be in a position to "name the price for his Consent".

Except where <u>Assignment</u> or <u>Sublease</u> are absolute leasehold rights the landlord's consent, be it qualified with language as to reasonableness or not, should always, either implicitly or explicitly, be at least partially based on his review of any prospective new tenant or sub-tenant – as to their overall credentials, financial position, stability, and the nature of their operations. The landlord who rented his warehouse to a tenant who stores general merchandise might not be too keen on a sub-tenant with a heavy manufacturing operation.

A tenant may Execute a lease in his Individual / Personal Capacity; as a Legal Entity (LLC, Corporation), with only the Entity being responsible under the lease; or as an Entity with a Personal Guarantee as to all or certain of the leasehold obligations.

Leases may be in Writing or Verbal, for a month-to-month or other stated Term; or they may be in the form of "Quasi-Leases" (i.e., Lifetime Estates, Reversionary Interests, or Estates In Occupancy); and Granted by deed, will or other instrument. The Statute of Frauds, whose particulars differ in various jurisdictions, requires that leases of a certain duration must be in writing to be valid.

Lease Forms also differ from State to State but for the most part share certain common elements and boiler-plate. There are various Forms relative to specific types of leases (i.e., residential, commercial), which themselves by their actual language may be slanted in favor of either landlord or tenant – "Landlord's" or "Tenant's" Leases. Addenda and other Content which are supplementary to a printed Form (the "fill in the blank pages"), Customize leases; and an Addendum may be far-reaching and modify, contradict, or supersede given clauses in the basic Form.

Leases should be read and not merely glossed over. Moreover, the practice of too many attorneys, landlords and others of embracing technology to the extreme and spitting out regurgitated standard and rogue Forms on their computers often does away with the basic old-fashioned pre-printed Lease forms, which have clarity and whose point headings serve as recognized guides. This trend makes it important to carefully scrutinize all pages of the form.

It is wise to use Local or Statewide pre-printed Lease and other standard document forms and supplement them with an Addendum containing any customized terms. The reams of computer-generated paper which pass for Documents today, many generated by amateurs and replete with flaws, often lead to confusion, trickery, omission and impropriety; needless work for the diligent; needless risk for many; and unwarranted fees for the professionals who hit the start button on their printer and make believe they are "crafting" Documents.

Depending on their Duration, Assignability, Option Rights and Financial and other Terms, Leasehold Rights (Rights Under A Lease) may constitute very Valuable Assets for tenant or landlord. A lease may have a monetary value as a commodity (sometimes being the most valuable asset of a tenant's business), and it may possibly be sold or assigned to third parties or used as collateral by either the tenant or landlord. Restrictions or conditions on a tenant's ability to Assign or Sublease will obviously affect the "value" of its Lease. Where a Lease is an asset of value to the tenant, upon the sale or other closure of the tenant's business operations (even through Bankruptcy), or other transfer of the demised premises that Value should translate into a dollar or other form of Profit / Compensation for the tenant. Bankruptcy Estate auctions frequently realize sizeable proceeds from the sale of <u>Valuable Leasehold Interests</u> with unfulfilled terms.

Similarly, where a landlord can successfully deny a "valuable" Assignment or Sublease the Value will inure to his, instead of the tenant's, benefit. It can be an opportunity for the landlord to "Recapture" or "Retrieve" otherwise potentially "lost" future rental Profits which he may have "partially" or "temporarily" bargained away when he originally negotiated the lease-terms.

To the extent a landlord may thus escape what to him are otherwise unfavorable lease terms and re-rent to a new tenant on better terms, he denies his original tenant a possible windfall. The original tenant will have thus been pushed out, he will have no ability to pass on and profit from his "valuable lease" and the landlord will retain any new benefits.

Developers typically give large or "<u>Name</u>" <u>Tenants</u> (usually retail or food), so-called <u>Anchor Tenants</u>, favorable rental and other terms in order to secure their major leases, even prior to commencement of construction or Rehab, and then use the leases or commitments to draw other tenants, to show their ability to re-pay a mortgage, or as collateral to persuade lenders to grant construction and permanent financing on a project.

<u>The Payment of basic Lease Rentals and Utilities and the Performance of Repair and other Obligations</u> will involve a variety of arrangements.

In a <u>Gross Lease</u> rental payments are fixed and the landlord pays real estate taxes, real estate insurance and utilities, and repairs and maintenance (assuming damages are not caused by the tenant). In a <u>Net Lease</u> there is a fixed base rental figure and the tenant also pays all or some of the other expenses (i.e., real estate taxes, real estate insurance, utilities, repairs and, where applicable, Common / Shared / Condo Or Use fees).

A Net Lease may have the tenant paying any such "cost" items in their entirety; or paying a fixed portion of any such "cost" items; or only their increases over and above a stipulated dollar amount (or base) or only their increases over a given base year or month. Whether paid to the landlord or directly to third party payees by the tenant, this is all "added rent". And again, the Net Lease may or may not impose any range of repair or maintenance obligations on the tenant, regardless of what it says about who oversees the work. It may be general or specific in delineating a tenant's obligations for repairs and maintenance.

A Hybrid Net Lease, The Combo., might, for example, have a schematic which sets the tenant's base rental, makes the landlord responsible for taxes and utilities, has the tenant paying insurance, and places the maintenance burden on the tenant.

In most Apartment leases a Gross or basic Net version will be the norm with the landlord typically paying everything except utilities and bearing responsibility for maintenance and repairs which are not the fault of the tenant. In the typical one family Home lease the norm is a Net version which makes the tenant responsible for utilities and has either party solely or partially responsible for repairs and maintenance.

Aside from the labels of Net or Gross it should be noted that any type of Lease, Lease Extension or Lease Option, may incorporate Formulas which will, from time to time, establish its Base or other Rental amounts. Rent may be set as a stated sum or as a schedule of changing amounts. It may be a sum made subject to upward or downward revisions based on a formula or Index (variable). Or it may be set entirely as a variable figure based solely on a formula or Index.

Current or future Rentals may be the product of a base adjusted by the Consumer Price Index (CPI). Rentals may be set as an "amount to be calculated" according to some schematic using local rent comparables. Rent may be tied to or be a combination of a base plus a percentage of a tenant's business or sales volume at the demised premises. Or Rent may be stipulated as a function of virtually any escalation clause or criteria imaginable.

Especially where the demised premises are a particularly "valuable" property and initially carry a low or under-market rental the landlord should take care to protect himself in Lease Extensions and during possible Inflationary economic climates. Unless there is no choice when a Lease is made (and some seemingly stupid Deals are actually smart and necessary when agreed to during difficult times), the days when a landlord would expose himself to long term Extensions without the benefit of having inflationary or cost of living increments or other formulas built into the Lease, should be considered pre-1980's history.

By way of aside it should be noted that once - "shrewd" CPI - based Rental formulas which were built into many Leases and Extensions in the inflationary '80's turned into disasters when the Federal Government decided that one way to "beat" inflation was by changing the components, the calculations, if you will, of National and Regional Consumer Price Indices. The Government artificially tamped down the "rates" of increase, and thus made some of the inflationary spiral of the period "disappear" by magic!

When inflation subsides due to actual workings of the marketplace, the landlord whose leases are predicated solely on CPI gets hurt – Just one of the reasons why I have long preferred to stagger rental figures in longer-term leases and base Extension increments on a "General Local Comps Approach".

As a practical matter where a lease's stipulated rental was set at or is the product of a formula which later proves to be well above market rates and the landlord has a quality commercial or industrial tenant he wants to hold onto, he will probably have to adjust his "rent entitlement" downwards, anyway. But where he has a set below-market rental figure or a below-market figure which is the product of a flawed formula, he is stuck.

Indeed, I have made many downward adjustments to industrial lease rentals in poor rental markets when formulas in leases and extensions pushed rents to over-market numbers. The leases looked good on paper but I had to make deals if I wanted to keep decent tenants, notwithstanding the "attractive" albeit unrealistic option and extension figures which I "had".

During Good Economic Cycles landlords who own strip malls, shopping centers, and isolated retail locations will often be able to reap large Profits, and in a way become "silent partners" with their tenants, when under their lease all or a portion of the rent is stipulated as a product or a percentage of the tenant's sales volume.

Whatever the Deal, Gross or Net; Assignment, Sublease or Something Else; CPI or Otherwise; a landlord typically best serves his own interests by Being Reasonable and Not Going For The Last Dollar. And this is particularly so with short-term rentals where he might want a renewal and when leasing "junk" properties. In most other cases the market and intuition should be the Guide but bear in mind the landlord will usually get more in valuable trade-offs and future performance when he leaves something on the table for his tenant. And this will make things a lot less complicated. When you consider the Bigger Picture, the Overall Yields / Returns / Gains / Market Swings and Strategies in Flipping and Holding, a few extra Rental dollars made at the expense or sacrifice of more significant Potential pales in comparison.

HUD Section 8 Residential Rental Assistance is a terrific benefits program for both landlords and tenants. Subject to local quotas of availability and other rather benign conditions, Section 8 has historically been a boon to many residential landlords, particularly in depressed and urban areas. Under the Program the Government pays most or almost all of the rent on sliding scales; rents may be market level, and most Section 8 Tenants are, to the satisfaction of their landlords, usually happy and cooperative – as they typically live virtually free!

In terms of rent Pay Periods most leases will require that rent be paid on a monthly basis in advance – opposite to typical mortgage payments, which are usually monthly and sometimes bi-weekly, but by their terms payable in arrears for the preceding month or two week period.

When leasing to a "weaker" tenant, especially in a decent Market, the landlord may want to collect more than the standard one to two month Security Deposit, with the first month's rent to also be paid at signing or upon occupancy. Or he may require the pre-payment of more than the first month's rent, either at signing, upon occupancy or in stages over the initial portion of the lease term. (State laws typically restrict residential Security Deposits to one or two months' rent.)

By way of quick overview, some issues and recurring themes relative to the topics of Lease Terms and Extensions bear mention.

Deciding on the Legal and Business Matters of a Lease often involves a tension, a balancing act by the landlord. "How long should the property be tied up for in the Lease period or Extension? Does a long term really make sense? How will the answers to such questions affect the quality of any prospective tenant or the rental income? What are the best Plans for the property? Are a longer Lease and possible Extension necessarily the smartest options?"

Retail, Commercial and Industrial Tenants often require "longer" commitments – they may rely on a particular location for repeat trade and goodwill; they may need to make substantial investments to use the facilities; and moving, even where the tenant wants to, can be costly and disruptive to business.

Again, Lease Extension Options can be very solid when based on clearly stated terms. They have more value and wiggle room for a landlord when pegged to a Comparables Approach or some other flexible Formula. They are hollow for a tenant when their terms are premised on a future "hoped-for" agreement with the landlord. When based on certain prior performance or compliance as a pre-condition, they leave an opening for questions and "interpretations" by the landlord.

When a <u>Lease Term</u> expires, whether there was an <u>Option</u> to extend which was not consummated or there was no Option, in most jurisdictions a <u>Holdover Tenant</u> who thereafter tenders rent which is accepted by the landlord will, by operation of law, automatically establish a new Month-to-Month Tenancy. Continued payment and acceptance will perpetuate this new relationship. It may be terminated by either party in accordance with local procedures, usually by written notice to the other served at least one month prior to the next recurring rent due date.

<u>Just as Leases may contain Options to Extend, they may also have (any) variety of Forms of Options to Purchase the demised premises</u> – and, as with Lease Extension Options, the presence or absence of clear defined financial and other conditions precedent may, in an Option to Purchase, impact its value and any chance it will ever lead to an actual sale. Crucial – the Value of an Option is a function of its financial and other terms and its clarity and certainty in defining how and when it may be exercised. Options may thus represent valuable contractual rights and privileges or be meaningless words.

<u>In Negotiating a Lease</u>, either landlord or tenant may bargain for a recital making any type of <u>Option Clause Assignable or Non-Assignable</u> – and again, if it is to be Assignable, the landlord should consider making it so only upon certain additional conditions. This is another way for the parties to reach a Meeting of the Minds. The tenant can be given a Lease and Option, while the landlord might still hold something back, something that may be of a dollar and/or negotiating value down the road; namely, an Option Clause not automatically Assignable (transferable) with the lease.

The procedures for exercising an Option must be spelled out if future disagreements and legal entanglements are to be avoided. How it is to be sent (usually by certified mail, return receipt requested); when sufficient Notice of Intent to Exercise must be sent (deadline for receipt of the Notice); where and to Whom it must be sent (landlord, counsel); and in conjunction with what, if any, other Conditions / Acts the Notice is to be sent (i.e., additional deposit with Notice).

Overall Lease Provisions and Issues, some additional matters: In Drafting a lease, save for those situations where the landlord must specifically bar certain Uses of the premises either due to his own reasons, due to an existing or contemplated "non-compete" clause in favor of a neighboring tenant, or because the new tenant is being granted a certain exclusivity of Use as against neighboring tenants, it is best to not grant permission for any specific "Uses" or to even discuss Uses per se.

Except for those leases which involve non-competes or exclusivity, complete the section entitled "Use" as follows: "The tenant may do anything permitted by the applicable Zoning Codes and other Governmental Laws, Rules and Regulations, as they may, from time to time, allow."

Unless you "have to", do not tell the tenant, through his lease, that he "can" do something. It is easier to tell him what he cannot do. The landlord is not the Code Official. He is not the final arbiter. And while some professional "drafters" like to be wordy, often for their own agenda (sometimes contrary to the best interests of their client), in our Litigious Society very often the more you write the greater the potential for lawsuits and other problems.

In Law one word can lead to a Pandora's Box – a panacea for the litigious tenant and the hungry lawyer alike. Do not restate "what" is permitted by Code or Environmental Regulations. Verbally discuss with your tenant what you understand to be permitted Uses, perhaps help him inquire with the municipality, introduce him to local Zoning people if it seems appropriate. Tell him to assure himself, to go to the source and check out the propriety of his intended Use. Save for any necessary Prohibitions on Use Grants (restrictions) your lease should be safe and simple; tell your tenant he can Use the premises "how they say he can Use it".

As alluded to earlier, in all but the Residential context the amount, method of holding, and disposition of any interest on Security Deposits are subjects for agreement between the parties. Whenever possible non-residential Security Deposits should be held as the landlord sees fit, and not in an escrow account: 20 tenants times $5,000.00 security each equals some working capital for your next venture. Depending on the tenant, the Market and prevailing interest rates, a tenant's request for interest on Security should be a matter of practical discretion. The actual amount of any annual interest may be more a minor bookkeeping headache than any real gain or cost for either party. Sometimes otherwise savvy tenants get picky about interest and a small concession here can often mean a lot in overall negotiations. It is more important to the landlord that he has the ability to use his pool of security deposits – no "Escrow".

Although a Landlord's Rights And Remedies upon Breach by a Tenant may sometimes seem time-consuming and lacking in punch (versus a tenant's Rights and Defenses, especially in residential cases), notwithstanding frustrations in the process the Landlord's Rights, particularly Eviction, are quite viable.

Again, try to select a Decent tenant. Be Responsive, Be Fair, Give him some Latitude (perhaps extensions for late payments where the relationship and Market justify). But Be Prudent, Firm, Present and Diligent. And should you get hit now and then with a bad tenant or difficult eviction, redouble your efforts and attention in the subject property and elsewhere, and understand this is all part of the game. Investments and businesses have their problems. But if you Buy Low, Buy Right, and Function Prudently in your Dealings, a hit here and there should not really matter in the long run.

In addressing Environmental Concerns lease provisions should demand strict tenant compliance with all standards and inspections during, at the conclusion of, and after the rental has expired. This includes clean-up and remediation, ensuring proper standards of operation, preventative compliance, and facilitating inspections and filing Reports. Security Deposits should be adjusted to reflect a tenant's environmental risks and exposures. To achieve an additional layer of comfort and protection, in certain situations it is wise to incorporate into lease payments the cost of an owner's / landlord's environmental insurance policy.

Real Estate Salespeople and Brokers are sometimes vilified as vultures with little concern for the landlord's interests. Of course this describes some of them. Stick with the good ones. They can prove invaluable. Commission terms should be reduced to writing and ultimately memorialized in the lease or by separate agreement. But also honor any verbal promise to pay a Broker. Cultivate good relationships with professional productive Brokers – as with Sales, in Leasing you will also usually wind up with a better Net in your pocket after deducting commission where you use a good Broker.

The question of How and When a Commission should be paid is common in leasing – especially where future rental payments "add up" and it is an extended term. (Mostly commercial, office, retail and industrial leases.) The Broker would like it all up-front and the Landlord would prefer to pay later.

Depending on many factors – strength of a tenant, desirability of the property, market conditions, dollar value of future rent and the current rent level *vis-à-vis* fair market, length of the lease, needs and position of the landlord, and the personalities of the parties – the Method of Commission payment on future rental income will, and should, vary from case to case. Broker and Landlord must make their competing interests mesh.

In "smaller" leases a total or substantial up-front commission payment on future rentals is the norm. Often payments are spread out in staged increments. Sometimes, most notably in "larger" transactions, commission on future rents is made subject to continued performance by the tenant. Any combination of payment arrangements which the parties agree to is of course their business, but the savvy landlord should understand that good Brokers do not want to show buildings, secure a tenant, help negotiate a lease, do everything that goes into making a Deal, and possibly forego another leasing opportunity for the tenant someplace else, only to receive little or nothing upon their tenant's occupancy and to further risk the possibility that the landlord may not even pay as agreed later on.

It is a balancing act: the Landlord risking payment today for a Tenant who may not pay him later and the Broker risking future non-payment of deferred commissions or just having to wait for his money. Heed local industry standards which may "govern" the Methods of Payment, and remember that your Broker can be a valuable asset down the road.

Regardless of when Commission is paid, there is often an issue as to its calculation: Should the Commission percentage be applied to the Gross amount of a lease or to some lesser Net amount? The landlord may claim that real estate taxes and insurance are not "income", but are merely pass-through expenses exempt from Commission. In Net Leases Commission is often paid only on the basic Net rental.

Similarly, Commissions on Extension Options and Options for additional space or Purchase of the demised premises are variously agreed to be paid either in a lump sum or in staged increments upon exercise, at closing, or during the term of the Option. And the Commission rate is often negotiated down for Extension periods and Purchases pursuant to a lease. Whatever the case, in Commission negotiations you must keep an eye on both the value or desirability of the Deal and future Broker relationships.

Insurance is always an important subject where leases are concerned. The landlord / owner must carry a Multi-Peril Comprehensive Policy covering his real estate and "himself" (the named Individual or Entity Owner), insuring against casualty loss to the premises and loss or injury to third parties due to fire or other casualty. The Policy should include general liability provisions, standard workmen's comp. and cover the landlord for loss of rent and use of the premises due to damage or destruction.

Policy endorsements for matters like Workmen's Comp. and Loss of Rent are relatively inexpensive and are obviously valuable in a multitude of situations – i.e., where a mechanic who did minor repair work for the landlord or tenant comes up with a claim for personal injury or when the building cannot be occupied for say six months due to fire and the landlord must still handle mortgage and other ongoing expenses. Riders to a basic Policy can protect against things like environmental mishaps caused by either tenant or third parties, losses occasioned by natural disasters such as earthquakes, and even manmade disasters like terrorism.

In Designated Flood Zones, so classified by Government Maps, an endorsement for flood insurance or a separate flood policy is always a wise choice and is indeed required by most primary lending institutions.

An Umbrella insurance policy does as its name implies: it provides an extended dollar limit of coverage against categories of potential claims which are already insured against by an underlying basic policy. Such coverage protects the named insured on the policy with regard to the subject property and other properties – be the insured an Individual or Entity Owner, the Owner of an Entity in title, or any Third Party.

Where the liability limit in an underlying policy, for example, is $500,000.00 and an umbrella raises it to $1,000,000.00, the insured will escape any personal liability should a claim result in a judgment or settlement of, say, $700,000.00. Absent the umbrella in such a case, the insured would have a $200,000.00 exposure. The umbrella picks up, to its own specified limits, where the underlying policy stops. Annual premiums on even substantial umbrellas are surprisingly small.

Some years ago I had an embarrassing and potentially very costly problem, partly of my own making and partly the result of an absurd jury verdict, in what was really one of those "classic cases". I was renting out a small one family owned in my Individual Name, which was basically breaking even as I waited for a more Opportune Market to Resell. I had gotten a Good Buy on the property, put next to nothing Down, and Assumed my seller's old mortgage – but I was sloppy in my paperwork.

My insurance policy on the premises carried low coverage limits and I had a lapse in my umbrella. I just had poor coverage at the time. Negligence, potentially very dangerous negligence.

My tenant was very congenial. Rent was always paid on time, and we had an informal arrangement with a modest cap whereby she would have her brother, a carpenter, fix most things "of necessity" and on the next rent day deduct what were always extremely fair charges for the work.

I finally sold the house, gave my tenant notice to move, she moved and left the place broom clean and current in her rent; I refunded the Security and heard nothing for almost two years – which in New Jersey is the Statute of Limitations period from the date of an occurrence within which an "injured" plaintiff must either settle his claim or file suit for damages in tort (negligence), if he is to preserve his claim and proceed through the Courts.

When I got served with the Complaint and Summons from the Superior Court of New Jersey seeking unspecified damages and costs for injuries, pain and suffering, medical bills and other losses occasioned by an "injury" which my former tenant's 20-year-old daughter had allegedly suffered in the house before they vacated, I was astounded. And I became more concerned than astounded when I realized how under-insured I was on the property. During her occupancy my tenant would tell me just about everything. She would even gently complain if the neighbor had a loud party. But never once did she say anything about her daughter's so-called "fall", let alone that anybody felt I, the landlord, was responsible due to alleged negligence or "poor" condition of the property.

Counsel for my insurance carrier called the suit "frivolous", not worthy of serious settlement discussions. Nevertheless, since the language in the Complaint indicated a potential claim for which I would be under-insured, by law my carrier had to advise me to retain private counsel on that portion of the claim which exceeded my policy limits. The case eventually went to a jury trial.

The plaintiff weighed over 300 pounds and the Emergency Room Report which she gave in connection with the "accident" quoted her as saying she and some friends had been "drinking…(and) horsing around in (her) bedroom" when she fell out of bed onto the oak floor and suffered a broken hip.

In Court, with her walker and rehearsed demeanor, she struck a sympathetic figure. And I was the out-of-town "slumlord". She claimed her fall was caused by "uneven" floors. She could not explain away her hospital statement.

Nobody could explain why neither she nor her mother never mentioned the "accident" or "condition" of the floor to me.

Sure, she had surgeries and a permanent problem, she suffered losses and endured pain and suffering. She had plenty of *prima facie* damages. My point at trial, however, was that her injuries were of her own making and not the result of my negligence and since there was no fault or liability the case should be thrown out.

Yet the jury awarded her almost $400,000.00 (my policy limits were $250,000.00); the Judge almost fell off his chair when he heard the verdict, and my carrier's lawyer was dumb-founded. If I had an umbrella I would have been in the clear, notwithstanding the low limits on my underlying policy. I was facing a large personal liability and serious legal fees on any appeal.

Probably because even he realized the jury award was not justified and could be overturned on appeal, the plaintiff's attorney agreed to compromise after negotiations with my insurance carrier for under my coverage limits and I was in the clear. But it was a valuable lesson – even though I should have never needed one in the first place: Carry Adequate Insurance On Your Real Estate – skimp on items that do not much matter if you have to, but have adequate insurance. And again, sound coverage should consist of a Comprehensive Multi-Peril Liability Insurance Policy with appropriate Riders.

When it comes to the real estate itself, coverage limits go to Replacement Cost. The issue is not fair market value or land value. Land does not burn, and its value should not be included as part of the insured amount. Limits of property coverage should be a function of the estimated replacement cost of a structure, the calculation that awards are based on. Under-Insurance will result in penalties or a pro-rata reduced compensation in the event of a claim; but Over-Insurance will not result in any "bonus" for the insured.

A Deductible is the threshold, the initial amount of a claim – as set forth in the policy – which must first be paid or absorbed out-of-pocket by the insured before benefits of the coverage will kick in. Insurance, as a System, was designed as a mechanism to Allocate Risks of Loss in Society. Submitting very small claims, "small" being relative to a situation, typically results in an insignificant net to the insured after any Deductible and will cause an increase in premiums. The Smart Owner will submit only claims of a "decent size". Generally lower Policy Deductibles tend to encourage claims and thus expand a carrier's ongoing exposures and costs. Carrying a Low Deductible will lead to a higher premium. Raise your Deductibles, and Lower your Premiums.

You do not "make" money on nuisance claims. Insurance should be used for the larger matters. Thus, particularly with investment property where rates are normally higher than for owner-occupied dwellings, carrying a $500.00 or $1,000.00 Deductible is silly. It will result in higher premiums; and if you were to submit, for example, a $1,500.00 claim, in the long run you would lose more than you would "gain". And where you do actually have a more substantial claim which merits submission, the Repair or Replacement Cost will typically just as easily absorb a $2,500.00 Deductible as it will absorb a $500.00 Deductible. Compare premiums for identical Policies and for variations in the Deductibles. Many owners maintain needlessly over-priced policies because they carry rock-bottom Deductibles or simply do not shop around.

Also try to avail yourself of premium payment installment plans. A mortgage held by an institutional lender will typically require the first year's premium to be paid in full prior to closing; and most lenders will escrow insurance monthly and remit payment to the carrier on policy anniversary dates, meaning you are in effect continually pre-paying.

Inquire about the strength and stability of particular carriers – shop and compare. There are State Funds which back up "most" defunct carriers, but getting a claim paid where there has been a bankruptcy or State takeover of a carrier can take years, and will usually result in only a partial payment of the actual claim amount.

Insurance policies may list pre-existing risks or problems with a property as Exclusions from coverage (i.e., property loss or third party claim); or, as the result of routine inspections, a carrier may direct its insured to remedy sub-par conditions within a given period of time or risk cancellation of the policy. Carriers can be picky in identifying conditions which they deem to be in need of upgrade or correction. They run ever-greater risks in our Litigious Society; it is an everyday occurrence for people with known pre-existing back problems, for example, to see an "accident waiting", perhaps a broken or icy sidewalk, and suddenly "fall" and "sustain" serious injury. At the inception of a policy and periodically thereafter, most carriers will inspect the insured premises with an eye on its physical condition and the operations of any tenants.

Even where a lease requires the tenant to carry liability or workmen's comp. or other insurance naming the landlord as co-insured, either generally or in connection with specific work which the tenant may do, it is wise for the landlord to still maintain his own coverage. The tenant's policy should be a second layer of protection. And where a lease requires landlord's or tenant's interests to be covered through a policy carried by the tenant, the lease should compel the tenant to furnish a copy of the policy and proof of premium payments. Where a tenant is required to provide or pay for primary coverage which is for the exclusive benefit of the landlord, i.e., fire and casualty, the lease should stipulate that he pay the premium to the landlord, who in turn should actually secure the coverage.

An owner's carrier may also require a tenant to have its carrier insert qualifying, limiting, or hold harmless language into the tenant's own policy.

Also insure yourself Personally and Individually where you own in the name of a Legal Entity, which will be the primary insured, as in given circumstances you may still have liability exposure. With environmental issues or at-risk tenants, the "cover" afforded by the Entity Owner's responsibility could be pierced as a matter of law and liability extended to reach the Individual behind the Entity Owner.

The notion of "piercing the corporate veil" took hold many years ago in cities like New York, where wealthy individuals would operate a business, like a fleet of taxicabs, and shield their assets by dividing them up and placing them in multiple companies and carry woefully low levels of insurance coverage. With each cab in a separate corporation, in serious accidents injured third parties would receive very small awards and be left in dire straits as the shell corporate entity owning the cab had no other assets, and the owner would fold or bankrupt the corporation after the claim and stand in the background with impunity since he did not personally own the cab. The law evolved under the premise that absent "adequate" coverage or in other "grievous" cases, as a matter of Public Policy the "veil could be pierced" and the claimant could seek redress by going after the Individual behind it all.

Public Policy, in part designed to Allocate Risk and avoid fraud and other wrong-doing, dictates that an Insured Party must have an <u>Insurable Interest</u> "in that which is insured". For example, the Common Law and Public Policy will not permit recovery where a neighbor decides to go out and buy a life insurance policy on some 95-year-old who lives down the street and with whom he has no "proper connection" which would give him an Insurable Interest in this person. And one cannot buy a policy on real estate belonging to somebody else and someday try to collect if there is a loss.

Today, more than ever before, carriers tend to investigate proposed insureds before binding new coverage. Such caution is typically a product of a "poor" economy; enhanced risks inherent in dealing with insureds who are suit happy or financially unstable; a pervasive climate of mistrust; rising levels of insurance fraud; and the ease of snooping. Many carriers run credit checks, verify references, and even review financials and bank accounts. The issue is Risk. Insurance is the Allocation of Risk. The carrier underwrites the Risks of its insured. It does not want an insured to itself be a further Risk. The carrier is in business to take in more premium dollars than it pays out in claims.

An owner should also understand the role of the <u>Insurance Adjuster</u>. Often regarded as vultures who sit around listening to police scanners or waiting for some runner to call in a tip so they can hurry to the scene of a fire or some other problem and convince a distraught owner or other victim to sign an Authorization with a 10 to 20% Commission Agreement giving the Adjuster the exclusive right to negotiate their claim with the carrier, Adjusters have long had the reputation of being unsavory characters.

In some States they are licensed and, in truth, many Adjusters are fair and often obtain much more favorable payouts for their clients than many could negotiate on their own. Their Commissions are negotiable and the wise owner will Prudently check and choose a reputable Adjuster should the need arise. The Right Adjuster who knows his client is not a fool can perform very valuable services.

Some Adjusters do prey on the vulnerable, the less savvy owner, the elderly, the poor and the less educated; sign them up at a high commission, negotiate a quick inferior settlement with the carrier, get their piece, and maybe even set the owner up with a slipshod contractor who will take the lion's share of their proceeds and leave them with pocket change and shabby repair work. Such Adjusters will typically shy away from the investor or deal with him on more businesslike terms. I once had a client call me, as the fire was still raging in her home, saying she did not know what to do, who to go with – she said she had more cars out front from Adjusters than there were fire engines!

For even the Non-Organization more private type landlord and speculator, "<u>Affiliations</u>" with trade groups can be valuable. These groups help keep their members abreast of changing laws and local regulations, market and industry trends, developments pertaining to Property and Management, and new products which might be appropriate for Rehabs or Maintenance. Group affiliations open up important Learning Opportunities – seminars, guest speakers, sponsors. They provide a forum to meet competitors and colleagues and possible future Partners or Financiers. They help Explore Ideas, shed light on what others in the Field are Thinking and Doing, and provide a Network and a Lobby – all to Improve your Endeavors and your Bottom Line.

And Yes, as a Landlord what you Learn and Do, your Directions and Timing, all Relate to the Larger Paramount Issues and Concerns of Holding; Refinancing / Leveraging; Rehabbing; Converting a Property to a Higher and Better Use; Gaining / Profiting in All of its Diverse Forms; and ultimately, Reselling or Passing the Property on to the Next Generation; in short, Your Efforts to Realize All of Those Gains and Yields which are at the Heart of and which are the Underpinnings of the Real Estate Game, And Thus Our Economy.

CONCLUSION

THAT'S WHY THEY CALL IT, <u>REAL</u> ESTATE.

www.ingramcontent.com/pod-product-compliance
Lightning Source LLC
Chambersburg PA
CBHW061503180526
45171CB00001B/23